Studies in the Prophecy of Jeremiah

Works by G. CAMPBELL MORGAN, D.D.

THE ACTS OF THE APOSTLES
AN EXPOSITION OF THE FOUR GOSPEL NARRATIVES
THE ANSWERS OF JESUS TO JOB
THE CORINTHIAN LETTERS OF PAUL
THE CRISES OF CHRIST
GOD'S LAST WORD TO MAN (HEBREWS)
GREAT CHAPTERS OF THE BIBLE
THE GREAT PHYSICIAN
HOSEA: THE HEART AND HOLINESS OF GOD
THE PARABLES AND METAPHORS OF OUR LORD
PREACHING
SEARCHLIGHTS FROM THE WORD
STUDIES IN THE FOUR GOSPELS
       The Gospel according to Matthew
       The Gospel according to Mark
       The Gospel according to Luke
       The Gospel according to John
STUDIES IN THE PROPHECY OF JEREMIAH
THE VOICE OF THE DEVIL

Studies in the Prophecy of Jeremiah

By
G. CAMPBELL MORGAN, D.D.

Fleming H. Revell Company
Old Tappan, New Jersey

U.S.A.
FLEMING H. REVELL COMPANY
OLD TAPPAN
NEW JERSEY

OLIPHANTS
BLUNDELL HOUSE
GOODWOOD ROAD
LONDON S.E.14

Reprinted 1969

Printed in United States of America

Contents

Studies in the Prophecy of Jeremiah

I

THE AGE AND THE WORD OF JEHOVAH

Preparatory Readings: Jeremiah 1 : 1–3; 2 Kings 22–25; 2 Chronicles 34–36 : 21.

" The words of Jeremiah . . . to whom the word of Jehovah came."—JEREMIAH 1 : 1, 2.

IN *The Cambridge Bible for Schools and Colleges,* Dr. Streane has prefaced his handbook on the prophecies of Jeremiah with a remarkable quotation from Lord Macaulay:

" It is difficult to conceive any situation more painful than that of a great man, condemned to watch the lingering agony of an exhausted country, to tend it during the alternate fits of stupefaction and raving which precede its dissolution, and to see the symptoms of vitality disappear one by one, till nothing is left but coldn ss, darkness, and corruption."

Nothing could be more apt than the selection of that paragraph to preface a study of the prophecy of Jeremiah, for nothing could be more accurate as a description of the ministry which Jeremiah was called upon to exercise in Judah.

No prophet of the long and illustrious line had a more thankless task than he, and none was more magnificently and heroically true to his sacred ministry.

Dr. Moorehead has given a graphic picture of the times in which Jeremiah exercised his ministry:

STUDIES IN THE PROPHECY OF JEREMIAH

" It was Jeremiah's lot to prophesy at a time when all things in Judah were rushing down to the final and mournful catastrophe; when political excitement was at its height; when the worst passions swayed the various parties, and the most fatal counsels prevailed. It was his to stand in the way over which his nation was rushing headlong to destruction; to make an heroic effort to arrest it, and to turn it back; and to fail, and be compelled to step to one side and see his own people, whom he loved with the tenderness of a woman, plunge over the precipice into the wide, weltering ruin."

This gives us the key to the book of Jeremiah, and introduces us into the true atmosphere; these prophetic utterances of the prophet of strength and of tears, constituted the word of Jehovah to a decadent age.

This is in itself a remarkable and suggestive fact, and as such, is worth our most careful consideration. The fact that having spoken, and been disobeyed, God should continue to speak; the fact that He should persistently speak, when there was no immediate response; the fact that He should continue to speak when He knew there would be no response; and, that under such circumstances, and at such a time, He should speak in such terms as He employed in these prophesyings of Jeremiah; these are among the most interesting and remarkable things in our Old Testament Scriptures.

In these meditations it is not our purpose to consider the whole prophecy by way of analysis or full exposition; but to listen for the accents of the voice Divine, and attend to the messages which came through Jeremiah, remembering that in them we have the word of God to His people in an age of failure.

We take first the paragraph at the commencement of the book, constituting, as it does, the title-page.

The title-page shows that the particular age in which the messages were delivered, was that of the last forty years of the history of Judah. The central declaration of the paragraph, " The word of Jehovah came," reveals the supreme value of the book.

Our present theme then is that of the nature of the age; and that of the fact and the purpose of the word of Jehovah in such an age.

The nature of the age we will attempt to understand; first, by recalling the kings, and the character of their reigns; secondly, by reminding ourselves of three epoch-marking events of the period of the ministry of Jeremiah; and that in order that we may understand the condition of the people to whom these messages were sent.

During the period of Jeremiah's prophesying, there were five kings, but Jeremiah mentions three only, probably because the other two sat upon the throne of Judah for so brief a period. Josiah reigned eighteen years after Jeremiah commenced his ministry, and he was followed by Jehoahaz who only reigned for three months. Then Jehoiakim reigned for eleven years, and was followed by Jehoiachin, who reigned for only three months. Zedekiah followed, and reigned for eleven years. The two brief reigns Jeremiah does not name; and so in this paragraph we have the three names, Josiah, Jehoiakim, and Zedekiah.

Josiah came to the throne in a remarkable time. If we look back to the hour of his accession, thirteen years before Jeremiah commenced his ministry, we see in the distance the light and the glory of the wonderful reign of Hezekiah; but removed by more than half a century from the time of Josiah. During the reign of Hezekiah, there shone and flamed over Judah the glorious light of the ministry of the great Isaiah. Immediately after the death of Hezekiah, Manasseh succeeded to the throne, and the nation was plunged with terrific suddenness into the uttermost corruption. The nation was involved in almost every form of heathen abomination, and all the corruptions issuing from such practices. Manasseh was followed by Amon; and then Josiah succeeded. He was conscious of the terrible condition of the nation; and after a time cleansed the temple, and attempted to restore the Divine worship. In the process of that cleansing, the book of the law was discovered. This was followed by more thorough reform, which, nevertheless, so far as the nation was concerned, was a reform entirely upon the surface of things, never finding its way into the depth of the national character. The people were simply swayed by the popularity of the king, and there was no return to God on their part.

Then came the death of Josiah, and he was succeeded by Jehoahaz, who reigned only three months, and was succeeded by Jehoiakim, first a vassal of Egypt, and then a vassal of Babylon. Jehoiachin followed for three months, and was succeeded by Zedekiah, whose reign was a period of religious darkness, moral corruption, political intrigue; during which the nation moved rapidly downward, toward the catastrophe which at last overtook it. Throughout this whole period Jeremiah uttered the word of Jehovah, and was mocked and scoffed at, persecuted and imprisoned, a man of loneliness and of tears.

The three remarkable events that must always be borne in mind if we are to understand the period were: first, the battle of Carchemish between Judah and Egypt, in which Josiah died; secondly, the battle, again at Carchemish, between Egypt and Babylon, when Babylon won its victory over Egypt, and all that region passed under the sway of Babylon; and finally, the fall of Jerusalem itself. Jeremiah exercised his ministry in a period when these epoch-marking events succeeded each other, events of world-wide interest and influence.

Now let us consider carefully what all this really meant. Who were these people? We must begin there. It is only as we do so, that we shall understand the depth of this degradation. I answer my question by quoting from an apostolic description. When Paul was writing his letter to the Romans and contrasting the Jew and the Gentile for Gentile readers, he asked what advantage the Jew had, what were the things that gave the Jew peculiar privilege, position, or favour; and he answered his question by saying that to them belonged the adoption, the glory, and the covenants; the law, the service, and the promises; the fathers, and the Messiah. The *adoption;* that is, the Divine election, the fact that God had chosen them as His own, for definite and specific work. The *glory;* that is the Divine presence, manifesting itself among them in those olden days, by the mystic shining of the Shekinah light between the cherubim on the mercy-seat, and in many other ways, in the course of their history. The *covenants;* that is the covenants of the wilderness, the original covenant with Abraham, and successive covenants made in hours of need; all which constituted the Divine fellowship. The *law;* the Divine instruction, meeting the needs of the people, conditioning their life, so that it might harmonize with His good and acceptable and perfect will. The *service;* that ritual of worship, the pattern of which had been given to them so particularly by the servant of God; and constituted the method of their approach to Himself. The *promises;* declaring the Divine intention for them, and for the world through them. The *fathers;* the whole of their history so far back as Abraham. The *Christ;* the Divine prophecy and intention for the world, to be fulfilled through them.

Judah represented all these things. They were the people of the Divine election, the Divine presence, the Divine fellowship, the Divine instruction, the Divine mediation, the Divine intention, the Divine history, the Divine prophecy for the world. These are the people whom we see moving surely, swiftly, awfully toward doom. It is only as we see this height, that we are able to sense the situation to which the prophet spoke, or to apprehend the depth of the degradation to which this nation of Judah had passed.

Let us attempt to see the depth by glancing on in this prophecy to the second chapter, where we have a summary of the whole story, in verse thirteen: "My people have committed two evils." We do not understand that unless we lay emphasis upon the first word, "My people." It is the height of privilege which reveals the depth of degradation and failure. "My people have committed two evils; they have forsaken Me the fountain of living waters, and hewed them out cisterns, broken cisterns, that can hold no water." They had forsaken Jehovah. That was the first evil, the fundamental evil, the evil out of which all other evils had sprung. Every evil that cursed them nationally, socially, and politically; blighting, blasting, and mildew; grew out of this fundamental thing: they had forsaken Jehovah the fountain of living waters. Then, with fine poetic satire the prophet described what they had done, they had "hewed them out cisterns, broken cisterns, that can hold no water." In other words, the nation as a nation, forsaking God, had given itself to policy, instead of obedience; to the manipulation of its own affairs of state, to the attempts to play off one nation against the other, in the hope of securing their own safety. The nation that had forgotten God, the fountain of living waters; had been hewing for itself cisterns, broken cisterns, that could hold no water.

There is no darker page in all the history of the people of God than this, for Judah had the solemn warning of the northern kingdom of Israel, as they had been swept away into captivity. They had heard the tremendous appeal of Hosea the prophet to Israel. While preaching to the northern kingdom, he had ever and anon uttered a message to Judah in the south: " Ephraim is joined to idols; let him alone." This was not the doom of Ephraim. God was not saying, I am going to

[14]

let Ephraim alone. It was Hosea's message to Judah. The northern kingdom of Israel was joined to idols, and Hosea said to the southern kingdom, Let Ephraim alone, let there be no league between the north and the south, for the north is corrupt.

Judah had received that message. She had seen Israel, joined to idols, carried to captivity. She knew that upon the northern border of her territory was a barren land, because a people had forsaken God. Yet, in spite of this, she forsook the fountain of living waters, she hewed cisterns to herself, she prosecuted policies and intrigues and manipulations, and she forgot God; swiftly and yet more swiftly she ran resolutely from God, and out toward the darkness; until the hour came when the Chaldeans captured her city, and she also became a people scattered and peeled.

Yet, during all that period, the word of Jehovah came insistently and persistently. This speaks to us of the faithfulness of God amid the unfaithfulness of His people. As we read the prophecy of Jeremiah, we find a phrase, occurring in other books of the Bible, but never in the same way or the same connection. It is the phrase, "*rising early.*" Jeremiah is the only one who used this phrase of God. Eleven times over, at different stages in his ministry, as that ministry is recorded for us, we find him speaking of God as rising early. Of course it is but a figure of speech, but it is a figure of speech intended to impress upon the soul something that needs to be remembered. "Rising early"; and the word means quite simply to incline; then to incline the shoulder in order that a burden may be put upon it; until finally it was used only of loading up either beast or man, to start a journey in the early hours of the morning. Rising early, bending the shoulder to the burden, and starting!

Now Jeremiah took that old phrase, and used it of God. He declared that He came to His people, rising early and speaking to them, three times; rising early and sending to them, six times; once, rising early, protesting to them; and once, rising early, teaching them, that is teaching by discipline, goading. The phrase, so often recurring in the prophecy, is in itself illuminative. It gives us a picture of the attitude of God; His people rushing away from Him, forsaking Him, forgetting Him; but He, never rushing away from them, never forsaking them, never forgetting them; rising early, bending His shoulder to the burden, and hastening to speak, to send, to protest, to teach.

This fact does more than reveal the faithfulness of God. There was a reason for this coming of the word of Jehovah, during that dark age. It constituted a Divine Self-revelation in times of darkness, and for times of future darkness. We are inclined to say, What was the use of it? God knew that the people would not obey. He told Jeremiah so. Then why did the word of God persistently come? If there be no other reason, it came in order to give us this prophecy; in order that through all subsequent history, and in every hour of darkness, we may return to it, find what God thought, what God felt, and discover wherein these men failed. In the fact of the coming of the word of Jehovah by Jeremiah I have an Old Testament exposition of the New Testament word of the apostle John, when he wrote his Gospel, "The light shineth in the darkness; and the darkness apprehended it not," could not extinguish it. The light that shines in the darkness of to-day, if to-day will not have it, is light for some other day, in order that men may be saved from a similar darkness.

The immediate purpose of this coming of the word of Jehovah is most poetically set forth in this first chapter in one verse. In the tenth verse, in the commissioning of Jeremiah, Jehovah is reported as saying to him, " I have this day set thee over the nations and over the kingdoms, to pluck up and to break down, and to destroy and to overthrow, to build and to plant." Do we really see how remarkable a word that is? Jeremiah? Jeremiah the priest of Anathoth? Jeremiah, whom priests will laugh at, and false prophets buffet, and kings despise? Yes, of him Jehovah said: "*I* have set *thee* over the nations."

The man to whom the word of Jehovah comes is the man of value. "In the fifteenth year of the reign of Tiberius Cæsar, Pontius Pilate being governor of Judæa, and Herod being tetrarch of Galilee, and his brother Philip tetrarch of the region of Ituræa and Trachonitis, and Lysanias tetrarch of Abilene, in the high-priesthood of Annas and Caiaphas." Seven notable men all needed to mark an hour, but none of them needed for anything in the hour that was of value. In that hour, "The word of God came unto John." Luke uses all these dignitaries; emperor, tetrarchs, governors, and high priests, simply to indicate the time when the word of God came to a man named John. The word of God passed emperor, passed the tetrarchs, passed the priests, and found a man rough and rugged, an ascetic of the desert, and came to him. In the higher heights, for the recording angels, writing human history, the epoch-marking fact was nothing at Rome, nothing in the palaces of the tetrarchs, nothing in the courts of the high priests, but the fact that the word of God came to a man. The same principle is discovered in the words to Jeremiah, "I have set thee over the nations and over the kingdoms."

The purpose of the word of God to him is revealed in four words that speak of destruction, and in two that speak of construction. Four of destruction, "to pluck up and to break down, and to destroy and to overthrow." Two that speak of construction, "to build, and to plant."

Our English translation hardly carries over the poetic imagery of the Hebrew words. "To pluck up," literally to tear away, to tear up something growing. "To break down"; that is to raze to the ground something that has been erected. The next figure returns to the plant; "to destroy," that is, the plant taken up by the roots, is now left to perish. The next, "to overthrow," goes back to the figure of the building, and means to break in pieces, to grind to powder that which has been torn down. Thus two poetic figures merge in the prophet's declaration; the figure of that which is planted, and the figure of that which is built; and the method is that of alternation. Is this thing planted? Then thou shalt tear it up. Is it built? Then thou shalt tear it down. Is it planted? Then that which thou hast torn up, thou shalt leave to perish. Is it built? Then thou shalt break the stones to pieces. This is the destructive work of the word.

Then follow the words "To build, and to plant," which suggest the constructive side of the prophetic ministry. Verily "The waster seems the builder too." That is always the twofold activity of the word of God. The word of God is for the plucking up and destruction of the plants which are not of God's own planting. The word of God is for the breaking down and the overthrowing of the buildings of which He has not laid the foundations. But the word of God is not for ultimate overthrow and destruction. It is for construction; it is for planting according to His will, and for building according to His line and His plummet.

Thus this lonely man in a decadent age,—the word of God burning like a fire within him, terrifically conscious that he was doing nothing if his work were measured by human statistics—was rooting up and planting, flinging down and building up; for the word of Jehovah is never void of power. The men of the age saw the prophet in the dungeon, saw him escape the dungeon, saw him in Egypt, and thought his mission a failure. Yet that word of God by Jeremiah was part of the work of God, and contributed to the ultimate victory.

The lessons of this background of history may very briefly be expressed. A great history is a grave responsibility. If Judah, the last remnant of the Hebrew national life, had the adoption, the glory, the covenants, the service, the promises, the fathers, and the Christ; then their responsibility was all the graver. Any nation that has a great history has a grave responsibility. For a people to boast in the glory of the past, and to deny the secret that made the past, is to perish. To forget and forsake the fountain of living waters, Jehovah, is to perish. The word of Jehovah persistently heard and disobeyed, ceases to appeal. I sometimes wonder if that is not the peculiar peril of our own time. We have said that we have been neglecting the Bible, but why? Because we have known it so well, and have not obeyed it, and it has become an idle story to us.

The lessons of the foreground are that God still continues to speak, whether men will hear, or whether they will forbear; and that the word of God is the only thing not void of power in a decadent age; it destroys, it preserves. It is possible that the word of Jehovah may be uttered, and men may not detect it as the word of Jehovah, and so may murder the messenger. We need to pray, not merely that the word of Jehovah may come to us, but that we may know it when it comes, lest we also perish by the way, and that, with the blood of the messenger upon our hands.

II

THE INSTRUMENT

Preparatory Reading: Jeremiah 1 : 4-19.

" Then said I, Ah, Lord Jehovah! behold, I know not how to speak: for I am a child."—JEREMIAH 1 : 6.

THESE words reveal the mental attitude of Jeremiah, in view of the sacred and solemn responsibility to which he was called. There are two matters for our consideration; first that of the man himself as he is revealed in this chapter; and secondly and principally, that of the Divine method with him, in order that he might be the instrument through whom the word of Jehovah would be spoken.

It may be said that such a meditation as this would be fitting for those who are called to the public ministry of the Word. It is well therefore that we remind ourselves that all the people of God are called to the proclamation of the Word of God in this age. When the Spirit rested on Eldad and Medad, and they prophesied, Joshua appealed to Moses to forbid them, and he replied, "Art thou jealous for my sake? Would that all Jehovah's people were prophets." The day when all the Lord's people were enabled to become prophets dawned after Messiah had come, had accomplished His sacred ministry, had ascended on high, leading captivity captive and receiving gifts for men; and having received the Holy Spirit, He had poured out the Gift constituting the Christian Church; thus calling every member of the Christian Church to the sacred business of prophesying and equipping them for the service. "In that day," said

Joel, " I will pour out My Spirit upon all flesh, and your sons and your daughters shall prophesy . . . upon the servants and upon the handmaids . . . will I pour out My Spirit." That prophecy, Peter claimed as fulfilled at Pentecost. Therefore there is a pertinent application of such a study as this, to all those who bear the holy name, and wear the holy sign; for we are all called to be the Lord's witnesses, His prophets, the instruments through whom He proclaims His word to-day.

Jeremiah was a young priest, living in Anathoth, one of the priestly cities. He was the son of Hilkiah. There are differences of opinion as to who this Hilkiah was, but a comparison of this passage with the story in the book of the Kings makes it extremely probable that the father of Jeremiah was the high priest, who in the reign of Josiah, discovered the book of the law. That book was discovered five years after Jeremiah had received his call to prophetic ministry, and the quotations from the first five books of Moses, found in his messages, show how his mind was saturated with its teaching.

Another matter to be remembered is that Jeremiah's uncle, Shallum, was the husband of Huldah the prophetess, to whom the deputation was sent in the days of Josiah, to inquire as to the proposed reformation.

Again, Ahikam, the son of Shaphan the scribe, protected Jeremiah when all the elders of Judah were against him; and there can be little doubt that this was the man who helped Hilkiah and Josiah in the work of reformation.

Thus in days of decadence in the national history, Jeremiah was born, and lived in an atmosphere created by those elect souls who knew the ways of Jehovah, and who strove, according to their light, to serve Him in circumstances of grave difficulty.

So much for the facts concerning the man suggested by the title-page. Now let us attempt to see him as he is revealed in this story of his call to prophetic ministry.

The fact that this passage prefaces the prophecies, is in itself suggestive. In the book of Jeremiah we have the account of a spoken ministry, and of a written ministry. When these messages, which he had delivered over that long period of forty years, were gathered together and written, probably by Baruch, Jeremiah prefaced them with the account of how he was called to prophetic work, and thus revealed himself to us. The story demonstrates the fact that he was a man living in fellowship with God in the midst of the dark age. The word of Jehovah which is to be delivered to an age, to nations, to men, always comes to souls prepared to receive it, by acquaintance with the Secret Place. When God has need of the proclamation of His word, He must find as an instrument, one who in his own personal and private life has become familiar with the voice of God. The call is often sudden, but it is always spoken to a man who is already in the Divine secret, knowing something of the ways of God. The word of Jehovah came to him, and he was listening, or he had not heard the word.

The story is one of reverent familiarity with God, and of reticent boldness. He is seen shrinking from the work, and yet ready for it; always shrinking, never shrinking; always trembling, never trembling; always shrinking when talking to God about his work, never shrinking when talking to men about his God; always trembling when in the Secret Place he waited the whisper of the voice Divine, never trembling when he thundered forth the secret that he had heard.

Now let us fasten our attention upon the man as revealed in the actual words of the text: " Then said I, Ah, Lord Jehovah! behold, I know not how to speak: for I am a child." That was his response to an almost terrific word; " Before I formed thee in the belly I knew thee, and before thou camest forth out of the womb I sanctified thee: I have appointed thee a prophet unto the nations." It is only as we dare to let our imagination help us that we can understand this. Should such a word of God come, in the whisper of the night, in the matin of the morning, borne into the silent recesses of the soul of some one of us; how terrific, how appalling it would be! How should we answer? This man cried: "Ah, Lord Jehovah! behold, I know not how to speak: for I am a child." That was the cry of weakness, not of unwillingness. I *know not how to* speak; not I *will not* speak. It was a cry born of the consciousness of the awful dignity of the position to which God was calling, of the supreme and overwhelming majesty of having to deliver the word of God to the nations. It was the recognition of a destiny from which there could be no escape, and the sobbing declaration of inability to fulfil the destiny. Jeremiah heard the call of God as that of his Supreme Lord, Who was the mighty God. In the very name he used there was a revelation of his sense of destiny, "Ah, Sovereign Lord Jehovah!" That was the response of willingness, expressing itself in an almost agonized cry of weakness.

When God called Moses to his work, he said, "I am not eloquent," and God patiently dealt with him. Moses persisted in his rebellion until "The anger of Jehovah was kindled against Moses." The anger of Jehovah was not kindled against Jeremiah. The Divine answer was full of grace, full of tenderness, an answer to his sense of weakness, assuring him of sufficient strength. From that moment the man went forward to the most difficult, the most hopeless, the most heroic ministry, of any of the Hebrew prophets.

Thus we see him, a young priest, born and reared in the atmosphere of elect souls who believed in God; himself reverent and familiar with God, knowing the secret of fellowship; called, and answering the call with the cry that told of his weakness, and yet realized his destiny.

STUDIES IN THE PROPHECY OF JEREMIAH

The supreme glory of this story is its revelation of God's method with Jeremiah; and because we cannot cover all the ground fully, and yet do desire to see the whole movement accurately, let me at once, by the use of four simple words, indicate the method of God in the preparation of the man who was to be the instrument for delivering His word. The method was that of ordination, revelation, illustration, and exhortation.

As to his ordination God said four things to him: "I knew thee . . . I formed thee . . . I sanctified thee; I have appointed thee." The first three had reference to pre-natal ordination. The last, "I have appointed thee," referred to his actual and personal ordination.

The word in this declaration of ordination which carries the mind furthest back, is not the word "I formed thee," but that which in statement comes second, "I knew thee." "I knew thee" before "I formed thee"; and so "I formed thee." Therefore also "I sanctified thee," separated thee, before thou wast born, to this very ministry. Now upon the basis of My foreknowledge, of My creation, of My sanctification, I have appointed thee!

What strength is here in spite of all weakness, that God shall say to a man, "I have appointed thee," and that because "I sanctified thee" to this work before thy birth; and "I sanctified thee" to this work before thy birth because "I formed thee" and "I knew thee." In thy very being is the stuff I need for the doing of this work, for thou art in thyself My handiwork; I formed and fashioned thee according to the pattern of My foreknowledge of thee!

If Jeremiah really heard that, and Jeremiah believed that, then we need not be surprised either at his fear or his courage! Here was a man going now to prophetic ministry under this supreme, awe-inspiring, courage-begetting conviction that the responsibility was on God,

Who knew him, formed him, sanctified him, appointed him! That was how he became like a brazen wall to his enemies; that is what filled him with courage as the days ran on, those drear dark days, and made him sing his songs of hope, when he was in the dungeon!

The method of God was not only this fore-ordination; but the fact that He revealed it to the man. When there came out of Jeremiah's soul the cry of his conscious weakness: " Alas, supreme Lord and mighty Jehovah! I know not how to speak; for I am a child "; then God is seen accommodating Himself to the man's weakness in the most wonderful way. He said, I am a child. Jehovah said to him, " Say not, I am a child: for to whomsoever I shall send thee thou shalt go "; the strength of thy going is to be in My sending. He said, " I know not how to speak." God said to him, " Whatsoever I shall command thee thou shalt speak." At the moment you feel you never can, because you are but a child; you will do it, because whether you are a child or not, I am sending you! Then He spoke the final and inclusive word, " I am with thee." Link that to the revelation of ordination, and the Divine assurance is complete; " I knew thee, I formed thee, I sanctified thee, I have appointed thee, I am with thee."

Then God touched his mouth. How? Who can tell? In this hour of revelation Jeremiah was very much out of himself; away from the consciousness of the near things, the material things, the sensual things; high lifted above them. Then God touched his mouth, and He said: Thus My words are in thy mouth. Jeremiah had said, I cannot speak. God replied: Thou needest not speak of thyself. I have put My words in thy mouth instead of thy speech. The words of Jehovah were to take the place of the speaking of Jeremiah. These words were to be the only powerful things in that degenerate age. They were to be destructive and constructive. The words that were to pass the lips of

Jeremiah, being the words of God, communicated by the touch of His hand, and the supremacy of His will, would be for tearing up and flinging down, for destruction; but they would also be for building and for planting.

God went further yet with him in preparation. He passed beyond the facts of ordination and revelation, to illustration. He asked him, "What seest thou?" And he answered, "I see the rod of an almond-tree." As a matter of fact, he did not use the actual word for almond-tree, but the figurative word. Some translators have rendered the passage thus: "What seest thou?" . . . "I see a rod of an *awake* tree." . . . "Thou seest well, for I am *awake* in the matter of My word." Or, "I see the rod of a *watch* tree." "Thou seest well, for I *watch* over My word."

The almond-tree is covered with blossom before the time of leaf; and in ancient use was the symbol of the spring-time. The word of Jehovah was not precious in those days. As the days passed on, Jeremiah would increasingly feel as though the word of God had lost its power, and Jehovah said to him ere he began to proclaim the word of Jehovah, I am watching over My word; even though the death of winter is over all the land, I watch over My word.

Yet again God asked His servant, "What seest thou?" and he replied: "I see a boiling caldron; and the face thereof is from the north," that is, so that evidently soon its hot, seething, scorching, blasting contents will be poured out over this southland. It was a figure of speech absolutely true to the political situation at the moment, for in the north four great nations were fighting against one another, and evidently to the eye of the true statesman—and the prophets of God were always statesmen—the hour was approaching when one of them would gain the mastery over the rest.

Then God said to him, "Out of the north evil shall

break forth upon all the inhabitants of the land." Thus Jeremiah learned another secret. God did not reveal to him that war was raging among the nations in the north; he knew that. He did not reveal to him that in all probability the caldron would overflow the southland. The revelation was that God was presiding over the tumult; that the things that would come to pass were under His control.

These are the things that the prophet of God must know. First that the word of Jehovah is the blossoming almond-tree, full of life; and that God will care for it on the darkest winter day. Secondly, that all tumult and strife and clash of arms are under the Divine government.

Then followed the word of exhortation. "Thou therefore." That word *therefore* is the word I want to have emphasized in this chapter. That is the word I would bring out in letters of red if I could, so that whenever my eye glanced at it, I should be arrested. "Thou *therefore!*" Wherefore? Because God is watching over His word; because God is presiding over all the tumult and the strife of the nations! *Therefore!* "Gird up thy loins, and arise, and speak!"

The abiding condition for the proclamation of the word of Jehovah, on the human side, is that of the consciousness which found utterance in the case of Jeremiah in the words of our text. It is the man who says: "Ah, Lord Jehovah! I know not how to speak: for I am a child," who is the instrument God can use. That cry of the prophet was born of his sense of the solemnity and supreme importance of the word which he was called to deliver. If a man thinks lightly of the word of God, he can preach easily; but such preaching is valueless! If the word of God is a light matter, or a matter not particularly vital, then there is no burden, no travail, and no agony! When the word of Jehovah is a fire in the bones, an agony in the soul, a terrific thing;

then a man says, " Ah, Lord Jehovah! I know not how to speak: for I am a child." That is the finest of all fine revelations of competence, a child; just a child; folly against subtlety, frailty against strength. That is what God wants.

If this first chapter of Jeremiah is to do what God means it to do for us, it will not discourage, but encourage us. It is the little child who shall lead in millennial glories. It is out of the mouths of babes and sucklings that God ordains His mighty strength. Not to the wise and prudent, but to the souls conscious of inability, He communicates ability, for the proclamation of His word.

Therefore the abiding right to proclaim the word of Jehovah is the conviction of Divine authority. The Divine ordination and the Divine revelation of that ordination to the soul of a man; these things are necessary, if we have to preach to thousands, or talk to tens, or deal with one soul, about the word of Jehovah.

Finally, the abiding condition for proclaiming the word of Jehovah on the Divine side, is that of the consciousness of the sufficiency of God for all He appoints. Lord, I know not how to speak! Thou wilt speak exactly what I give thee! Lord, I am only a child! I am with thee! As we hear these words spoken to our souls, then we dare not adventure forth in our own strength; but we dare in His strength!

III

THE CHALLENGE OF GOD

Preparatory Readings: Jeremiah 2-4:2; 2 Chronicles 34:3-7.

"Thus saith Jehovah, What unrighteousness have your fathers found in Me, that they are gone far from Me, and have walked after vanity, and are become vain?"—JEREMIAH 2:5.

JEREMIAH'S solemn call to prophetic ministry came to him in the thirteenth year of the reign of King Josiah. From that time until the death of Josiah, eighteen years later, he exercised his ministry in circumstances of comparative peace. After that, tumult broke upon him. In eleven chapters, beginning with the second, and ending with the twelfth, we have the notes of his ministry during this earlier period.

In order that we may understand the bearing of this upon our meditation, let us rapidly review the history. Josiah began to reign when he was eight years old. In the eighth year of his reign, being then sixteen years old, he began to seek after God. Four years later, in the twelfth of his reign and the twentieth of his age, he began his first campaign against idolatry in Judah; and crossing the borderline, he passed through the cities of Manasseh and Ephraim and Simeon, even unto Naphtali, that is through the ruins of the cities of the northern kingdom of Israel, whose people had been carried away into captivity. There, among the remnants of the families of Israel, he carried on the same iconoclastic mission, breaking down idol shrines. In the thirteenth year of his reign, the year following, Jeremiah commenced his ministry. Five years later the book of the law was discovered, in the hour when Josiah was leading a new campaign at the very centre of Judah's life, in the cleansing of the Temple.

Round these facts we may group the prophecies of the eleven chapters in the book of Jeremiah, commencing with the second, and ending with the twelfth. Chapters two to six contain the notes of prophecies delivered during the first five years of his ministry, before the finding of the book of the law. Chapters seven to nine contain messages delivered in connection with the cleansing of the Temple, and the discovery of the book of the law. Chapters ten to twelve record the messages which Jeremiah delivered in connection with the more drastic reform which followed upon the discovery of the book of the law.

The historic background, then, of the words of our text is that of Josiah's earlier campaign against idolatry; and the character of the age is revealed in a flash in one statement of the prophet: "And yet for all this her treacherous sister Judah hath not returned unto Me with her whole heart, but feignedly, saith Jehovah" (3:10). It was a time of reform, but the reform was superficial. The king was perfectly sincere. Zeal for Jehovah of hosts possessed his soul, and he was determined to abolish idolatry, and to restore the people to the ways of God. The king moreover, was popular. His people loved him, and they followed him because this was his way and his will; but there was no depth in the national reformation. It was an age when evil was suppressed by legislation, but the heart of the people was alienated from God. A sincere and godly and high-souled young king attempted to enforce righteousness, but was quite unable to do it. The people followed him externally, superficially, but there was no turning of the heart to God.

The words of our text constituted the challenge of

Jehovah to His people at that time. " What unrighteousness have your fathers found in Me, that they are gone from Me, and have walked after vanity, and are become vain? " Everything that followed, during this period in the ministry of Jeremiah, was of the nature of argument, warning, and appeal. This was the central enquiry of God.

Let us first attempt to understand the facts causing the challenge as they are referred to in these words: " your fathers . . . are gone from Me, . . . have walked after vanity, . . . are become vain." In the second place we shall consider the challenge in itself: " What unrighteousness have your fathers found in Me? "

First then, the facts causing the challenge. Here, as so constantly, Holy Scripture is its own interpreter; and if we take this enquiry of Jehovah out of its setting, we shall surely miss its tremendous note and fail to hear the underlying passion of the Divine heart. This challenge of God followed immediately upon an affirmation:

" I remember concerning thee the kindness of thy youth, the love of thine espousals; how thou wentest after Me in the wilderness, in a land that was not sown. Israel was holiness unto Jehovah, the firstfruits of His increase."

" What unrighteousness have you found in Me that you have gone far from Me, that you have walked after vanity, that you have become vain? "

This reading of the affirmation, side by side with the challenge, reveals the fact that the challenge grew out of the affirmation, and that the conditions described therein were the exact opposite of those obtaining in the early days.

They may be placed yet more distinctly in contrast.

" I remember concerning thee the kindness of thy youth, the love of thine espousals."

" Your fathers . . . are gone far from Me."

" How thou wentest after Me in the wilderness, in a land that was not sown."

". . . And have walked after vanity."

" Israel was holiness unto Jehovah, the firstfruits of His increase."

". . . And are become vain."

The condition causing the challenge can only be understood as we go back to the height of the estate from which the people had fallen. The days of old were described in plaintive language, thrilling with emotion, warm with a tender affection, as Jehovah made use of the most sacred figures of speech, speaking of Himself as the Lover, and of His people as the loved. " I remember concerning thee the kindness of thy youth," that is; I remember concerning thee the attitude and the activity of affection that characterized the beginning of thy history. I remember concerning thee, that bowing of the face upon My bosom, which was the abandonment of love, and the outward expression of it. I remember concerning thee the love of thine espousals, the answer of thy virgin heart to the wooing of My love. But now everything was changed. " They are gone far from Me." This was God's view of His people. They were away from Him. Love had failed, and all the tokens of love were absent. This figure of speech constantly recurs in the Scriptures. God reveals the true nature of His thought of His people in the language of love, employing the highest consciousness of human love as illustration; " I have betrothed thee unto Me for ever." In the tragedy and agony and sob and travail of Hosea's great prophecy delivered to Israel, the figure employed was that of God's attitude toward His people as Husband, while the sin of the people was that of the infidelity of the wife. The heart must interpret this sob and this agony. God is seen bending over His people, and saying: I remember for thee the kindness of thy youth, the love of thine espousals; but thou art away from Me,

[32]

thou art at a distance, there is failure of love, and absence of all the tokens of love!

The result in the case of the people is revealed in the second contrast. They who walked after God in the wilderness in a land that was not sown now walked after vanity.

These people were thus taken back in imagination to those days at the beginning of their national consciousness and history, when He led them forth by a high hand out of Egypt to the wilderness, a people to Himself. They followed Him then independently of advantage; into the wilderness, into a land that was not sown. In those days they followed Him for His own sake; and for very love of Him were content to follow Him even into a barren land, a land not sown. Now they were seeking advantage, by compromise and policies, hewing out to themselves broken cisterns unable to hold water; and thus they were losing advantage, while they sought it. In the days when they sought no advantage, but love of God, He guarded, kept, delivered, and made them great. Now at a distance from Him, seeking their own advantage by policies and intrigues and ways of cunning, they had " become vain."

The final contrast is as remarkable as the others. Israel was holiness to Jehovah, sacred to Him, clean to Him, separated to Himself; and therefore Israel was guarded in that strength of character, against all the forces that could be against her, but Israel had become vain, void, foolish, the prey of her enemies.

The whole picture is a revelation of the lost strength of character, and the futile strength of circumstance. In the old days the nation had been true to God, answering His call out of love, following Him even into the wilderness contentedly, because He was God. Those were the days of her strength. Before she was organized into national consciousness or constitution, before any army had been raised, before any policy had been formulated, when in her youth and affectionate regard for God she followed Him, then had she been strong and safe. But now she was trusting to the circumstance of the hour, attempting to strengthen her borders by intrigue, and alliances with other peoples; entering into negotiations for alliance with Egypt, and hoping to win the favour of Assyria; and all this because she had lost her strength of character.

That consideration of the condition of the people is of value because it helps us to understand the challenge of God. In effect God, through His servant, demanded of the people that they should declare the reason of this deflection. Why have you left Me? Why have you gone after vanity? How is it that you have become vain? And He made the challenge personal as to Himself in the remarkable words of this text: "What unrighteousness have your fathers found in Me?" God challenged His people to read their history in the light of His relationship thereto, and His relationship to themselves. He challenged the king and the rulers, the princes, the priests, and the prophets, to go back over all the history from those days of their youth when He made them a nation, and they were strong in their love of Him; and to say wherein He had failed. As though He had said to them: What covenant have I broken that I have made with you? What deceit have I practised in My dealings with you? What promise have I disregarded in My guidance of you?

For the moment, we have the amazing picture of God taking the high line of argument that suggests the loyalty of His people, and His own disloyalty: If you have turned from Me Who loved you so; if you have abandoned Me and wandered to a distance, who once bent upon My bosom, and leaning there were strong; there must be a reason for it! Is it in Me? What covenant have I broken? What deceit have I practised? What promises have I disregarded? What unrighteousness have you found in Me? It was the challenge of wounded love. It was the challenge of conscious faithfulness. It was the challenge of the God of absolute integrity and fidelity to covenants. Why have you left Me? What unrighteousness have you found in Me? The very method of the enquiry serves as an exclusion of the idea that their deflection could be due to faithlessness on His part.

The challenge has a deeper note; and by its suggestion we are led to the heart of the matter, and discover why these people had turned their back upon Him. There is light upon the enquiry in a following paragraph:

" Pass over to the isles of Kittim, and see; and send unto Kedar, and consider diligently; and see if there hath been such a thing. Hath a nation changed its gods, which yet are no gods? but My people have changed their glory for that which doth not profit " (2: 10, 11).

In these words the attention of the people was directed to the nations outside. They were charged to observe the fidelity of these people to their gods; and to put that into contrast with their own infidelity to God; and yet these were false gods. The God of Israel was the true and faithful God, but His people had abandoned Him, and in doing so had abandoned their own glory, and that which profited them.

This fidelity to false gods, and unfaithfulness to the true God is extremely modern. If we glance at the religious world, we find that the most glaring infidelity exists in the Christian Church; men of other religions are far truer to their religious conceptions than we are to ours. For instance, the followers of Mohammed are far more loyal to him than we are to Christ. I suggest this immediate application in order that we may understand the prophecy; and I refer to this paragraph in order that we may understand the mystery of this departure from God. The reason may best be stated in the form of a paradox. This very fact of the failure of the ancient people of God, and of the Church, is a revelation of the supremacy of Divine religion, over every other form of religion. The gods to which men were faithful were the gods which they had made for themselves, gods which they had evolved out of their own consciousness. When a man makes a god according to the pattern of his own being, he makes a god like himself, an enlargement of his own imperfection. Moreover, the god which a man makes for himself, will demand from him that which is according to his own nature. It is clearly evident in Mohammedanism. Great and wonderful and outstanding in his personality as Mohammed was, yet the blighting sensuality of the man curses the whole of Islam to-day. Men will be faithful to those gods who make no demands upon them which are out of harmony with the desires of their own hearts.

When God calls men, it is the call of the God of holiness, the God of purity, the God of love; and He demands that they rise to His height. He cannot accommodate Himself to the depravity of their nature. He will not consent to the things of desire within them that are of impurity and evil. He calls men up, and ever higher, until they reach the height of perfect conformity to His holiness. God's call to humanity is always first pure, and then peaceable; first holy, and then happy; first righteous, and then rejoicing.

That is why Israel failed. Her departure from God was due to the fact that she declined to respond to His call to the highest. Wherever you find a people turning back from God, it is not that they are unconscious of His holiness, but that they are conscious of it; not that they are unconvinced of the high ideals of His requirements, but that they are convinced. This principle finds its central focussing in the life of Jesus. When He began to talk to His disciples in mystic language about eating His flesh and drinking His blood, they said, This is a hard saying, and many of them went back, and walked no more with Him. Why did they go back? Because they did not understand Him? No; but because they did understand Him, and they were not prepared to follow. Why has any nation which has seen the glory of God drawn back? Not because it did not understand, but because it did understand. Not because it failed to apprehend the glory; but because it apprehended the glory, but was not prepared to pay the price. Not because there was unrighteousness in God had Israel left Him; but because there was righteousness in God, and Israel was not prepared to follow. God calls to the highest, and so calls that there can be no mistaking Him; and if men fall back after a period of following, it is not because of mystery, but because of light which they are not prepared to follow.

Observe finally the purpose of this challenge of Jehovah. This is revealed in the course of the prophetic messages. "Wherefore I will yet contend with you, saith Jehovah, and with your children's children." . . . "Wilt thou not from this time cry unto Me, My Father, Thou art the Guide of my youth?" . . . "If thou wilt return, O Israel, saith Jehovah, unto Me shalt thou return." These outstanding words show that the purpose of the challenge was not condemnation, but deliverance. The burning, searching word of God, that shames the soul of a man, is not intended to bow him down and crush him; but again to lift him to the heights, to lift him to love, to call him to the realization of that which is highest and best.

A meditation such as this carries its own message. Departure from God is the secret of national degeneration. Whatever nation has received the special favour of the light of the Divine revelation, remains great as she walks in that light. If such a nation turn her back upon the light because of its brightness, decline to follow because of the glory of the ideal, then nothing can save her. The reason of such departure from God is always that of refusal of the highest, and reversion to the base. Its issue is always vanity; vanity which may express itself as pride of place and power created by confidence in circumstance, and hope in the cunning of policy. When a nation has come to such confidence, having once seen the glory of the face of God, that nation is on the sloping declivity to unutterable ruin. When a nation, to which God has given the revelation of the supreme truth that character is strength; and that the character which is strength, is that which results from response to Him, and His law of holiness and love; when such a nation turns her back upon God, it is because she is not prepared to pay the price of the high and the holy; and in such an action she resolutely turns back to the base and the low.

In proportion as a nation is in danger of doing that, then let it be recognized that there is only one way of salvation, that of return to God.

How is a nation to come to God? By remembering that righteousness must come before revenue; by remembering that purity is more important than pleasure; by recognizing the fact that the health of a people is more than the wealth of a few; by understanding that God is before mammon. In proportion as a nation shall recognize these things and return, that nation shall be restored to strength. Though her fidelity may lead her for a while into the wilderness, a land not sown, even there shall she be God-guarded. But if she forget, then all her treaties, and policies, and defence of circumstance, will not avail her. God's challenge to us to-day is this, "What unrighteousness have you found in Me, that you forget Me?"

IV

THE VERDICT OF MEN

Preparatory Readings: Jeremiah 4: 3—6; 2 Chronicles 34: 3-7.

" Refuse silver shall men call them, because Jehovah hath rejected them."—JEREMIAH 6: 30.

THIS is the last note in the prophetic ministry of Jeremiah during the earlier reforming campaign of king Josiah. As we saw in our last meditation, the true condition of the people is revealed in one clear declaration to be found in the third chapter and the tenth verse, " Judah hath not returned unto Me with her whole heart, but feignedly, saith Jehovah." The reformation under Josiah was perfectly genuine so far as the king was concerned, but so far as the nation was concerned, it was a mere following of a popular king, with no return of heart to God.

Three movements characterized the messages of the prophet during that period: first, an impeachment of the people; secondly, a call to them to return to Jehovah; and finally a clear foretelling of judgment. The first two of these notes we found in the section under review in our previous consideration. In this, the note is that of judgment. It is announced; its reason is declared; its instrument and process are described.

The prophet first declared that judgment was determined on. He appealed to the people to repent, and that not in external manifestation, but actually, and in heart. The people are described as panic-stricken, because of their imminent peril. In a parenthesis the prophet's anguish is revealed as he saw the judgment approaching.

He nevertheless continued his message, and described the swift attack of the foe, again earnestly appealing to Jerusalem to turn from wickedness. After this description his anguish was again manifested in a great lament. He was pained at his very heart, as he saw destruction coming, and the more so, as he recognized that it was the result of their own sin. The picture which spread itself before his vision was that of widespread devastation. Notwithstanding his sorrow, he declared that the judgment was inevitable because the word of Jehovah had been uttered; and he warned those of the anguish which must be their portion in the coming day of visitation.

Having thus declared that judgment was determined on in the Divine economy, the prophet with great care declared the reason of that judgment. This was first that of the utter corruption of conduct which prevailed. Among the people not a man was to be found who was truthful and just. Disappointed in his search, he turned to the great men and to the rulers, but they also had "broken the yoke and burst the bonds." Therefore judgment was now inevitable, and pardon impossible. The second reason was that of their unbelief of the very message which had been delivered. They had declared that the punishment announced would never fall upon them. The declaration of judgment was then repeated, and the terror of it described. When it fell, if they should inquire why Jehovah had visited them, the reply would be, because they had forsaken Him. Finally, the reason of judgment would be the revolting and rebellious heart of the people. They were not ignorant but obstinate. They had eyes but they saw not; and ears, but they heard not; they had deliberately flung off the fear of God. The greed of gain had been their curse, and had expressed itself in persistent rebellion. The whole reason was graphically summarized by the prophet as "a wonderful and horrible thing."

Prophets, priests, and people were united in their sin, and there was no alternative other than that of judgment.

This judgment the prophet then proceeded to describe. A fierce and relentless foe, yet acting under the word of Jehovah, was described as coming against Jerusalem. The prophet declared that the city would be taken, and described the thoroughness of the judgment under the figure of the gleaning of a field. All ages would be affected, and the whole land as well as the city involved.

And once again he declared the reason of this judgment to be the complete corruption of the people, their false sense of security, and their utter absence of shame. He made his appeal to the past to bear witness, but they would not attend. He made his appeal directly to the present, but they would not hearken. Therefore the sentence was inevitable. Returning to what he had already said, he again foretold the coming of the foe from the north, and the suffering of the people which must follow. This message concluded with an account of the word spoken to the prophet by Jehovah, in order to strengthen him. His position among the people was that of "a trier," or as the margin has it, a tower, that is one who tested them; and at the same time he was the one and only fortress for the troubled people. Yet his ministry would be fruitless, for the people were grievous revolters. Thus everything moved to this final declaration, that the ultimate verdict even of men outside the covenant, would be that this nation was refuse silver, because God had rejected it.

In this final outburst we find one declaration, two revelations, and three facts. For the interpretation of the one declaration, we need the two revelations, and the three facts. The one declaration is that men will call the people whom God refuses, *refuse silver*. The revelations of the text are those of a people rejected by

God and scorned by men. The three facts which the text suggests are: first, that which is not declared within the text, but without which the text would never have been written, and the condition which the text describes would never have obtained,—the people's refusal of God; secondly, God's consequent refusal of the people; and finally that when a privileged people refuse God, and He refuses them, then all other men count them reprobate, refuse, worthless.

Let us examine these three facts, in that order. First, the people's refusal of God. The master-thought of the text is revealed in a word twice repeated. In the Revised and Authorized Versions we are in danger of losing sight of this fact. The Revised reads " *Refuse* silver shall men call them, because Jehovah hath *rejected* them." The Authorized Version reads " *Reprobate* silver shall men call them, because the Lord hath *rejected* them." In the Hebrew the word is the same in each case, and this is realized if we read, " *Refuse* silver shall men call them, because Jehovah hath *refused* them." The value of noting this repetition is that it directs our attention to principles of importance. The Hebrew word literally means to spurn, to contemn, to despise. It occurs no less than eight times in these earlier messages of the prophet; (2:37), " Jehovah hath *rejected* those in whom thou trustest "; (3:3), " Thou *refusedst* to be ashamed " ; (4:30), " Thy lovers *despise* thee "; (5:3), " They have *refused* to receive correction: they have made their faces harder than a rock ; they have *refused* to return " ; (6:19), " As for My law, they have *rejected* it." And finally (6:30), " *Refuse* silver shall men call them, because Jehovah hath *rejected* them."

In these passages the word runs through the music like a minor note; and reveals the selfsame facts;—the people refusing God; God refusing the people; and men refusing the people who are refused by God.

In the first we have a declaration of God's contempt for the political intrigues of His people. They had been attempting to enter into an alliance with Egypt, as on a previous occasion they had made an alliance with Assyria. "Why gaddest thou about so much to change thy way? thou shalt be ashamed of Egypt also, as thou wast ashamed of Assyria. . . . Jehovah hath rejected those in whom thou trustest."

The next reveals Judah's contempt for chastisement. God had chastised her, had visited her with dispensations in order to her restoration to Himself; but she refused them, she held them in contempt.

The next records how, after charging Judah with infidelity to Jehovah and harlotry with other nations,—a terrific figure, yet common in the prophetic writings,—the prophet said, "Thy lovers despise thee." Judah was held in contempt by her allies, by Egypt and by Assyria, and by those through whom she was trying to make herself safe.

The next points out the fact that Judah held the correction of God and His instruction in contempt; and that consequently they would not repent.

The deepest word reveals the secret of Judah's failure; she had refused the law, rejected it, held it in contempt.

Thus we come to the culminating declaration, Men shall call her refuse silver, because God has refused her.

From that rapid survey it is evident that the underlying fact was that Judah had refused God, had rejected Him, had despised Him, had come in some way actually to hold Him in contempt. Moreover it must not be forgotten that these prophecies were uttered in an hour of reformation, in an hour of revival in religion. There can be a pernicious and deadly hardness of heart in the midst of emotional revival. Josiah was at this time prosecuting his earliest campaign of idol destruction; the people were following him, demonstrating with him, approving him; and the casual onlooker, the man not instructed of the Spirit of God, would have rejoiced in the national return to the ways of God. Yet, as a matter of fact, deep down in the national heart there was a contempt for God; and the expressions of this contempt are clearly marked in the passages I have read.

The dispensations of God produced no shame in the national heart. There was no sense of the sin of their own courses. The name of God was upon their lips, the reformation was the work of their hands, the destruction of idols was the occupation of the day; but in their heart there was no shame for their own sin; and God's dispensations, prophetic and judicial, failed to produce such a sense of shame. It was an hour of form devoid of any spiritual or moral power.

Consequently, the corrections of God produced no repentance, no change of mind, no change of heart, no turning back to those attitudes of the early days, when they had followed Him; recognizing His love, and yielding themselves to Him with full purpose of heart.

The final expression of their refusal of God was that His law was despised, rejected, refused, held in contempt.

These expressions of attitude demonstrated the fact of a lost love, a lost faith, and a lost obedience. In our last meditation we dwelt upon the lament of the heart of God, the wail of wounded love: " I remember concerning thee the kindness of thy youth, the love of thine espousals; how thou wentest after Me in the wilderness, in a land that was not sown." The nation had lost that love; the nation had lost the faith that proceeds out of such love; and the nation therefore had lost its loyalty. The nation had cast God off, practically, actually, inspirationally. His name was still upon her lips; a reform in honour of Him was in progress, and idols were being destroyed; and the people with chant and song

were following the king; but in their heart they were
away from God, they had refused Him.

That leads us to the observation of the second of these
facts, that of God's refusal of the people. That is named
in our text. Its main declaration is that men will refuse
the people; but that refusal is declared to result from
the fact that God will refuse the people.

Why did God reject Judah? God rejected Judah because He is a God of truth. God is a God of things as
they are. He sees things as they are. His estimate is
the estimate of the facts. Therefore to God a thing
which is contemptible in itself, is contemptible. God
never puts good for evil, or evil for good. His judgments are righteous judgments, that is judgments from
which there can be no appeal, because they utter
the absolute and actual facts of the case. Let me
quote once again that very remarkable declaration
in the prophetic writings concerning God's appointed
King, that He shall not judge by the sight of His
eyes, or the hearing of His ears, but with righteous
judgment. This is a most startling declaration; for
men judge by the sight of their eyes, or the hearing of their ears, and they can none other. Every
court of law in our own land, and in all civilized lands
carries on its procedure upon the basis of things seen
and things heard; and beyond that no earthly tribunal
can go. But God does not judge by the seeing of the
eye or the hearing of the ear; that is, not upon the report of witnesses, not upon evidence received, and sifted.
He needs no jury to sit with Him, and help Him to the
final understanding of any case. All things are naked
and open to the eyes of Him with Whom we have to
do.

When God looked upon the nation of Judah at this
time, He saw its reforming practices under the inspiration of the popularity of its king; but He saw the deeper
fact; He knew that the nation had become contemptible,

void, empty, worthless in all the deepest things that make for the strength of national life; and God's rejection of the nation was merely His acceptation of the fact that the nation had destroyed itself. In consonance with His holiness and His justice, and the fact that He is true, He could none other.

There is an illustration of all this in the passages we have already referred to. At that time Judah was attempting to make a political alliance with Egypt. A little while before she had made alliance with Assyria, and had been cruelly disappointed. Now, said the prophet, " Why gaddest thou about so much to change thy way? thou shalt be ashamed of Egypt also, as thou wast ashamed of Assyria."

This led up to the declaration, " The Lord hath rejected those in whom thou trustest." Why did God hold these political associations in contempt? Because they were contemptible, because they were worthless. It is not that God said: I alone will help Judah, and will permit none other to help her. That is not the idea. It is rather that of Judah turning from Him, Who was able to help her, and Who ever had helped her; and attempting to strengthen herself by making political alliances with people who cared nothing for her, but only for themselves, and who presently would break their alliance in order to serve their own ends; and therefore God rejected their confidences because they were unworthy. He held them to be contemptible because they were contemptible. When He rejected Judah, He rejected her not to make her contemptible, but because she was already contemptible; because by her attitude toward Himself she had sapped her own strength, and all the essential things of greatness in her national character had ebbed away, and were lost.

Not with gladness, but with sadness; not with any satisfaction to His own heart, but with a wail of lamentation and woe; God, the God of infinite truth, Whose judgments are absolutely righteous, rejected that which in itself had already become contemptible by reason of its own choices.

Therefore it must also be recognized that the reason of the rejection of the nation was that God is a God of love. To contemn love is to be contemptible. To trust in vanity is to be proved vain, and love demands reality. To refuse patience is to be proved worthless and love seeks value. We have false ideas of love, and sometimes when we have climbed to what seems to us to be the highest height, we are in danger of missing the profoundest value. Love, said Shakespeare,

> ". . . is not love,
> That alters when it alteration finds."

And if that be true—and how true it is—it has its chief exemplification in the God of the Bible. Yet it is also true that by reason of what love is in itself, love demands worth. It sees worth when no other eyes can see it. It goes after it when every one else has thought it impossible. In those matchless words of Paul, " Love hopeth all things, endureth all things. Love never faileth." But all the quest of love is for the perfecting of the loved one, and if it be conceivable,—and alas! in national life it has been illustrated, and in individual life also,—that at last love shall be so persistently contemned and refused and flung back, that the one contemning becomes so worthless that there can be no remaking, then love must acquiesce in the judgment of truth, and declare that that man or that people is rejected because that man or that people has already rejected love.

The Divine refusal of a man or a nation is never capricious. It is simply the Divine acceptation of that which a man or a people has deliberately chosen. The attitude of God toward a contemptible people is inevitable, not because He assumes it, but because the people have chosen it. God is the unwarped conscience of the universe. Whatever other conscience is seared, hardened, robbed of its sensitiveness, that of God is never seared, or hardened, or robbed of sensitiveness. If a nation turns from following Him to follow vanity, turns from the recognition of Himself and dependence upon Him, to trust in Egypt or Assyria, or human alliances alone, then that nation by such choice does devitalize itself, cut itself off from the true resources of power and greatness. This, God knows, and of necessity acts upon the basis of it. We cannot warp the Divine conscience. We cannot bribe the Divine holiness. No nation can play tricks with God. Or as Russell Lowell put it quaintly, and yet with terrific force in his " Biglow Papers ":

"   .   .   you've gut to git up airly
Ef you want to take in God."

That is a supreme truth. God is not seen in this page of history, sitting upon a throne, capriciously rejecting a people. He is seen, the unswerving conscience of right in the universe, declaring the truth concerning a people, and adopting toward that people the attitude which they have made necessary by their own choice. Such an attitude on the part of God is irrevocable, within His own will. He waits with infinite patience, but when there is no answer He rejects, and He rejects because that which He rejects is already rejected. He only hardens Pharaoh's heart when Pharaoh has hardened his own heart.

All this leads us to the final word; the real declaration of the text. It needs no argument. It needs illustration only. The attitude of the nations toward Judah illustrated the truth. Into what profound contempt the ancient people passed when God rejected them. At this moment the attitude of the world toward the Jew is that of contempt. Even though the world does not understand its own attitude, that contempt is a fulfilment of this declaration: "Refuse silver shall men call them, because Jehovah hath rejected them."

The great principle is one we need to ponder. The attitude of the nations of the world toward a Christian nation which wanders from its Christianity, is always that of contempt. Or to bring the matter within the compass of a personal illustration: the man of the world holds the Christian man who has turned his back upon God, in supreme contempt. Let there be a Christian man, whether in public life or in private, whether judged by national standards, or by social, who wanders from God, and turns his back upon Him, and does things unworthy of the name he bears, and the profession he makes, until he himself has lost his sense of communion, and the old joy is absent, and the old light of unsullied holiness is no more seen in glance, or found in action; then the man of the world says, Reprobate silver! Such a man, refusing God, and refused of God, is held in supreme contempt by the world.

In that fact there is discovered something that ought to fill the heart with hope and joy. The underlying human conscience is true to God, and bears testimony to God; and even though it be unintelligent testimony, it is nevertheless powerful testimony. Deep down in the human heart, beneath all its waywardness and its wickedness is something that is true to God; and the common human conscience always vibrates in harmony with the conscience of God, even though men violate it.

Right down beneath all the sins of humanity, there is that which acquiesces in the decisions of God. When God pronounces His august and awful sentence upon a man or a nation, that he or it is reprobate, refuse; the common human conscience agrees. "Refuse silver shall men call them, because Jehovah hath rejected them."

V

THE ABUSE OF TRUE RELIGION

Preparatory Readings: 2 Kings 22:3-7; 23:21-23; 2 Chronicles
34:8-13; 35:1-19; Jeremiah 7-8:3.

*" Trust ye not in lying words, saying, The temple of
Jehovah, the temple of Jehovah, the temple of Jehovah,
are these."*—JEREMIAH 7:4.

IN order to a correct appreciation of the force of
these words, we need the historic background. As to
this, there are two suggestions; first, that the words were
uttered by Jeremiah in the reign of Jehoiakim; secondly,
that they were uttered in the reign of Josiah. The former view is based on the fact that in the twenty-sixth
chapter of the prophecy we have the account of a similar
charge to the prophet, which is there distinctly dated as
in the reign of Jehoiakim. The only reason for identifying the messages is that of this similarity. In each
case the prophet was charged to stand in the temple
precincts; as we read in the seventh chapter, at the *gate*
of Jehovah's house, or as the twenty-sixth chapter
says, in the *court* of Jehovah's house; and in each case
the burden of his message was the same. This similarity
is however no proof of identity; and to treat this message as belonging to the days of Josiah, is to follow the
natural sequence of the book. We find in his reign the
exact conditions described in the prophecy; and from
that standpoint of interpretation therefore I shall approach the text, and consider its meaning.

In the eighteenth year of the reign of Josiah, that being the fifth of the ministry of Jeremiah, the temple was
repaired. During the process of that work, the book of

the law was discovered by Hilkiah the priest. The finding of this book had a profound effect upon the king, revealing to him as it did, the distance to which the people had departed from the ways and the will of God. As a result of the discovery of that book of the law, he immediately commenced a yet more drastic reformation.

Now in the reading of these particular chapters of our prophecy (7–9) it is quite evident that two matters were occupying the thought of the prophet; and that, because these selfsame matters were at the moment preeminent in the attention of the nation. I refer to the matters of the temple and of the law. The first part of them, chapter seven, and so far as the third verse in chapter eight, is occupied with the temple; while from the fourth verse of the eighth chapter, to the end of chapter nine, the special burden of the prophetic message is that of the law of God. I propose now only to consider the first part of this particular section; and everything of value in the prophetic message is focussed in the words of the text: "Trust ye not in lying words, saying, The temple of Jehovah, the temple of Jehovah, the temple of Jehovah, are these."

One can imagine the repaired temple, the gathering multitudes of the people, coming with apparent gladness to the observance of the feasts; and in all probability to that one special observance of the Passover in the reign of Josiah, which in many senses was the most remarkable in the history of the nation. If in imagination we see that temple, so long neglected, now repaired, its doors and its courts opened, and the thronging worshippers crowding through the courts, the arresting and remarkable thing is that of the young prophet-priest from Anathoth, who is seen standing in the gateway, facing the multitudes of the people, and rebuking them, in the act of worship, and for the act of worship. He was a lonely man in very deed; a solitary and yet heroic figure; a man responding to a Divine commission which must have taxed his courage to the utmost. In the very hour of worship, in the gate of the very temple which had been but recently repaired and restored, he said to the people, " Trust ye not in lying words, saying, The temple of Jehovah, the temple of Jehovah, the temple of Jehovah, are these." That is the key-note of this particular message; and it must be interpreted by the context.

Let us then consider: first the attitude of the people at this time; secondly, the truth concerning the people as the prophet declared it; and finally, for our own instruction, the inter-relation of these two matters of the outward attitude of worship, and the actual fact of sin.

I have already said sufficient perhaps to indicate the attitude of the people, and yet let us consider it a little more closely. In the second book of Chronicles we have the account of how the temple had been repaired, of how the king had appointed Hilkiah the priest, Shaphan the scribe, and others with them, to this especial work of repairing the temple. We have the account of how a fund had been provided for the renovation by the people, quite willingly. We discover also that the fund was made over to the workmen, and we have this significant declaration that they did the work faithfully, and did the work well. We must not lose sight of these things. The more we study this time, the more we are impressed with the fact that to all outward seeming, to the eyes of the ordinary observer, it was a period of remarkable religious revival. To lose sight of that fact, is to miss the terrific impact of this prophecy, especially this early part of it. The work had been done faithfully; it had been carried out successfully.

Not only was the temple thus repaired; the forms of worship were observed. It was at this time that Josiah's great Passover was kept; and I can most readily dismiss this by quoting the actual words of the chronicler concerning this particular Passover:

" And there was no Passover like to that kept in Israel from the days of Samuel the prophet; neither did any of the kings of Israel keep such a Passover as Josiah kept, and the priests, and the Levites, and all Judah and Israel that were present, and the inhabitants of Jerusalem."

It was a great religious festival, a remarkable occasion, in which priests and Levites, the people of Judah, and remnants of Israel gathered from the cities across the border line, were assembled. Vast masses of people were engaged in the one business of worship, by observing that Passover which was intended to remind them of their relationship to Jehovah; of how they were a ransomed people from slavery, by the stretching out of His strong right arm. These people were rejoicing in the existence of that temple. They were rejoicing in the observance of that feast. They were rejoicing in the restoration of the outward forms of a true religion. When the prophet said to them in the words of my text, " Trust ye not in lying words, saying, The temple of Jehovah, the temple of Jehovah, the temple of Jehovah, are these," he was in all probability simply repeating what they themselves were actually saying; and the picture is so true to Eastern colouring, that we can almost imagine we hear the actual words passing the lips of the rejoicing people. There stood the temple restored. There were the priests in their offices, the Levites in their courses, and the singers in their places; all the order of worship was restored; and the vast multitudes gathered, in all probability broke out into exultation in these very words, " The temple of Jehovah, the temple of Jehovah, the temple of Jehovah ! " They were exulting in the restoration of the house of God. They were exulting in the restoration of the true religious order. They were exulting in the things of a restored religion.

This rejoicing was based, moreover, not merely upon the fact that the temple was repaired and that the order

[53]

of service was restored; but upon the fact that they believed that this restoration was an excellent thing for the nation. That fact is seen more clearly a little later when, in the midst of an almost terrific indictment of the people, the prophet described their attitude as that of those who stood in the house of God and said, "We are delivered." They trusted in the temple in that they believed that its restoration meant national safety. They believed that in the restoration of worship, according to the pattern which had been given to their fathers, in the priestly order and the Levitical course, in the songs of the sanctuary and the magnificence of the Passover feast, there was safety for the nation. They were perfectly accurate in their intellectual apprehension of the relation which exists between the religion of a people and national safety.

It was to people in that attitude of mind, that the young prophet-priest from Anathoth came; and standing in the gate of the house of Jehovah he halted them, and thundered against them the fiercest denunciations of sin. As we have seen the attitude of the people and the character of the hour, we desire to see why this prophet was thus sent to them, and why his message was that of severity.

There is no need that we dwell upon these things now in detail. The reading of the prophecy is enough. Let me but summarize. Jeremiah first of all declared that these worshipping people were at that very time sinning against their fellow men; they were guilty of theft, of murder, of adultery, of perjury. They were rejoicing in the restoration of the temple and the order of worship, and that because they believed that in that restoration there was the secret of national safety, and yet they were guilty of theft, of murder, of adultery, and of perjury.

Now all this is almost incredible; but we need to remember that the prophets of God always described things by their right names. These sins have many modes of expression, but when the Divine messenger refers to a particular sin, he names it for what it is, and not by the new names by which men hide the ugly facts.

I think it is quite conceivable that these people were actually guilty of these sins in their most vulgar forms: but if not, they were guilty of them in other forms; just as to-day many a murderer may sit in the house of worship, who if you called him a murderer would be angry, because there is no actual blood upon his hands; but in the view of God the blood of men is on his garments; for if he has wronged men, and trampled on them to gain power and wealth, he is a murderer in the sight of God; and the prophet of God will name him a murderer. The prophet will never speak of dishonesty in business as " business acumen "; he will name it theft.

The young priest came up from Anathoth, trembling and astonished at the awfulness of his commission, saying out of the agony of his soul, "Ah, Lord Jehovah! behold, I know not how to speak: for I am a child." When from that inner presence chamber of the awful purity of God, he turned to gaze upon the sins of men, he named sins for what they were in themselves. Thus we have this ghastly picture of people sinning against their fellow men, wronging their fellow men; and yet trusting in the temple, and thanking God for the restoration of national religion, because they thought it would give them national safety.

Not only had these people sinned against their fellow men, they had sinned against God. The sin against men is always the outcome of sin against God. Here again we have a yet more startling situation. These people, rejoicing in the restoration of the temple, were nevertheless guilty of burning incense to Baal, of offering sacrifices to Moloch, and of worshipping sun and moon and stars. Moreover, as we study carefully these words of the prophet, revealing the condition of the people, we find evidences that the people imagined that because these abominations were forms of religion, they were therefore of value. When they worshipped Baal they imagined that in some sense they were worshipping God. When they offered the sacrifices of their own children to Moloch, making them pass through the fire, they imagined that in some sense they were placating God. The word of God to them was, "They have built the high places of Topheth . . . to burn their sons and their daughters in the fire; *which I commanded not, neither came it into my mind";* a statement showing that the people had somehow come to imagine that all these things were of value, and according to the mind of God.

These people were convinced of the fact, and of the power of Jehovah. They believed in God. Hence their exultation when the temple was repaired, and the order of worship was restored. They imagined, however, that this conviction *about* God was a safeguard; and that the presence of the temple was an insurance against the attacks of their foes. They said in effect: The temple of Jehovah is erected, therefore we are safe; The worship of Jehovah is restored, therefore no peril can overtake us and harm us. They had become superstitious; they had descended to the lowest level of idolatry, that of fetish worship. They had come to imagine that there was some kind of magical value in a temple, and a form of service, by which they were guarded from all the perils that they had seen confronting them. They cried: The temple of Jehovah, the temple of Jehovah, the temple of Jehovah! We are delivered, we are safe, because the temple is with us. They failed exactly as that man fails to-day who thinks that unless he reads a few verses of his Bible in the morning, *something will happen* during the day, and who reads the few verses of his Bible in order to be safe. That is a descent to the lowest and most ignoble form of superstition. These people were living in rampant sin against their fellow men; and yet were rejoicing because the temple was built and the order of service restored. They imagined that somehow God would take care of them because they had repaired the temple and restored the order of worship.

It was against that attitude that the prophet was commanded to protest, and he did so with vehemence, and with passion. His words ring with infinite satire: " Trust ye not in lying words, saying, The temple of Jehovah, the temple of Jehovah, the temple of Jehovah, are these." Having said this he declared that the temple had really become " a den of robbers." This was a very carefully chosen figure of speech; a den of robbers is a safe lurking place for those who despoil their fellow men. Therefore it must be destroyed for the sake of the men who were despoiled. Said the Lord: I will destroy this house that you trust in, as I destroyed the place at Shiloh which was consecrated to My worship, when it was disgraced and had become degenerate; because you have forgotten the things for which it stands!

Religious observance also becomes a blasphemy under certain conditions, an opiate dulling and deadening the spiritual sense when it ought to be an inspiration, lifting ever higher and nearer God. Then it ought to be ended, for the sake of those who themselves are being deceived.

There is a yet deeper note in this prophecy. It is that religious conviction may itself become a curse. Unless it be answered, unless it be obeyed, religious conviction does but react upon the soul of a man, or a nation, for its deadening, and for its destruction. A religious conviction about God, which becomes an assurance that if certain things of external form are observed, safety is insured, prevents repentance and makes shame impossible. If the nation is religious in its deepest life, unless it is religious also in the activities of its life, it is but persisting in disobedience to an inward conviction; and presently that conviction will no longer appeal; but will become a solace which is false, a refuge which is a refuge of lies.

The whole teaching of the prophecy, thus focussed in the satire of the text, is first of all that the essential value and proof of religion is that of the effect it produces on conduct. It is not enough to say that the act of worship in the sanctuary is worthless, unless it harmonize with all the life of the other days; the act of worship is not worthless merely; it is forceful; powerful, but in an evil way, for it reacts upon the soul, making it more and more impossible for man or nation to be truly religious. Failure to obey truth is infinitely worse than no knowledge of the truth, for such disobedience reacts upon heart and soul and conscience. The essential value and proof of religion is that of its effect on conduct toward God, and conduct toward men. These are interdependent. A man's conception of God is ever revealed in his attitude toward his fellow men. There is no more profound and wonderful word on that subject than the word of James, the supremely ethical writer of the New Testament: " Pure religion and undefiled before our God and Father is this, to visit the fatherless and widows in their affliction, and to keep oneself unspotted from the world." In that sentence, of the severest ethic, nevertheless thrilling with the tenderest emotion, James puts the ultimate form of the expression of godliness in the phrase, " To visit the fatherless and widows." How much that includes, and how much it excludes! The man who accepts that as the highest expression of religion cannot be guilty of theft, and murder, and adultery, and perjury. If these things are permitted, then the presence of the worshipper in the sanctuary is a blasphemy, a profanation, a blasting, a blight, a mildew. Sacred places, sacred days, sacred observances, are all subservient to the matters of right relationship with God and our fellow men; and are only valuable as expressions of the deeper things. If they are made occasions by which we escape from these higher obligations, then they at once become vain and pernicious. The temple without the Deity is nothing. The day without the truth is vanity. The celebration of Christmas day by men who forget what incarnation means is vanity, blasphemy, and a curse. The observance of a rite apart from the life of which the rite is the symbol, is death; and the process to a yet deeper death. Therefore the prophet, standing in the gate of Jehovah's house, amid the worshipping people in Judah, charged them to put no trust in that temple; declared to them that the facts of the temple erected, of the worship restored, were nothing, until they did themselves amend their ways and turn back in conduct to God, and express their right relationship with God, in right attitudes toward their fellow men.

We have moved far since the days of Jeremiah. The light in which we live is a clearer, brighter, more wonderful light. This country is often called a Christian country. There are some senses in which we are inclined to deny it. There are some senses, however, in which it is profoundly true. This is a Christian country. It is a Christian country because it is what it is to-day, through Christianity. We owe everything to Christ; all the noble ideals which we cherish, all high aspirations that move us in our national life, are attributable to Him. Every conception of the necessity for men being able to live their lives in circumstances that make possible the fulfilment of their profoundest aspirations, has come to us through Jesus Christ.

Let us then remember that the measure in which the Nation departs from Christianity is the measure in which it ceases to be Christian. It is for those of us who name the Name, and wear the sign, and profess that closer allegiance to Christ expressed in membership of the Christian Church, to bear this thing perpetually in mind; to watch our own age, lest there be within us this selfsame paralysis that was revealed in Judah; a rejoicing in certain external manifestations of religion, while all the time, in our attitude toward our fellow men, we reveal the fact that we are far away from fellowship with God. The measure of a nation's Christianity is the measure of its right relationship to men; the measure in which, within its own borders, the sins that wrong humanity are stamped out. We are in danger of being lulled into a false security because evidences are constantly given of the fact that in the heart of the national life there is religion. If the nation is religious at its heart, it is a tragedy, unless the nation becomes religious in its will. As long as theft, and murder, and adultery, and perjury, in their newer and more subtle forms are rampant, then let us mourn and lament before God; and let us give ourselves to a passionate endeavour to turn the heart of the people back again to Him, that there may be the realization of true religion in the national life.

What then shall we do? The call of God on the ancient page makes its appeal to this hour as surely as to the hour in which it was uttered: "Amend your ways and your doings; if ye thoroughly execute justice between a man and his neighbour; if ye oppress not the sojourner, the fatherless, and the widow, and shed not innocent blood in this place, neither walk after other gods to your own hurt: then will I cause you to dwell in this place." Such is the Divine call to us who name the Name, and rejoice in the religion of our land.

VI

NATIONAL STRENGTH. FALSE AND TRUE

Preparatory Readings: 2 Kings 23:1–2; 2 Chronicles 34:29–30;
Jeremiah 8:4—9.

" Thus saith Jehovah,
    Let not the wise man glory in his wisdom,
    Neither let the mighty man glory in his might,
    Let not the rich man glory in his riches:
But let him that glorieth glory in this,
    That he hath understanding and knoweth Me,
    That I am Jehovah Who exerciseth
        Lovingkindness,
        Justice, and
        Righteousness, in the earth:
For in these things I delight, saith Jehovah."
                              —JEREMIAH 9:23, 24.

THIS paragraph is complete in itself, and indeed
stands in contrast to the prophetic burden in the midst
of which it is found. Contrast is the right word, for
there is no conflict. The conditions in the midst of
which the prophet was speaking were the exact opposite
of those which he described as giving delight to Jehovah.
In themselves these words are full of force and beauty,
and constitute one of the passages of these old prophetic
writings which have impressed themselves upon the mind
and heart of men. They are constantly quoted, even
though their setting is not always recognized. As a
matter of fact they are characterized by great and grave
solemnity, and this is at once seen when the words immediately preceding, and those directly following, are
taken into account.

Before uttering these particular words, the prophet

had been describing the desolation of the people as the result of the judgment of their sin:

" For death is come up into our windows, it is entered into our palaces; to cut off the children from without, and the young men from the streets. . . . The dead bodies of men shall fall as dung upon the open field, and as the handful after the harvestman, and none shall gather them."

Then, following the words of our text, we find others in which he again, in the name of Jehovah, declared that Judah would be punished, in company with Egypt, Edom, Ammon, and Moab, because the house of Israel was uncircumcised in heart.

In the process of the repairing of the temple, the book of the law had been discovered by Hilkiah the high priest. He had delivered it to Shaphan, the scribe, who carried it to the king, and after reporting the completion of the temple work, read it in his hearing. This reading filled the king with consternation, as he became conscious of how far the people had failed to keep the word of the law, and to do according to all that was written therein. After consultation with Huldah the prophetess, Josiah gathered together the elders of Judah and Jerusalem, the priests and the Levites, and all the people; and himself read in their hearing the words of the book of the covenant, which had been found in the house of Jehovah. In order to an understanding of the consternation of the king, it is interesting to compare the instructions of that particular book with the conditions obtaining in Judah at this time. It is necessary that we should carefully distinguish between the book of the law, and the book of the covenant. In all probability the book of the law was that of the entire Mosaic economy; but the book of the covenant was a part of it, and it was this book of the covenant that Josiah read publicly to the people. We find it in our Bibles in the twenty-first, twenty-second, and twenty-third chapters of Exodus; and the words of this particular book were written by Moses immediately after the enunciation of the Decalogue, and were read in the audience of the people under Mount Sinai before the giving of the full priestly code. The laws contained in this particular book had to do with personal life, with property, and with the State. Now in these chapters of Jeremiah we have a revelation of the fact that the people in their actual conduct were holding these very laws in supreme contempt. Evil practices of every kind were rampant; the poor were oppressed; justice was not being administered. While this was so, the people were not only trusting in the fact that the temple existed, as we saw in our previous meditation, they were also boasting in their possession of the law. They said, " We are wise, and the law of Jehovah is with us." The prophet referred to this vain boasting, and in one sentence revealed the secret of the failure of the people as he said, " But, behold, the false pen of the scribes hath wrought falsely." In other words, the people had received through their teachers false interpretation, and this was due to the false living of the scribes themselves. Jeremiah charged these men with covetousness, with the practice of injustice, and with creating a false sense of security in the mind of the people as they said, " Peace, peace," when there was no peace. The result of all this in the life of the nation was that of false national conceptions. The people were placing their confidence in policy, in might, in wealth; and were neglecting lovingkindness, and judgment, and righteousness.

All this enables us to see the force of this particular text. In it the prophet focussed national teaching of the most important kind. He revealed to these people and to nations for all time, three matters: first, false national securities; secondly, the true elements of national strength; and finally, or rather centrally, the true secret of national greatness.

[63]

STUDIES IN THE PROPHECY OF JEREMIAH

False national securities. " Let not the wise man glory in his wisdom, neither let the mighty man glory in his might, let not the rich man glory in his riches." The true elements of national strength; "lovingkindness, justice, righteousness." The secret of national righteousness; "Let him that glorieth glory in this, that he hath understanding and knoweth Me . . . saith Jehovah."

Every nation has something in which it glories, that in which it takes pride, and ultimately, that in which it confides. To discover what that is, in which a nation glories; to discover what that is, in which a nation puts its confidence; is to discover the inspiration of all its activities, and the reason of all its attitudes.

There is one matter here, to which I desire to draw attention briefly, by way of introduction. It is that in this particular word of Jeremiah the national is illustrated in the individual. The prophet was speaking principally to the nation. Yet when he turned aside, to speak of these central matters, his appeal was individual: " Let not the wise *man* glory in his wisdom; Let not the mighty *man* glory in his might; Let not the rich *man* glory in his riches." A nation is the sum total of its people; and even in those days of long ago, before the clear light in which we live had shined upon humanity, these prophets recognized that the place upon which the emphasis of responsibility is to be laid is not upon king, or governors, but upon the individuals that make up a nation. If that was true in those olden days, it has a more pertinent application to us. In these days of representative government, the strength of a nation depends more than ever upon the individual character of its citizens. The nation puts the government into power, and the nation is ultimately responsible therefore for its acts. National sins fall back, as to responsibility, upon individuals.

Let us consider these false securities to which the

prophet referred. " Let not the wise man glory in his wisdom." In this word the prophet warned the nation against glorying, or taking pride, or putting confidence, in human wisdom. The idea of wisdom is that of understanding, and that of knowledge. I use these two words, because when we reach the central declaration of the text, it is this: " Let him . . . glory in this, that he *hath understanding,* and *knoweth* Me . . . saith Jehovah " ; and this is no careless repetition of words, but a very careful use of them, indicating two aspects of one great fact. " Understandeth Me " ; that is, has the capacity for knowing Me; " Knoweth Me," that is, uses his capacity and observes Me, watches for Me. So that wisdom here, taken in the abstract, is perception, as a faculty, and as an activity. The wise man is the man who has the faculty of perception, and who employs that faculty. Wisdom here therefore is the understanding and the knowledge of things and of affairs; and in this particular application, the prophet referred to political wisdom, political acumen. Behind the scenes, through all these days of Jeremiah's prophesying, as in those earlier days of Isaiah's prophesying, there was political intrigue, attempts to so arrange national matters as to ensure internal peace. The statesmen were attempting to play off—forgive the modern phrase, I am at a loss for a better—one *great power* against another, in order to ensure their own safety. The wise man therefore was the man who had a knowledge of affairs, and of things, and was carefully watching.

Now, said the prophet, " Let not the wise man glory in his wisdom "; let not the wise man take pride in his wisdom; let not the wise man put confidence in his wisdom. And why not? Because human wisdom is necessarily partial. It is partial in its observations. It is therefore and necessarily partial in its deductions. Consequently it is uncertain.

The force of this passage is the greater if we remember that the word of Jeremiah at this point did not refer merely to mistakes that men had made. He was not, for the moment, dealing with the fact that their political wisdom had been unutterable folly. All that was undoubtedly in the prophet's mind; but for the moment he left the fact of past mistakes, and spoke in the most general terms, as he declared, " Let not the wise man glory in his wisdom." His wisdom may be of the highest possible to the human mind. He may be diligent; he may be sincere; he may be honest in his attempt to discover the facts. His capacity for understanding may be keen, and his devotion to the exercise of that capacity may be constant; nevertheless, not in that human wisdom does a nation find its strength, for it is for ever partial. All the facts of things, or of situations, can never be discovered by the cleverness of the human mind. The foundation of such wisdom is not strong enough therefore upon which to build. It must inevitably break down sooner or later.

Let us pass to the second of the warnings: " Neither let the mighty man glory in his might." Here again most evidently the thought of the prophet was that of material force, both defensive and offensive. Let me take the thoughts that lurk within the two words defensive and offensive, and attempt to express them in another way. What is material force? What is the might of a man in the material realm? It has two qualities. The first is that of the unyielding grip; and the other is that of the irresistible blow. Those are the two exercises of merely material force, the ability to hold that which is possessed; the ability so to strike as to destroy. " Let not the mighty man glory in that."

And why not? Wherein is the weakness of material force? In the first place, material force is weak because it is limited to its own kind. Material force is only strong against material force; it has no power to resist moral force. Consequently, its strength is determined, not by itself, but by the strength of that to which it is opposed. It is negatived by other kinds of force.

There is no need for me to illustrate in this hour. The late war gave us one of the most marvellous exhibitions in human history of the terrific force of a moral ideal. Moral force is mightier than material; the force of a moral ideal, the ideal of right and truth, though the end seem long in coming, is always mightier than merely material force. Consequently material force is doubtful. Therefore, " Let not the mighty man glory in his might."

And again : " Let not the rich man glory in his riches." Now what is wealth? The idea undoubtedly here is that of material possession. Things possessed, of the kind which other people need. I did not say that other people ought to have those possessed by their fellows. There are material things that do not constitute wealth, because there is no value in them to other men. Again therefore wealth is that which procures other things to the man who possesses it. " Let not the rich man glory in his riches."

And why not? Because material wealth is only current in the material realm. Just as there are forces mightier than the physical, so there are facts that material wealth can never procure or ensure. The strength of material wealth is that of quantity only, and therefore it is fluctuating.

If national strength is based upon human wisdom, that wisdom is partial, it cannot encompass all the facts of the case. If national strength is built upon physical might, that might is limited to its own kind, and may at any time be mastered by a superior force in that kind, or by force of another kind which is mightier than it is in itself. If national strength is founded upon wealth, that wealth is only current in the material. The nation is the aggregate of the human personalities composing it; and human personalities in the last analysis are neither body nor mind, they are spirit; and spiritual strength cannot be built upon the foundations of material possession.

Yet that which is perhaps more startling in the text, is the prophet's revelation of the true elements of national strength. Over against these false confidences, he named the things in which God Himself takes delight; and consequently the things which give Him delight in men and in nations. They are the things which He Himself exercises in the earth; and therefore in so far as men exercise them, they fall into line with Him, and find the true secrets of national strength. What are they? Lovingkindness, justice, righteousness.

Lovingkindness. Here, as so often, we really touch the heart of the matter by feeling our way into the first intention of this word, and then observing its perpetual use. The first intention of this great Hebrew word, lovingkindness, most surely persists through all its varied use on the page of the Old Testament. Lovingkindness is the stoop which is prompted by love. It is the bending down, and the bending over, which is love-inspired. Lovingkindness is not merely an attitude of mind; it is the activity that springs out of an attitude of mind. It is love in action. Lovingkindness is not love in action toward those who are on a level with the lover; it is always love in action toward those to whom the lover must bow and bend and stoop to reach them. Lovingkindness is the stoop prompted by love toward all who lack. Lovingkindness is pity; lovingkindness is patience; lovingkindness is power communicated to those who are in necessity of any kind.

According to this prophetic word that is the first element of national strength.

Wherein is the strength of lovingkindness? It conserves the strength of the nation. It restores what otherwise were refuse, and it consolidates a people. Whatever view we may have of practical politics—whatever that phrase may mean—if we climb to the heights and imagine a nation wherein lovingkindness shall abound, and be the inspiration of life, we cannot escape from the conviction that such a nation would be strong indeed. Lovingkindness strengthens the things that remain, gathers all waste material and transmutes it into true wealth. Within the life of any nation, by the ministry of that lovingkindness, which is a stoop prompted by love toward all lack, in pity, patience and power, the true strength will be realized.

The next element of strength in the national life is that of justice. This follows lovingkindness, and indeed results from it. What is justice? The Hebrew word is one of the most variously translated in the Bible, and I sometimes think one of the least understood. Justice is not punishment. It may include it, but if it do, in that case punishment is chastisement, and not revenge. Justice is the administration of affairs in strict equity; it is government according to truth; it is that adjustment of relationships which is equitable and right. The true strength of a nation is found in its judgment, in its method of administration, if that method of administration be that of truth and justice and equity. Wherein lies the strength then of justice? It satisfies the deep, profound, underlying conscience of men, and of the nation. It secures the true and best conditions for human life. It silences that complaining in the streets which is the gravest peril that ever threatens the life of a nation. Not bombardment from without, but restlessness within, is the most terrible of all national perils.

What is righteousness? Absolutely, it is found in God, and is straightness; God in action; no perversity, no iniquity, no crookedness. Relatively therefore, righteousness is conformity to God in action. Frank W. Gunsaulus has well said: That is great statesmanship which discovers the direction in which God is moving, and sets itself to remove the obstacles to His progress.

That is righteousness in the national life. God's attitudes and activities are righteous. Righteousness in a nation is conformity to those attitudes and activities. Righteousness in a man is conformity to the Divine mind and action. If righteousness in national life is conformity to the Divine action, it is always that of truth toward man. What then is the strength of righteousness? It links with God; it energizes all life; and it defies all destructive forces.

Finally we return to the centre of our text, and discover there the central secret of national strength. The true reason of glory, that is, of pride, that is, of confidence, is the understanding, and the knowledge of God. That nation is truly strong, and has found the secret of true confidence, that has a capacity for the knowledge of God, and that sets itself to the use of that capacity.

God is all-wise; God is Almighty; God is all-sufficient. "Let not the wise man glory in *his* wisdom"; but let him glory in that he understands and knows God Who is all-wise. "Let not the mighty man glory in *his* might," but let him glory in God Who is Almighty. "Let not the rich man glory in *his* riches," but let him glory in God Who is all-sufficient. God is all-wise, and therefore His attitude toward man is that of lovingkindness. The old French proverb, often quoted mischievously, nevertheless has within it a great truth, "To know all is to forgive all." The very all-wisdom of God enables Him to be loving, and impels Him to activities of lovingkindness and compassion that you and I are incapable of, save only as we are in fellowship with Him. The Almightiness of God enables Him to the exercise of judgment in meekness. The stronger a man is, the more gentle he is toward the weak. The Almighty is the all-meek, and His judgments are the judgments of truth and of patience. God is all-sufficient, and therefore righteous. But is that a true sequence? Yes, if you are thinking of national things. The moments when a nation fails in righteousness are the moments when a nation is not sure of its revenue. In proportion as there is all-sufficiency, there is no bribery. Men cannot bribe God. Among the lower reasons for this is that there is nothing you can offer Him that is not already His. In proportion as a man or a nation are conscious that their ultimate possessions are in God, you cannot bribe them, for they will measure the passing years by His abiding eternity; and will be content ofttimes to wait, in the consciousness of strength, upon the foundation of righteousness, even though the immediate necessity be that of poverty and shame and difficulty.

The supreme matters therefore in national life are those of an understanding of God, of the knowledge of God which is the exercise of the capacity; and ultimately therefore that of obedience to that which is revealed to the capacity. To know Him is the life of the ages, as our Lord Himself did say: " This is life eternal, that they should know Thee the only true God, and Him Whom Thou didst send, even Jesus Christ." To seek His Kingdom first, is to find all else ultimately supplied, as He also said: " Seek ye first His Kingdom, and His righteousness; and all these things shall be added unto you." To delight in Him is to be His delight, for to delight in Him is to seek lovingkindness, judgment, and righteousness; and these are the things wherein He does delight.

The nation turned back to God may for a while appear, in the counsels of men, weak and foolish, and be in danger of suffering defeat; but that nation turned back to God, has turned back to life and strength, and the things that make for her abiding.

VII

SUBSTITUTES FOR GOD

Preparatory Readings: 2 Kings 23:3–24; 2 Chronicles 34:31–35:19; Jeremiah 10–11:17.

" Thus shall ye say unto them, The gods that have not made the heavens and the earth, these shall perish from the earth, and from under the heavens."
—JEREMIAH 10:11.

KING JOSIAH reigned over the kingdom of Judah thirteen years after his great observance of the Passover Feast. In the records we have very few details of that period.

The immediate result of the finding of the book of the law was that of a covenant which the king made with all his heart and with all his soul, to confirm, or to perform, the words of the covenant written in that book. The recorder says: "And all the people stood to the covenant" (2 Kings 23:3); while the chronicler in the book of Chronicles writes: " He caused all that were found in Jerusalem and Benjamin to stand to it" (2 Chron. 34:32).

This new covenant made between the king and his people in the presence of the newly discovered book of the law, was followed by yet more drastic measures on the part of the king, for the suppression of idolatry; and this was outwardly successful, at least for a time, for the chronicler declares, "All his days they departed not from following Jehovah, the God of their fathers" (2 Chron. 34:33).

It is evident, however, that idolatry was never wholly

suppressed, and that during the later years of the reign of Josiah the national deterioration continued. Even the king became involved in the political deflections, and ultimately met his death in a battle in which he ought not to have been present.

The prophecies of Jeremiah contained in the tenth, eleventh, and twelfth chapters correspond to that period. The first movement deals with idolatry, and in it we may have the notes of his prophetc messages during the campaign against idolatries, intended to strengthen and defend the action of the king. That movement is found in the first sixteen verses of chapter ten.

The second movement is characterized by a sudden foretelling of judgment, the wailing of the people, and the cry of the prophet in his distress. That is contained in the tenth chapter, verse seventeen to the end.

The third deals with the broken covenant, in which the sins of the fathers had been repeated by the sons. That is to be found in the first seventeen verses of chapter eleven.

The last movement tells the story of how the prophet was afflicted; and how he was strengthened by Jehovah for the continuation of his ministry.

In our present study we shall confine ourselves to the first of these movements, that dealing with idolatry; and our general theme is that of the contrast which the prophet drew between idols and God.

When men lose the consciousness of God they do not lose their sense of the need of God; and consequently they substitute the false for the true. It should be recognized that the making of an idol follows, and is the result of, the loss of the consciousness of God, rather than precedes, and causes it. Disloyalty darkens the apprehension of God, but does not destroy the necessity for a god; and it is in such dark hours, resulting from disloyalty, that men set about the business of making gods for themselves. This is the story of Judah. It has

[73]

often been repeated in human history. I propose only one illustration, and that still by way of introduction. In the onward sweep of the French Revolution, that sharp and bloody medicine for a much longer and more terrible disorder that had preceded it, men battling against the tyranny and oppression of their fellows, forgot God, and deified reason. It was then that Robespierre decreed the existence of a supreme Being, in order to find a firm base for authority. Gardiner says:

" For a moment expectation prevailed that this recognition of a Supreme Being would be followed by a revival of sentiments of humanity. The case proved otherwise."

Of course it did, because the Supreme Being decreed was the creature of Robespierre's brain, not the Creator. Nevertheless the act was a revelation of the fact that when men have lost the vision of God, they have not lost the necessity for God; and that they must create a god of some kind, if they have lost the God Who created them.

In this teaching of Jeremiah the contrast between false gods and the true God is vivid, and its value is permanent; for if the form of the idols changes with changing times, the essential matters abide for all time.

We shall consider the contrast then, by observing the teaching concerning substitutes for God in three particulars; those namely, of their origin; their nature; and their worth.

So far as I have any right to differentiate as to the values of different passages of Scripture, I should say that with one exception, this is the most remarkable passage on the subject of idolatry in the whole Bible. The one perhaps greater is Isaiah's, from which in all probability Jeremiah quoted.

Concerning the idols that men were substituting for God, Jeremiah takes one instance only, referring to it

twice in the course of his argument. He first referred
to it as a tree, a tree killed. That is the first thing; it
is a dead tree. Secondly, it is a tree fashioned by human hands into some form, according to the mind of
the artificer. In the third place, it is a tree decked with
silver and with gold. Finally, the prophet referred to it
as with nails and hammer fastened down, in case it
should sway!

A little further on, still dealing with the same subject,
but speaking of the wise men of the age, in comparison
with God, he referred again to these idols, and in an
exclamation said, "The instruction of idols," or the
teaching of idols; and then dropping into the singular
number, evidently looking upon some actual idol, he exclaimed, "It is but a stock!" "The instruction of
idols; it is but a stock"; it is but the work of the artificer, and the goldsmith; they brought their silver from
Tarshish, and their gold from Uphaz; and then they
clothed it—the stock, the chunk of wood—in purple and
blue! It is impossible to read these passages without
being conscious of the satire that breathes through them.

Let us look again. Imaginatively let us watch men
doing what the prophet described. First the tree must
be cut down. A dead tree is necessary for the making
of an idol. The dead tree is then formed, decorated,
clothed, and fastened securely down, lest it sway! As
we have been attempting to see the process, let us see
the man carrying it out. What is he doing? Why is
he doing what he is doing? I watch the forming and
fashioning of the tree; I watch the laying on of the
gold and the silver; I watch the fastening down with
nails and hammer lest it sway; I watch the decking of
it in blue and purple. Why is all this being done?

There is in the heart of that man a great human desire, a great need, a great demand, a great craving; and
his activity in the making of his idol, is that of his attempt to create something to answer the clamant cry

of his nature. He is making out of something inferior to himself, that which is to answer the deepest cry of himself. Though millenniums have passed away, and the sons of Judah are no more employed in this way; and though we are far enough removed from the physical idolatries of other parts of the world, I see in all this something very near, and very real. I am watching a man attempting by physical and mental dexterity, to answer the clamant and agonizing cry of spiritual need. That is idolatry.

In every case Jeremiah puts these idols into contrast with God. God is the enthroned King. God is the everlasting King. God, as he says at last, is the Former of all things. The tree is cut down; the tree is formed; the tree is covered with gold and silver; the tree is decked in blue and purple; the tree is nailed down. God is the King of all things; God is King from everlasting to everlasting; God is Former, Framer, Fashioner of the man tinkering with the tree, of the gold and silver, of the blue and purple, of everything! Mark the graphic contrast. They are fashioned; God fashions. They are made; God makes. They are less than men, and must for ever be; He is more than men.

Let us now consider the teaching of the prophet as to the nature of these substitutes for God. The first word on this subject is that in which the prophet said: "They are like a palm tree, of turned work." The English revised version gives an alternative reading in the margin, "They are like a pillar in a garden of cucumbers." That marginal note in its difference from the actual words of the text, reveals the difficulty of the text. Admittedly it is not easy to decide the exact meaning of the prophet; but I turn to the book of Baruch. There I find Baruch's quotation of this very passage; there the words are given as, "Like a scarecrow in a garden of cucumbers!" I am not going to dogmatize about this matter, but I certainly believe that this is what Jeremiah

[76]

actually said. It is so entirely in keeping with the spirit of the whole movement. A little further on he described them as "The work of skilful men"; a description which was at once a suggestion of their inferiority, and a satire on the men who made them.

The final reference to their nature is that on which the prophet said: "There is no breath in them." I doubt if in all this prophecy, or in any other prophecy, there is one brief sentence more comprehensive, more inclusive, more exhaustive, more full of satire, more flashing with light than that, as a revelation of what idolatry is as to its nature.

The nature of idols then may thus be summarized. They are first contemptible, like scarecrows in gardens of cucumbers. They are secondly subservient, the work of cunning men; and consequently subservient to the men who make them. Finally, they are unresponsive, there is no breath in them. Take your dead tree, frame and form and fashion it in some outward, external, superficial sense in the likeness of a god or a man; lay on gold and silver; deck and drape it with blue and purple; fasten it with nails and hammer lest the wind should blow it about. Then lay your head upon its bosom, and wait to feel the heaving breast that speaks of breath. There is no breath in them!

Here also we have a revelation by contrast. God is fear-commanding, duty-demanding, trust-inspiring, principally because there is breath in Him, there is Spirit in Him, there is life in Him. Idols are dead, or impersonal. I add the word impersonal of set purpose, for there are idols which we cannot describe exactly as dead. They are in certain senses living things, but they are impersonal. They make no response to individual agony, to individual aspiration. God is living, and in an infinite mystery that baffles all attempts at explanation, God is personal. A man who knows Him, may live with Him, and talk to Him, and listen to Him; have all His heart to himself, all His wisdom for his guidance, all His strength for his comradeship; and yet never impoverish any other man, who has the same need and the same relationships. This is indeed a mystery, but it is also a demonstrated fact, in the experience of millions of men and women who have put their trust in Him.

The idol is altogether false, for the tree becomes a god in proportion as men hide the fact that it is a tree. They kill a tree, and then try and make it look like something else; then they hide it with gold and silver, blue and purple; at last the fact of the tree is forgotten, and that which is now a god is at its heart, wood; it is a lie. The living God is altogether true. To deny Himself must be to cease to be. He cannot deny Himself. They are false things; He is true Spirit.

Now let us ask what is the value of these idols; what are they worth? The prophet answers, first as to power, then as to intelligence, and then as to influence. Their value as to power is revealed in two statements; first, "They . . . speak not"; and secondly, "They must needs be borne, because they cannot go." As to intelligence, "The instruction of idols, it is but a stock." In other words, the instruction, the wisdom, the philosophy of idols, is wooden! When we come to the influence they exert, we touch the deepest note of the tragedy. They are in themselves vanity, and therefore they are a work of delusion; and the word delusion there misses something of the tragedy of the actual word—they are a work of mockery. In their silence they laugh at the men who made them. In their inability to speak they utter contempt for the men who created them. When men have formed and fashioned them in answer to the clamant cry of their spiritual life, when they have thus by dexterity of fingers attempted to meet their need, the silence and the immobility of idols is the awful mockery which answers the makers. This is true of every substitute that man sets in the place of God.

[78]

Idols are unresponsive burdens that men have to carry if they go anywhere. They are vanity, which a man worshipping, does himself become brutish and foolish. They are disappointments, which react upon the soul of the man who makes them, in shame. The goldsmith is ashamed of his molten image; and worse than ashamed, he is in despair.

All this is flung again into clearer light by the revelation of God that runs through the chapter. God is great, and His name is great. God is true, and living, and His voice is heard. God is the Former of all things, the ceaselessly active One, the ultimate Reality in all experience.

The abiding difference between idols and God, is that they are carried, while He carries. This is taught by Jeremiah, but if we want to find it most clearly taught, we must turn to Isaiah's prophecy. A man makes his idol. He must then carry the thing he has made. God makes a man. God carries the man He has made. That is the difference between false and true religion everywhere. False religion is the religion you carry. Christianity is idolatry to some people, because they carry it. True religion is the religion that carries you, that bears you, that strengthens you, that upholds you. Idols are of the earth, and under the heaven: God is over the heaven, and the earth is of Him. They are a mockery: He is the portion of His people. They perish; He cannot perish; and He possesses those who put their trust in Him, so that neither can they perish.

I have largely confined myself to an examination of the passage itself, to a meditation upon its statements. I can imagine that in the heart of some one there is a feeling that this is a work of supererogation, and of very little practical value, because we are not doing this kind of thing now. Men are not taking trees, and making idols of them. Yet spiritual intelligence will realize that there is a difference between that which is essential, and the forms in which it expresses itself; and will realize that this fact of idolatry persists. Even though the ancient forms, so far as we are concerned, have passed away, men are still finding substitutes for God.

What is God to a man? Either *He* or *that* to which a man renders worship; either the person, or the thing, whether the thing be material, or mental, matters nothing.

What then, is worship? Let us be quite simple. What is this old word, worship? Let us feel our way into the fabric of it. Worship is the response to worth. What then is worship? Homage, and service, rendered to that which a man considers to be worth such homage, worth such service. Then if I want to know what a man is worshipping, I have to see what he pays homage to, what he serves; for a man may recite the name of a God, and never worship Him at all. When Israel had been carried away captive from the Northern part of the kingdom, that wonderfully sagacious politician, the king of Babylon, colonized the country with people from other places. With what result? They were superstitious, and had a haunting fear that the God of the land would trouble them. They built altars to Him, and it is written, " They worshipped Jehovah, and served their own gods." They built altars to Jehovah, and served their own gods. Their real worship was not that of the altar built, but that of the homage rendered; and it is always so.

There is widespread idolatry in our own country. There is the worship of power, that is, the worship of Mammon. Or let me amend what I have said. The worship of Mammon is the worship of power; for the worship of power may be larger than the worship of Mammon, but the worship of Mammon is never larger than the worship of power. By Mammon I mean gold and silver; wealth. No man really worships wealth; he worships that which wealth can do, the power wealth confers upon him. Or there is the worship of beauty; and perhaps most widespread, the worship of sensation. These are expressions of idolatry, and the man who gives himself, with all his mind, and all his heart, and all his soul to the service of power, beauty, sensation, is an idolater. He is worshipping, and he is worshipping a god that he has made for himself; and every man who is doing this—I care not what his name may be, what the creed he recites, what his family history, what his ecclesiastical relationship—has lost the vision of the one true, and only God. He may still recite His name, he may still affirm himself Christian, but his religion is to be tested by his worship, and his worship is his homage, and his service; and the man who flings to the eternal God the remnant of a week, on a Sunday, and for the rest of the week worships power, or beauty, or sensation, is an idolater; with the added iniquity that he is not honest enough to give himself utterly to his own idolatry.

All modern substitutes for God may be tested by this old rough word of Jeremiah. I call it a rough word, because he was dealing with the first methods of idolatry, those purely in the material. Far more subtle forms of idolatry prevail to-day. We may take this old and rough word of Jeremiah, and place its measurement upon modern idolatry; and we shall find how correct it is. All substitutes for God are limited, and unsatisfactory, because they are less than the man who created them. Because a man makes his god, his god is less than he is himself, and therefore never can satisfy the cry of his heart. They are dead things, and there can be no communion with them. They are utterly worthless in the day of visitation and calamity, of need and of heartbreak, for there is no breath in them, no response. It was this that Paul felt, when in the midst of the decadent philosophies of that day and hour, and in the midst of the effete systems of idol worship, he saw Athens, full of idols. We read that little sentence,

" full of idols," and perhaps hardly recognize how literally it was true. Athens was crowded with idols. You could not walk its streets, or enter into its homes or halls, without seeing actual effigies everywhere; all of them deified. When these Athenians had exhausted the list of men, they turned to other things, and raised an altar to rumour, and an altar to sentiment, and an altar to an unknown god. Paul was in a paroxysm as he saw the city wholly given to idols. Standing on Mars' Hill he said: Some of your own poets have told you that you are the offspring of God. It is not reasonable therefore to make your gods of gold and silver. Why not? Because if you are the offspring of God, your God cannot be less than you are yourselves. Yet all substitutes for God are less than the men who make them.

Wherever a man puts a substitute for God before mind and heart and will, to command homage, and to inspire conduct, he is creating for himself the uttermost agony; for whensoever there shall come to him the hour of need, it may come with the clash of strife, with the swift stroke of suffering, with the benumbing influence of bereavement, it may come in a thousand ways; but when it comes, then what are these things to which he has given his strength? Scarecrows in gardens of cucumbers! Then let us to the Lord our God with contrite hearts repair.

VIII

THE STRENGTHENING OF THE PROPHET

Preparatory Readings: 2 Kings 23:25-37; 2 Chronicles 35:20-
36:5; Jeremiah 11:18-13.

*"If thou hast run with the footmen, and they have
wearied thee, then how canst thou contend with horses?
and though in a land of peace thou art secure, yet how
wilt thou do in the pride of the Jordan?"*
—JEREMIAH 12:5.

THESE were the words of Jehovah to Jeremiah. It
is impossible to understand their meaning save in the
light of the context and in that of the historic background.

As we saw in our previous study, the last days of
Josiah were days of deterioration in the life of the
nation. He met his death in battle at Megiddo, when,
in spite of warnings, he went to fight against Pharaoh-
Necho, king of Egypt. He was immediately succeeded
by Jehoahaz, whose mother's name was Hamutal. His
reign was short, lasting only three months, and it was
wholly evil. His appointment was not acceptable to the
Egyptian king. He was taken captive, and Jehoiakim,
the son of Josiah, was made king of Judah by Pharaoh-
Necho, the king of Egypt. In return for this appointment Jehoiakim taxed the land, and paid tribute to
Egypt. In a little while Nebuchadnezzar defeated the
Egyptian king, and Jehoiakim became the vassal of
Babylon for three years, after which he rebelled against
the king.

The period to which these particular chapters, beginning at the eighteenth verse of chapter eleven, and running through the thirteenth, belong, was that of the transition period covered by the last days of Josiah, the three months' reign of Jehoahaz, and the beginning of the reign of Jehoiakim. They were dark and troublous days. Warned against alliance with Egypt as a false confidence, Josiah impetuously went to fight against Egypt, and met his death. Judah almost immediately passed under the power of Egypt. Babylon was already moving against Egypt, and Judah was necessarily involved. The people under the evil influences of Jehoahaz, the usurper; and that of Jehoiakim, the vassal king, were becoming more and more corrupt. Evidently the work of proclaiming the Word of Jehovah would be beset with more and more difficulty. In the light of these facts let us glance at the context as it reveals the prophet, and so illuminates our text.

Jeremiah, although he had been prophesying in Jerusalem, would still seem to have been living in Anathoth, and there he was in peril. This fact was revealed to him, as he declared, by Jehovah. A plot had been formed against his life. He made his appeal to his God, and was answered by the declaration of the Divine knowledge of the plot, and of the fact that the severest punishments would be meted out to the men who were plotting against his life. The prophet then poured out his soul, his vexed and troubled soul in questions to God. Why is it, he asked, that the wicked prosper? "How long," he enquired, "shall the land mourn?" The answer of Jehovah indicated the fact that the things he had seen, and the trials through which he had passed were as nothing to those which awaited him. Those to come were by comparison as horses to footmen, as the swellings, or the pride, of Jordan to the land of peace. Concerning His own people Jehovah declared that He had forsaken them, and with this statement of the case, and the necessity for it the prophet declared that he was necessarily in agreement. He saw the judgment impending. He recognized its righteousness. Jehovah declared to him that the evil neighbours of the prophet would be plucked up with Judah; but that there would yet be a way of deliverance for them, that He would visit them in compassion.

The account of this time of communion between Jeremiah and Jehovah ends with the story of how Jehovah gave him two signs; one for himself, and one for the people. The sign for himself was that of the girdle which he was to wear, then to hide by Euphrates, then to seek in order to gaze upon its worthlessness. The significance of the sign was clearly declared to him. The girdle was the emblem of the house of Israel and the house of Judah. The second sign was a spoken one, in the form of a proverb, " Every bottle shall be filled with wine." This he was commanded to utter in the hearing of the people, and told that their obvious retort would be, " Do we not certainly know that every bottle shall be filled with wine?" In answer he was commanded to declare that God would fill the rulers with drunkenness, and dash them one against another.

The account closes with the cry of the prophet to the people to hear the last charge of Jehovah which is a call to the king and queen mother, Jehoahaz and Hamutal; an announcement of the coming judgment, and its cause; the declaration of the hopelessness of the case; and a final pronouncement of doom.

That rapid survey enables us in some measure to realize the atmosphere in which Jeremiah was living at this moment. In the midst of these circumstances, and in the course of this communion between Jehovah and the prophet, the words of my text were uttered. The words consist of two figurative questions. The difficulty of the text is admitted. This is revealed in the fact that almost every expositor gives some different translation of this particular verse. You will have noticed the difference between the Authorized and Revised Versions. The former reads,

" If thou hast run with the footmen, and they have wearied thee, then how canst thou contend with horses? and if in the land of peace, wherein thou trustedst, they wearied thee, then how wilt thou do in the swelling of Jordan."

Isaac Leeser, the Jewish translator, in his translation according to the Massoretic text, renders the passage thus,

" If thou hast run with the footmen, and they have wearied thee, how then canst thou contend with the horses? and if in the land of peace, (wherein) thou trustest, (they wearied thee), how then wilt thou do in the swelling of the Jordan?"

Helen Spurrell, in her scholarly translation of the Old Testament, all too little known, renders the passage thus,

" If thou hast run with the footmen, and they have
    wearied thee,
Then how wilt thou be overheated with the horsemen?
And in the land of peace wherein thou securely
    abideth,
Then what wilt thou do in the swelling of Jordan?"

Rotherham's reading in *The Emphasized Bible* is,

" If with the footmen thou hast run, and they have
    wearied thee
How then wilt thou hotly contend with horses?
Though in a safe land thou art confident
Yet how wilt thou deal with the proud banks of the
    Jordan?"

And yet once more, Ball in the Expositor's Bible translates thus,

" If thou hast run but with foot-racers, and they have wearied thee, how wilt thou compete with the coursers? And if thy confidence be in a land of peace (or, a quiet land), how then wilt thou do in the thickets (jungles) of Jordan? "

The reading of these various translations reveals two things; first, that there is difficulty with regard to the latter part of the passage; and secondly, that the main ideas are the same in each translation. In the Septuagint Version, a word is found, which is omitted in our Hebrew texts. I have no question in my own mind that this word was originally in the Hebrew text. Now I will read the passage, inserting the word, and changing " though " for " if " in the Revised Version; and I think by so doing, we shall come in all probability nearest to the actual thought of the passage.

" If thou hast run with the footmen, and they have wearied thee, then how canst thou contend with horses? and if in a land of peace thou art *not* secure, yet how wilt thou do in the pride of Jordan? "

The word introduced is the word " not " before " secure." It is found in the Septuagint, and I shall proceed upon the assumption of the accuracy of that translation.

From these different renderings of a difficult passage we gather the simple and central thoughts, and these may thus be summarized. If a man is wearied when racing with footmen, how can he hope to win when he runs with horses? If a man lacks confidence in peaceable surroundings, then how is he going to fare when his course is among the jungles, and among the wild beasts?

This passage has nothing whatever to do with the question of how a man is going to die, if he does not know how to live. The phrase " the swellings of Jordan " has nothing to do with the thought of death, and that in spite of all expositions and hymns, about Jordan

[87]

being a type of death. Let us dispossess our minds of that idea, for if one thing is certain, it is that Jehovah had entered into covenant with His servant Jeremiah, that he should be delivered from death. There are experiences through which a man is called to pass, more terrible than death. There were hours when Jeremiah would have welcomed death; when his experiences lay among the swellings of Jordan, the pride, the thickets, the jungles where the wild beasts were, instead of in the land of peace, wherein he had been dwelling.

The questions as put to Jeremiah had a threefold value. They recognized his past experience; they revealed his future course; and they compelled thought and suggested their own answers.

We have in the text then, the method of God with His servant in an hour when it was perfectly evident that he was entering upon work more difficult, more dangerous, more terrible than anything he had ever had to do before; the method of God with His servant in an hour when wearied, filled with haunting fear by reason of the things through which he had passed, he saw that conditions were not improving, and he shrank from his task. How did God deal with that man?

First of all, by emphasizing his difficulty, by compelling him to a new consideration of his own weakness, by asking as from outside the man, the very questions that were haunting his own soul: "If thou hast run with the footmen, and they have wearied thee, then how canst thou contend with horses? and if in a land of peace thou art not secure, then how wilt thou do in the wilds where the wild beasts are?"

Let us examine these questions a little more carefully. In the first place, they recognized the past. His service already rendered was recognized; he had run with the footmen; he had rendered difficult service in a time of comparative peace, in the reign of Josiah. The questions also recognized his suffering. Both in the process of that service, and as the result of it, he was wearied. He was not secure, that is, he was haunted by fear, and restless. " If thou hast run with the footmen," was a recognition of all the service rendered during the years that were passed. " If they have wearied thee; and if in this difficult service in a time of comparative peace thy soul has been haunted with fear, and thou art not secure," was the gracious recognition of the man's actual suffering.

In the questions, however, there was more than a recognition of the past. There was a revelation of the future, or at least a suggestion concerning the future. There was yet severer service waiting for him. He who had run with the footmen would be called upon now to contend against horses. He would presently enter upon more difficult service in times of turbulence and upheaval, when there should no longer be the comparative peace of the reign of Josiah, during which reign the evil passions of the people were suppressed by the popularity of the king. He would be called upon now to exercise his ministry as among the wilds of the Jordan banks, the place of the thicket, and the ambush, and the wild beasts. Thus the questions constituted a call to this man to face the future, and to prepare for it.

So we come to that which is the supreme matter, the suggestion which such enquiries must inevitably have made in the mind of a man who had already run with footmen, had borne his testimony, and that a difficult one, even though in comparative peace, as these questions were asked him from without, coming to him from God. Being the very questions that had been haunting his own soul, they must have made certain very definite suggestions to him. The true preparation for the consideration is that of sympathy with the situation. Jeremiah was wearied; longing for peace, conscious of the national condition, having just discovered that his own townsmen in Anathoth had hatched a plot to take his life; feeling that everything was against him; heard these questions coming to him from God:

"If thou hast run with the footmen, and they have wearied thee, then how canst thou contend with horses? and if in a land of peace thou art not secure, how wilt thou do in the pride of Jordan?"

The very first suggestion of the questions was that of the confidence of God in Jeremiah. In the questions there was no suggestion that Jeremiah had failed in his past ministry. In the questions moreover there was a recognition of his actual experience. He was weary, he was haunted by fear; but he had run with the footmen, he had delivered his message. In those days at the beginning, when he was called and commissioned, he had cried out in the agony of his soul, "Ah, Lord Jehovah! behold, I know not how to speak: for I am a child"; and the answer had been, "Whatsoever I shall command thee thou shalt speak. . . . I have put My words in thy mouth." He delivered His messages, and there was no reflection upon his faithfulness in these enquiries. Now in the hour of his weariness, in the hour of his trembling, God recognized the experience, but had no rebuke for him, for his ministry had been fulfilled. The questions indicated a coming ministry of yet greater difficulty, and constituted a call to further and yet more difficult work. That in itself was an honour conferred. I realize the difficulty of explaining this, but if in imagination you will put yourself back into the place of Jeremiah, with all the weariness of a past ministry, with all the haunting fear of imminent peril, and then realize that God speaks to the soul with apparent severity, and yet suggests new work to be done, you will recognize immediately that God was expressing the utmost confidence in this man, and setting honour upon him in that He was entrusting him with yet more difficult work.

In the second place this Divine confidence in the man, in spite of the Divine knowledge of his trembling, was a call to confidence on the part of the man in God. God was saying in effect to him through his questions: There is more difficult work appointed for thee, and I have confidence in thee for I am calling thee to it. How will you do it? The enquiry was the suggestion that Jeremiah should answer the confidence of God in him, by placing his confidence in God. If God was prepared—I halt again because the language I am going to use is so terribly upon the plane of the human, but I know no better —if God was prepared to risk using this man, then let this man be prepared to risk everything upon God, and prepare himself for the new and more difficult service, by recognizing the reasons for the trust which God asked, as revealed in his past experiences, and in the bearing of the enquiry upon the experiences yet to come.

Again attempting to put ourselves in the place of Jeremiah let us consider some of the truths of which he would be reminded by these enquiries, as he had time to consider them in the light of all the facts.

I think one of the first would be that of the fact that God never calls a man to contend with horses until He has practised him with footmen; that God has never yet sent a man into the wilds of Jordan until He has trained him in the land of peace. It is a great principle, always obtaining in God's methods with His servants, and in all His dealings with His people. It is *the* truth which lies within that familiar proverb, which in many respects is a false proverb, while it yet endeavours to express a truth: "God tempers the wind to the shorn lamb." As a matter of fact God does nothing of the kind. The truth is that God tempers the lamb to the wind by giving the lamb its fleece. He never changes the course of His east wind, because men shear their lambs. Within the false method of expression however there is a truth. God tempers the individual to meet the circumstances. I do not know any illustration that may help us better than one which comes back to me from a tragedy of many years ago. After a terrible railway catastrophe in South Wales, when removing the débris, they found a mother dead, clasping in her arms a little child, unscratched. As they drew the mother out, dead, the little one looked up into the faces of the rescuers, and smiled. It was holding in its hands a little bag of sweets, and when in order to examine the child, they loosened the little fingers, and took the sweets away, the child cried. The child cried when it lost its sweets; but did not at all understand that its mother lay dead! To-day, if that little child is alive, it has forgotten the sweets, but it mourns the loss of mother. But God does not permit a little child of that age to contend with the horses of agony until He trains it by the footmen of its childish sorrows. That is always God's method. He prepares men for the terrific experiences of life and service, by the practices which are less terrific. " If thou hast run with the footmen, and they have wearied thee, then how canst thou contend with horses? " The first phase of the answer is that we are never called upon to contend with horses until we have been trained by running with footmen. God never sends a man into the wilds, where wild beasts are amid the jungles, until He has prepared him in the places of comparative peace.

But the questions would suggest more to the prophet than that. They would remind him that the difficulties of the past are intended to prepare for yet more strenuous service. The strength won out of conflict is for use in further conflict. In every hour of battle, when a man is bruised, and hardened by his bruising, he is being prepared for another battle that lies ahead, until the last field is fought and won, and the Kingdom of God has come. By all the training of present difficulty, God is preparing us, if we are in His will, and are prepared to follow Him, for yet more difficult service that lies ahead. Let that man who has not yet lost anything of the strength of his manhood, be very much afraid if somehow his life is becoming more easy in the matter of Christian witness and testimony. We ran with the footmen. It was a great experience, and a necessary one; and as we ran we were hardened, and so prepared for the more difficult work of running with horses. "Suffer hardship . . . as a good soldier of Christ Jesus," means infinitely more than be heroically determined to bear privation and difficulty. It means enter into the hardness, and realize its quality, in order to be yet more perfectly a soldier of Jesus Christ. The difficulties of the past are intended to prepare for more strenuous service. The strength won in the earlier conflict is preparation for the conflict yet to come.

And finally, there is another suggestion made by these questions. Victories won where they seemed impossible, are assurances that they will be won where they seem impossible. "If thou hast run with the footmen, and they have wearied thee, then how canst thou contend with horses?" In all reverence, how shall I answer God? Let me answer thus; because God is God, and because God asks the question, I will say: In my contending with horses, I shall also and again be weary; but I shall win, for I have already won by Thy strength in running with the footmen. That is the true answer. And when He asks me: If in the land of comparative peace I have not been secure, how shall I do in the wilds? then I shall say to Him, in effect; that because He is God, though in the wilds I shall oftentimes be assaulted by fear, yet I shall win, as I have won in the land of peace.

The one thing no man can take from us is the victory of yesterday, and its prophecy of victory to-morrow. The surprise of the past is the expectation of the future. Oh we are weary; yes, and haunted by fear; but let us look back! We ran with those footmen, as God commanded even though we thought we could not. We delivered our testimony in that land of peace even though it was difficult. Alas, how tremblingly, we know, as none can tell us, but we did it! The weariness is with us, the haunting fear is with us; but the past is with us also. Then by the witness of the past, we are ready for the horses; we are ready for the wilds of Jordan. Not that we are any less conscious of our weakness, but more conscious of it. Not that we have become callous, so that the fears of the jungles cannot assault our souls, for we trembled more than when He first called us. But

> " His love in time past, forbids us to think,
> He will leave us at last, in trouble to sink,
> Each sweet Ebenezer we have in review
> Confirms His good pleasure to carry us through."

So that if God shall bend over a man, and say to him with apparent severity, as though at the first He would rebuke him, " If thou hast run with the footmen, and they have wearied thee, then how canst thou contend with horses? " then let the answer of the man to his God be this: By the strength gained in contending with footmen will I now contend with horses; and by the God Who has given the lie to all my fears in the past, will I go forward to service in the wilds of Jordan.

Let us thus, if He be calling us to some new and difficult enterprise, while we are yet weary, and while our souls are assaulted with fears; let us thus answer Him; for every enquiry of God has at its heart an answer; and as we go forward in dependence upon Him, then horses cannot outrun us, and all the wilds of the Jordan cannot defeat us.

IX

SANCTUARY

Preparatory Readings: 2 Kings 24: 1–17; 2 Chronicles 36: 6–10; Jeremiah 14–17.

" A glorious throne, set on high from the beginning, is the place of our sanctuary."—JEREMIAH 17: 12.

THESE words constituted the prophet's affirmation of faith in a day of darkness, and in spite of great personal anguish. His prophetic messages at this time were burdened with the sense of impending doom, and vibrant with suffering. There are no clear historic notes, but we may safely consider them as belonging to the earlier days of the reign of Jehoiakim, when any hope of reform was dying out.

Their burden is that of God's determination to punish. The movement opens with a graphic parable of drought. The high and the low are alike affected. The ground is barren, and cracked for lack of rain; all life is suffering. The explanation of the condition described in the parable is found later on, when the prophet declared, " They have forsaken Jehovah, the fountain of living waters."

The parable is followed by the account of a remarkable time of communion between Jeremiah and Jehovah, in which the prophet poured out his soul in an agony of protesting prayer, and Jehovah patiently answered him, revealing the inevitability of judgment, resulting from the persistence of the people in their sin.

Then followed a new charge to the prophet in which he was called to a celibate life; and commanded to abstain both from mourning and from mirth. It was in answer to this solemn charge that the prophet uttered the words of this text, " A glorious throne, set on high from the beginning, is the place of our sanctuary."

Sitting amid the gloom, lamenting the suffering of the people, denouncing their sin with vehement earnestness, there was no ray of light breaking in the east. The outlook was one of utter hopelessness. The only illumination was the fiery red of imminent judgment. Then the prophet lifted his eyes, and the vision which greeted them is revealed in the text: " A glorious throne, set on high from the beginning, is the place of our sanctuary."

Since the days of Jeremiah all the externals have changed. Ideals, habits, manners, customs are different; but the essential stream of human history flows on. The sins of men to-day are more subtle, but none the less persistent. The judgments of God are of another character, but none the less sure. To those who speak His word to men, the hour is full of difficulty, and the heart often grows hot and restless. At such times it is good to lift the eyes; and to do so is to see the selfsame vision, and to be constrained to exclaim, as did the prophet in the days of long ago, " A glorious throne, set on high from the beginning, is the place of our sanctuary."

Beginning with the final word of our text let us consider first the meaning of sanctuary; and then, turning to the whole declaration of the text, we shall be prepared to understand its teaching concerning the true place of sanctuary.

The idea of sanctuary is certainly as old as human history. In the architecture of ancient Egypt sanctuary temples have been discovered, consisting of one single chamber, passing into which, men were protected. In the history of God's ancient people Israel, as we find it in the Scriptures of truth, we constantly have this idea of the temple as a place of sanctuary, as when a man, taking hold of the horns of the altar, claimed safety, and his claim was recognized. In olden time, in England every churchyard, and every church, offered sanctuary to men. Dean Stanley writing of Westminster Abbey as it was in the old days, said,

"The precincts of Westminster Abbey were a vast cave of Adullam for all the distressed and discontented in the metropolis who desired, in the phrase of the time, 'to take Westminster,'"

which simply meant, to take sanctuary.

That is the idea suggested by the word in our text. It is not that the prophet declared that we gather to the throne of God for worship; but that in relation to the throne of God we find sanctuary, refuge, safety, protection.

There is a twofold note in this conception of sanctuary, that of protection, and therefore that of peril; that of rest, and consequently that of unrest. Apart from peril and unrest the thought of sanctuary will never enter into the mind of man. Granted the peril, and granted the unrest, then desiring protection from the peril, and rest instead of unrest, man thinks of and desires sanctuary. From the midst of the circumstances of peril and unrest man cries out for protection and for rest; and thus proves at once his sense of conflict, and his desire for the realization of the highest purposes of his own life.

This idea is always connected with religion, in the mind of man. Whether the form of religion be high or low matters nothing. When man, conscious of unrest and of danger—unrest, it may be, resulting from his own folly, danger, resulting it may be from his own sin —whenever man thinks, from the circumstances of unrest and of danger, of the possibility of rest and protection, his mind turns toward religion.

That is singularly illustrated in the matters to which

I have referred. In that ancient Egyptian civilization, the place of sanctuary was not the place of the games, but the place of religion. In the economy of the Hebrews the place of safety for a man attempting to escape the result of his own wrong, was the place of religion. So also, in our own country, in those olden days to which we have made reference, rightly or wrongly, men associated the sanctified places with the sense of sanctuary and safety.

A threefold idea is contained within the thought of sanctuary when we thus relate it to the subject of religion. First there is the thought of purity, not upon the surface, not perhaps at the moment consciously in the mind of the man who is seeking sanctuary; but it underlies the whole conception of the possibility of safety. If we take the Hebrew word, we find that its very root suggests cleanness, and so purity, and so holiness.

Another idea involved is that of privacy, of seclusion, of getting into a place where we cannot be followed, where we shall be in quietness, and alone. I have gone back for illustration to ancient Egyptian history, and to Biblical revelation of Israel's history, and to our own history in days gone by, but there are many sights that meet the eyes of those who walk the ways of London which are eloquent, and yet they are so familiar that we miss their meaning. Sometimes when walking through Westminster Abbey, not in the hour of its sacred services, but in the hour of its quietness; or walking through St. Paul's; have you not seen tired, bruised men and women, sitting alone? The same is true in New York or any city, in the churches which leave their doors open, whether Catholic or Protestant. Never pass them without praying for them, for perhaps not at all perfectly understanding their own action, they have gone into the majestic stillness of those great buildings to be away from things, and to be nearer God. They are seeking sanctuary. Sanctuary is a place of privacy into which a man may go, and know that he will not be followed, that he can be alone.

Consequently the last and the simplest thought of the word is that of protection. Sanctuary, be it where it may, is the place into which one can run, and know that having passed the threshold thereinto, he is protected from all that is without; and consequently finds privacy; and thus inevitably is in the place of purity, and of holiness, even though he himself may be impure, he is enwrapped in the atmosphere of purity, in a place in which there is no lie, no deceit.

Even though the sinner may be there in his sin; his sin is sin there, whatever he may have called it outside. The holy of holies in the sanctuary of the Hebrews was a perfect cube, suggestive of regularity, integrity, exactness. Sanctuary therefore is a place having no complicity with the evil which makes sanctuary a necessity. It is a place of privacy, guarded by the fire of its holiness, from intrusion which is inquisitive or revolutionary. Sanctuary is a place of perfect stillness and quiet. Witness the sacred shrines of all religions, and the holy place of the temple of the Hebrew people; and the sense of awe and respect which ever does, or ever should characterize the attitude of men in any place consecrate to worship, whether the worship be false or true; for I maintain no truly Christian soul could pass within the region of a Mohammedan mosque without reverence.

Sanctuary is the sense of quietness and of peace; and that is in itself protection, for protection is the corollary of purity and privacy. Overcome in the conflict, bruised and broken in the battle, the spirit of man flings itself into that region; and by submission to its law of holiness and peace, becomes protected from all outside forces. Such are some of the simple suggestions of this word sanctuary.

To-day the strenuousness of life is more terrible than ever. The strain and stress have invaded places that once were characterized by immunity therefrom. We still sing,

> " Thou hast Thy young men at the war,
> Thy little ones at home ";

but it seems to-day as if even the home were invaded, and the little ones touched by the restless fever of the age. Never perhaps have men been feeling more keenly the need of sanctuary, not only in the things to which I have referred, but in all the larger outlooks of life.

Let us turn then to the declaration of the text: " A glorious throne, on high from the beginning, is the place of our sanctuary." The statement is not that the sanctuary of God is a throne, but that the throne of God is a sanctuary; and that is not a distinction without a difference. This text seems to me to be one of those highest notes of revelation contained in the Old Testament Scriptures. It strikes the deepest note in the music of the Divine revelation. It does not suggest that the sanctuary—with its order of worship, with its ritual, with its sacrifices, with its priests, all of which things were by Divine ordination—affects the throne of God, and so enables a man to reach God. It suggests that the throne creates the sanctuary, and consequently that man finds the place of his perfect quietness and rest and protection, not in the activities of the place or the hour of worship, but in right relationship to the God Who calls him to the activities of the hour of worship. It fastens attention upon the throne.

The throne of God—the fact of the throne, and the fact of God enthroned—is the revelation of the Bible. I do not hesitate to make that superlative affirmation, and to commend it to thoughtful consideration. The Bible has nothing else to say to men than that God is enthroned. Of course it reveals the laws by which He governs, and the principles of grace by which He deals with men; but the revelation of the Bible is massed here, is crystallized here. All its light is focussed into essential glory in my text: "A glorious throne, on high from the beginning, is the place of our sanctuary."

The throne is the supreme revelation of Scripture. In early Bible history the throne is unnamed, but it is ever present. All the pictures of the early times are pictures of men setting their lives into relationship with the throne of God, and thus finding peace, or rebelling against the government of God, and thus perishing. In the failure of the chosen people to recognize the abiding fact of the throne of God lay the establishment of the monarchy in Israel, that wholly evil thing. "They have not rejected thee," said God to Samuel; "they have rejected Me"; and out of that rejection began all their trouble.

It is at least a significant fact that the first mention of the throne of God in the Bible is to be found amid the story of the suffering of the peoples from the thrones of men, during the reigns of Ahab and Jehoshaphat. The devotional and prophetic books are full of references to the throne and the government of God. When we turn to the New Testament, we find that the one, supreme, master note of all the teaching of Jesus was that of the Kingdom of God. When we pass into the Acts of the Apostles we see the Son of Man, having passed to the throne of God. When we come to the last book of the canon, the book of Revelation, with all its mystic imagery, the central revelation is that of the throne; and the final interpretation of the throne is this, " A Lamb, as though it had been slain, in the midst of the throne." " A glorious throne, on high from the beginning, is the place of our sanctuary."

All this is suggestive. The throne is the centre of authority. It is that from which the law which governs life proceeds. It is the place of administration; not of the unfolding of law alone, but of its application to the affairs of men. The throne demands the principle of reward and punishment. The throne stands for arbitration, and the settlement of all disputes in the realm over which the King presides.

And now let us turn to the declaration of the text, that the throne of God is the place of sanctuary. The thought and the declaration of the text are almost revolutionary. We are much inclined to think that sanctuary means a place where we can escape from the throne of God. The text declares that sanctuary is to be found in the throne of God; that man's place of privacy, loneliness, seclusion, is never found until man finds the throne of God; that man is never protected from the forces that are against him, from himself, until he finds right relationship with the throne of God; that the safety of man is to be found in his government by God. Judgment is the supreme need of the race. The exercise of the Divine authority over human life is the last and final benediction that will ever come to humanity.

In that inspired outbreak Jeremiah declared that the throne is on high. In the Revised Version and elsewhere the statement reads, "*set* on high." This is not wholly inaccurate, but the word "set" has been introduced in order to interpret the meaning of the prophet; and as is so often the case, it somewhat robs the text of its roughness, and therefore of its grandeur. What the prophet said was this, "A glorious throne, on high from the beginning." This Hebrew figure of height runs through the Hebrew imagery, and is always indicative of safety. We find it in the Psalms, and in the prophetic writings. "Jehovah of hosts . . . is our refuge," is, quite literally, our high place. "The name of Jehovah is a strong tower, the righteous runneth into it, and is safe," or quite literally, "the righteous runneth into it, and is set on high." When the prophet Isaiah described the coming of the King and of the Kingdom, you remember his language, "Thine eyes shall see the King in His beauty; and a land of far distances." That is the ulti-mate promise. It was prefaced by the declaration con-cerning the man who submits to that King, and that Kingdom: "He shall dwell on high; his place of de-fence shall be the munitions of rocks; his bread shall be given him; his waters shall be sure."

Reverting to the threefold note which we have de-scribed as lying within this thought of sanctuary, we see the application of this. The throne of God is the place where man finds purity, because he is there set above evil; the place where man finds privacy, because he is lifted high above the tumult and the disturbance; the place where man finds protection, because he is lifted above all enmity.

> "I stand upon the mount of God
> With sunlight in my soul.
> I hear the storms in vales beneath,
> I hear the thunders roll.
>
> "But I am calm, with Thee, my God,
> Beneath these cloudless skies,
> For to the height on which I stand,
> Nor storms nor cloud can rise."

The throne on high is the place of sanctuary; and with all reverence, completing the figurative suggestion, I lis-ten to the words of God incarnate, "I, if I be lifted up from the earth, will draw all men unto Myself," a declar-ation which must never be measured by the Cross, but by the Cross and that which followed it, of resurrection and ascension and perfecting. The lifting up of the Son of man was the creation of perfect sanctuary for the sons of men.

"On high from the beginning," and once again the rhythmic beauty of the text arrests us. It is full of poetry. "The beginning" is another of these illustra-tive phrases of the Bible which are full of poetry and suggestiveness. In Dr. Parker's little volume, called *None Like It, a Plea for the Old Sword*, he says:

" ' The beginning,' the remotest date that has yet been suggested. Science has its slow rising and slow falling centuries. Yet ' the beginning ' is the dateless date which includes them all, and drowns them in a deeper sea. On that ocean millenniums are but tufts of foam."

That is interpretation by a poet of one of the most poetic phrases in the Bible.

" The beginning." It greets us as we open our Bible. " In the beginning God created." We find it in the book of Proverbs. While the seeds of the decay of earthly kingship were already scattered Solomon celebrated that wisdom by which in the beginning God wrought for the creation of His universe. We find in Isaiah's prophecy, uttered in the days of the decadence of man's kingly power, that wonderful declaration that from the beginning God has reigned. When John would introduce that pamphlet in which he grouped a few of the words and works of Jesus in order to the revelation of His true nature, he said: " In the beginning was the Word . . . And the Word became flesh." One day the Master used the phrase Himself; when correcting the false ideas of social life that had usurped the original Divine intention, He swept back beyond the law of Moses and said, " He Who made them from the beginning made them male and female." John used it again in the epistle which has as its key-notes light, and life, and love, " That which was from the beginning . . . declare we unto you." We find it finally in the book of the Apocalypse, the book of mystery and imagery and unveiling; where almost the last note is this: " I am the Alpha and the Omega, the first and the last, the beginning and the end."

This is sanctuary. The throne is settled in eternity.

We look back, and come to the ultimate, the limit, the place of the horizon, the beginning; there is the throne. In all scientific investigation of natural phenomena we reach a limit; there, says revelation, is the throne. If as students of economics we attempt to apply the high moralities to life, we come presently to some subtle question which baffles us; and then we discover a foundation in the beginning, before Moses. The law of Moses was but an accommodation to weakness, said Jesus, but the Divine purpose is from the beginning. " A glorious throne, on high from the beginning, is the place of our sanctuary."

The fixed point in the universe, the unalterable fact, is the throne of God. The laws which emanate from it, and the supreme Will that enforces these laws; the infinite and unchanging Wisdom that arbitrates amid all the conflicts; these are the things that make for peace; and it is only as a man, or a nation is in right relation to that throne that he or it can ever find true sanctuary.

In our present life, on every hand are mysteries that baffle and perplex. Oh, the inexpressible comfort of knowing that unseen by the physical vision, but surely apprehended by faith,

" Thy throne, O God, is for ever and ever.
A sceptre of equity is the sceptre of Thy Kingdom."

And yet again, the deeper comfort for individual life, when that life is immediately related to that throne by submission to its authority. That is sanctuary. Not escape from the throne, not hiding from God, not finding some place where He cannot find us; but hastening to the throne, submitting to its authority, yielding to its judgment, consenting to its verdicts, abandoning ourselves to its government; that is sanctuary.

In proportion as we know what it is thus to yield to that throne, we are indeed able to call God, " Father ";

for it is by submission to the throne that we discover the Father. "Seek ye first His Kingdom, and His righteousness; and all these things shall be added unto you," "For your heavenly Father knoweth that ye have need of all these things." To kiss the sceptre of the King, is to discover the heart of the Father. So we are able to sing,

> "Father, I know that all my life
> Is portioned out for me,
> The changes that are sure to come
> I do not fear to see:
> I ask Thee for a present mind
> Intent on pleasing Thee.

> "In service which Thy will appoints,
> There are no bonds for me:
> My inmost heart is taught ' the truth '
> That makes Thy children ' free.'
> A life of self-renouncing love
> Is one of liberty."

"A glorious throne, on high from the beginning, is the place of our sanctuary."

X

THE DIVINE SOVEREIGNTY

Preparatory Readings: 2 Kings 24: 18–20; 2 Chronicles 36: 11–13; Jeremiah 18–20.

" Then I went down to the potter's house, and, behold, he was making a work on the wheels."
—JEREMIAH 18:3.

CHAPTERS eighteen, nineteen and twenty of Jeremiah are closely connected in their teaching with chapters fourteen to seventeen. They are all concerned with the judgment which was decreed against the people of God on account of their sin. In the midst of the anguish which filled the prophet's heart as he contemplated the imminent peril, he had caught a vision of the true place of sanctuary, and he had exclaimed, " A glorious throne, on high from the beginning, is the place of our sanctuary."

In chapters eighteen and nineteen especially, that fact is emphasized. The sovereignty of God is insisted upon, and moreover, it is interpreted. Two signs were given to the prophet; the first was that of the potter's house, and this was intended for the prophet himself; the second was that of the earthen bottle, which had been fashioned in the house of the potter, but was dashed in pieces in the sight of the people, and this sign was intended for the people.

In the house of the potter Jeremiah was taught the secrets of the Divine government. " A glorious throne, on high from the beginning, is the place of our sanctuary," he had exclaimed, and rightly exclaimed; and

[107]

then in effect, God had said to him, In order to understand the operations of that throne, go down to the house of the potter, and watch him at work on the wheels.

So the prophet paused, to look upon that old and familiar activity, in which art and artifice so wondrously merge. For the instruction of his own soul, and for his preparation for the continuance of his difficult ministry Jeremiah was sent to the house of the potter. Afterwards in the valley of the son of Hinnom he revealed one activity of the government of God to the people, not that of the moulding, nor that of the remaking, but that of the marring, or breaking, or dashing in pieces.

The secrets revealed to him were those of the moulding, the marring, and the remaking; all which things he saw as he stood in the house of the potter. The activity revealed to the people was that of the Divine breaking of what He had already made, and there the revelation for the people ended at the time. But let us never forget to put these two things into connection. Standing in the valley of the son of Hinnom, in the neighbourhood of Topheth, he took the earthen vessel, and dashed it in pieces, and declared this as the Divine activity; and that it was the message for Judah at that moment. But in the house of the potter he had already heard another secret, and it was this, If the vessel be marred in the hand of the potter he will make it again another vessel.

We shall confine ourselves to the figure of the potter's house, remembering that its first and final application is national; but in order to our own profit we shall consider it in its simple individual teaching.

The figure of the potter and the clay has always been full of fascination. Perhaps it has not been so popular in the preaching of recent years as it formerly was. There is a note of severity about it, of which our softer age has been a little afraid. Yet it is noticeable that this figure is used in the Bible by the men mightiest in their personal thinking, in their spiritual apprehensions, and in the influence they exerted on their own age. It was the figure of Isaiah, the man who had the clearest vision of the throne of God. It was, as we see, the figure of Jeremiah, the man perhaps in all the long prophetic line, whose ministry was most heroic in that it was foredoomed to failure. It was used by Zechariah, to whom were given the most remarkable unveilings of the processes of the centuries. And it became a great figure in the teaching of Paul, the servant and the expositor of Jesus Christ.

But the figure contains a deeper note than that of its severity, which when discovered, explains and justifies the severity in the presence of which we are ever prone to tremble. That will be recognized if we remember again these very men to whom I have made reference. If the prophesying of Isaiah was characterized by thunder, how perpetually it trembled to the tenderness of tears. If indeed Jeremiah stood at times as a brazen wall, with an almost awful fierceness denouncing the sin of his people, his central word is this, "Oh, that my head were waters, and mine eyes a fountain of tears, that I might weep day and night for the slain of the daughter of my people!" If Zechariah made use of the figure to insist upon the sovereignty of Jehovah, his ultimate message is that of the glorious consummations in which peace shall come to men, and there shall be a realization of all the tender purposes of the heart of God. If Paul, in hard and logical argument borrowed the figure, it was Paul who wrote the mystic words, " I could wish that I myself were anathema from Christ for my brethren's sake."

All this seems to me to be significant, and a recognition of it is necessary to admit us into the true atmosphere for the consideration of the teaching of this wonderful figure, which here in Jeremiah comes out in all its simplicity and clearness of outline.

STUDIES IN THE PROPHECY OF JEREMIAH

There are three outstanding facts at which I think we should glance before attempting to consider the teaching conveyed. We shall best see these things, if we really allow ourselves to be children, quite simply. Very many of us have been to the house of the potter. It is an interesting fact that that very phrase is retained even yet to describe the actual place where the potter works. In the Potteries of England, where the first years of my ministry were spent, the place where the man sits at his work is still called the house of the potter. To watch him at his work, as I have often done in days gone by, is to discover that the essential things of the craft remain through all time, almost identical. I think I am right in saying that the only thing that has changed in the work of the potter to-day, from the time of Jeremiah is the form and fashion and shape of the wheel. There is still a man at work, and still clay that he works upon; the man is not improved, and the clay is no finer. There may be differences in the wheel, which also is parabolic; for the supreme things here are potter and clay; the wheel was necessary, but not supreme, presently to be set aside, while the potter abides, rejoicing in his work, and the work is perfected, glorifying the potter. Thus the wheel is done away. It was but the circumstance of the hour; and circumstances are always changing. That also is a parable.

Going down to the house of the potter then, these three things arrest our attention: the potter, the wheel, the clay. Of these things let us remind ourselves; first, that the potter is an intelligent and capable worker; secondly, that the wheels are proper instrumentalities under the government of the potter, for in this old-time potter's house, as in many a potter's house to-day, the revolving wheel is due to the pressure of the potter's foot, while his deft fingers manipulate the clay; and finally, that the clay is capable material; it must be clay; I will use the simplest word of all and say, it is the very stuff the potter wants, steel filings would be of no use.

Thus, standing in that potter's house, and looking at these things in all their simplicity, I take first of all the surface lessons. Jeremiah was sent to the potter's house. In the potter's house he beheld the potter working his work on the wheels. He saw a vessel suddenly crushed, marred in the hands of the potter; and then he saw that selfsame vessel moulded and fashioned again, until it was finished and perfected. Having looked at the man at his work, God spoke to his soul, and He said, "As the clay in the potter's hand, so are ye in Mine hand, O house of Israel."

The surface lessons of the potter's house are these: First, I watch the potter, and I learn God's interest, God's attention, God's power. What a help it would be to have a potter at work before our eyes at this moment! We should see him watching his work. If we watched him closely, we should detect in his eyes a light of keen interest in his work. As we watched him we should see power first restrained to the gentleness of an infinite delicacy, then crushing everything out of shape, and yet again moulding it back into exquisite beauty. That would be a portrait of God.

Then I cease to look at the potter for a moment, and I look at the wheels, revolving wheels; wheels turning, turning, and nothing more. How shall I describe the suggestiveness of those wheels? There is no better way than by borrowing Browning's words,

". . . this dance
Of plastic circumstance,
This Present, thou, forsooth, wouldst fain arrest
Machinery just meant
To give thy soul its bent,
Try thee and turn thee forth, sufficiently impressed."

The revolving wheel of the potter is the whirling wheel

of circumstance. I should be inclined to say that in the hour of worship, the Potter is not so busily occupied with us, as He is during the busy working days of the week. It is in the midst of the week, with its whirl and its strife, its drive, and its tension, its restlessness and its race, that God is able to do His best work with men and women. " This dance of plastic circumstance! "

Having thus glanced at the potter superficially and at the wheel superficially, I look at the clay; and two things impress me. The first is that of its wonderful capacity. Do not speak in any language that is derogatory of clay. What else can you find that will suit the deft fingers of the potter but clay? I repeat the thing I said a moment ago; it is the very stuff the potter wants. Man is the very stuff God wants in order to do something in the universe which He cannot do in any other way. What? Well, we are beginning to have gleams of light, but we hardly know yet. There are vaster secrets wrapped in humanity than humanity has ever yet discovered; higher and nobler purposes to be fulfilled through this strange race of which we form a part, with all its passion, and its power, and its doubt, and its grovelling, and its ascending, than we have ever dreamed. Let us think well of ourselves, when we think in God's presence. We are the clay, the very stuff God wants!

Now let us get back to the central matter. Contemplating this figure of the potter's house, or imaginatively standing by the side of Isaiah, of Jeremiah, of Zechariah, of Paul, of the seers of the ages, there are certain things that we must carefully observe. In this potter's house there is first of all discovered to man, a principle; there is secondly revealed to man, a purpose; but the ultimate, the supreme thing is neither the principle nor the purpose, but the Person of the Potter. The three are necessary to an understanding of the figure. Until I have discovered this principle, my life will be a failure. If however I have discovered the principle alone, then my soul will be filled with terror. I must also see the purpose. Moreover if I know principle and purpose only, I shall yet tremble, and wonder, and be filled with haunting foreboding. But, when presently I press through the principle and beyond the purpose, and discover the Person of the Potter, then the purpose will flame with light, and the principle that appears so hard and severe will become the tenderest and the sweetest thing in all my life.

What then is the principle? Let me attempt to express it briefly by saying that in this picture the principle revealed is that of the sovereignty of God, and the necessity for man's unquestioning submission thereto. I watch the revolving wheel, and I watch the potter at his work, and I am necessarily impressed with his right over the clay. It is an absolute right; his power over the clay is unlimited. I stand imaginatively in that potter's house all silent, I listen to the whirr of the wheels, and I watch the manipulating fingers of the potter; and I am impressed with his right and with his power; and for a moment, everything else seems to be as nothing. I glance from the potter to the clay, and I observe it lying plastic on the wheel, beneath his hand, with no wish, and with no right; but with infinite possibility; yet with no power within itself to realize the possibility that is resident within itself.

Infinite possibility! It is but a mass of grey, or half dirty white, material! Turn from the wheel, and behold on those shelves behind where the potter stands, the vessels of beauty and of glory. All that lay resident as possibility within the dull and shapeless clay; but there was nothing within the clay that was able to realize its own possibility. It once lay upon the wheel, a shapeless mass.

I glance once again at the wheel itself, and notice that it is under the complete control of the potter, having no effect upon the clay apart from the pressure of the pot-

ter's foot; but answering the pressure of the potter's
foot, bringing the clay constantly nearer to the potter's
hand, back, and back again; the revolving wheel presses
the clay into the potter's hand. Was there ever a picture so perfect, or so wonderful in the unveiling of these
profound things of human life?

Yet here one must pause for a moment. A difficulty
suggests itself, for no figure can in itself be final; and
a man is inclined to say as he watches the work: But
there is a great difference; that clay has no wish, nor
can it have a wish; that clay has no will, and I have will
power; I have been created by this very Potter, God,
with power to choose, to elect; and the disparity is
marked. I pray you look once again, and remember this,
that while that is so, you must take all your ratios into
account when you are dealing with an illustration. The
distance between God and man seems to be greater than
the distance between the potter and the clay. The difference between the Creator and that which is created
seems to be greater than the difference between any
form and fashion of creation. But this is false seeming.
The distance between God and a man is not so great as
that between the potter and the clay. That which seems
to indicate distance, really proves nearness. Between
the potter and the clay there is no link, of intellect, emotion or volition. The clay cannot coöperate with the
potter. In a man they are present. He is kin of God.
He can coöperate with God.

The will of man is free to choose its own master principle, and in no other way. The will of
man is not ultimately free, nor can it be. The will
of man is always mastered by some other force of
his personality; or as it has often been said in simplest language, No man ever yet did say, I will do anything, but that had he completed in speech the processes
of his mind, he would have had to declare, I will because; there was a reason behind his choosing. No man

is finally free; but God in the mystery of human creation has made man so that he may elect. The reason that shall drive him, the cause that shall master him, the principles that shall inspire him; he may elect; so far is man free, and no further. If we realize that, we shall see that the apparent disparity is more apparent than real; that allowing for infinite distances, between God and man, there is yet a very real nearness, and the picture is yet a perfect picture.

The principle revealed then is that God is absolutely sovereign over human life, and that man's wisdom lies in an unconditional and uncompromising surrender to the will of God; that man's highest wisdom lies in his accepting the figure of the clay, and ceasing to wish except as within the sphere of the Divine will; ceasing to choose save in answer to the Divine choices. All this is a preacher's argument! Then I pray you hear the whole philosophy in a poet's couplet:

> " Our wills are ours, we know not how,
>   Our wills are ours to make them Thine."

So sang Tennyson, and in that couplet there is the flash of a clear insight into the profoundest fact of human life. The Potter's sovereignty, His absolute right, His unlimited power; these are the first things I learn.

To leave the subject there, however, would be to do violence to the teaching of the figure, and to make the heart of men afraid. If some may not quite follow me there, then allow me to speak experimentally. If you simply tell me of God's sovereignty, and right, I not only tremble, I rebel. It is not enough to talk to me of sovereignty, of absolute right, of unlimited power; for even if this thing be true, that I am what I am by His creation, still I am what I am; and being what I am, I ask a reason for the pressure, an explanation of the pain, a vindication of the crushing. There is no irreverence in that. The Bible is the answer to that very essential cry of humanity, and this figure is the answer when we truly discover all its teaching.

So I pass from that discussion of the principle, to consider the next matter, that of the purpose. That which concerns me at the moment is not that this figure of the potter's house tells me what God's purpose is, but that it teaches me that God has a purpose. This is revealed when Jeremiah tells us that " He wrought *his* work on the wheels." I prefer the King James rendering here. Here is a sentence that seems to me to thrill with music, and be vibrant with the very poetry of eternity. " He wrought His work on the wheels." Then He is doing something. That is the first thing. The potter was not fooling with the clay, he was not playing with it, he was not amusing himself! It was work, it was serious; there was purpose in it. I do not know how that appeals to you, but as God is my witness, it brings great comfort to me, in the midst of life, with its problems, and pressure, with its oft-times agonies; God is not playing with me; " He wrought His work on the wheels." There he stands, there the wheel, there the clay! In his mind there is a purpose. What is it? The clay does not know, the onlooker cannot tell; the potter knows. I behold him with his hands on that clay, working; and presently the onlooker will know what was in his mind when he began his work; and lifting the figure into the higher realm, and admitting human consciousness, presently, the clay will discover that which it did not know at first; the purpose of the potter. But the thing of comfort is that when the potter took that clay and put it on his wheel, and placed his hand upon it, he meant something. To me this is a veritable gospel, it is comfort, it is the very essence of life! God means something! As yet I do not know what, even as to myself. As yet I cannot tell what, about this race of which I am a part; but He means something. Through this clash and strife about me, these strange aspirations of humanity, emerging into great songs in the centuries, and dying back into wails of unequivocal agony; God is not playing with humanity. He means something! There shall be a fair morn of morns, in which not I in my individual life alone, but the race will realize the purpose Divine; and God will be vindicated in that hour, for all the processes through which humanity has passed. That is my faith. That is my creed; and if I did not hold it, I could never preach again.

The Potter has a thought in His mind for the clay, and He alone is able to transfer His thought to the clay. The clay is ignorant of the thought in the Potter's mind, nor can know it, save as it plastically yields itself to Him, and lets Him carry out His great design. Mark the inter-relation between these things. That inter-relation as I see it, is one of the profoundest things in human life. Man gains in God, the One Who knows and understands the stuff, and Who can mould and fashion it to the ultimate purpose of His will. What does God gain in man? Does the Potter gain anything in that clay? Surely yes, a vehicle of vision, that through which He can give others to see that in His mind which cannot be seen save through such a vehicle. God gains in humanity, an instrument of revelation. Revelation to whom? Who shall tell? Paul, climbing the height, had some vision; and in his ultimate Ephesian letter he declared that in the ages to come, humanity, ransomed humanity, will be the instrument through which the wisdom of God, and the kindness of God are revealed to the principalities and the powers in the heavenly places. There is no reading that statement without dreaming dreams and seeing visions, without peopling those unborn ages with high intelligences who have never sinned, but who nevertheless could never understand the grace of God save as a ransomed people shall sing their passion song of blood in their presence.

Thank God for the conviction, that the principle of sovereignty demanding submission, is working to a purpose that shall be worthy of God Himself.

Finally we come to that which is central, for I am prepared to repeat the thing I have already said, that if I only discover the principle my heart is filled with fear. In the recognition of purpose, I find comfort, but humanity has been so fashioned, that it will inquire, what is this purpose; and there is foreboding until the eyes rest upon the Potter. If we are in the house of the potter, we can gaze upon the potter; but who can gaze on God? Yet that is the ultimate thing. If I am to submit myself to this principle, if I am to believe in the beneficence of this purpose, I must see God. " Show us the Father, and it sufficeth us." That is the most rational cry of humanity. I must see God. Who is this Potter of the universe? Absolute, supreme, moulding humanity like clay, working seriously toward a goal, who is He? That is the question, that is the question of all questions!

And now there remains little to say, for God has answered the cry. The Son of His love said to Philip, and He says to us, " He that hath seen me hath seen the Father ";

> " Would we view God's brightest glory,
>   We must look in Jesu's face."

In Jesus the great Potter came into view that we might see Him and know Him. I look again, and I watch Him at work in the potter's house. I watch that foot that turns the wheel, and I watch the hands that press the clay.

> " In His feet and hands are wound-prints."

Now my heart has found its ultimate rest. It is the

Person of the Potter which is the supreme matter of this
great figure of speech.

That being so, I am reminded that the potter's field
is last mentioned in Scripture in strange connection.
In Matthew's story of Judas I read: "They took
counsel, and bought with them the potter's field to
bury strangers in. Wherefore that field was called the
field of blood unto this day" (Matt. 27: 7–8). The
potter's field was the field or yard outside the potter's
house where the wreckage was cast. That they bought
with the blood-money of the Son of God. How little they
understood the significance of what they did. By the
mystery of His betrayal, by the mystery of His being
sold for the price of a slave, the vessel, marred in the
hands of the potter, may be made again—another vessel
as seems good to the potter.

XI

FALSE RULERS

Preparatory Readings: 2 Kings 24 : 18–20 ; 2 Chronicles 36 : 11–13 ; Jeremiah 21–23.

"Woe unto the shepherds that destroy and scatter the sheep of My pasture!"
"Behold, I am against the prophets."
—JEREMIAH 23 : 1 and 30.

HAVING observed the potter at his work, and learned therefrom the facts of the Divine sovereignty, Jeremiah had been sent to the valley of the son of Hinnom, there to dash in pieces a potter's vessel, as prophetic of the coming activity of that sovereignty in judgment.

Returning from Topheth he stood in the court of Jehovah's house, and repeated the prediction of imminent judgment. This brought him into the place of immediate persecution. Pashhur smote him and imprisoned him. On the following day, however, Jeremiah being brought forth out of the stocks, repeated his prophecy of judgment, singling out Pashhur for special attention, and declaring that upon him would fall the most severe judgment of God.

Out of the midst of these circumstances of persecution and of suffering the prophet poured out his own soul in the presence of Jehovah. Conscious that he had been compelled by the Divine ordination to declare these things of judgment, he complained before God that he had become the laughing-stock of the people, and that the word of Jehovah had made him a reproach and a derision. He had declared within himself that he would no more make mention of the Divine name, nor speak any more in that name; but the word had become a burning fire within him, and he had been compelled to utter it.

The tempest-tossed condition of the mind of the prophet at that time is seen in that after this complaint, there was a sudden outburst of confidence, as remarkable as the complaint had been; in which he declared that Jehovah was with him, that his enemies should not prevail over him; and he called for a song of praise, because of the deliverance which would be wrought.

Yet again that outburst of confidence was immediately followed by an outburst of fear. He cursed the day of his birth, and lamented the continuity of his life.

All this helps us to see how terrible were the sufferings through which Jeremiah passed in the delivery of his message; he was a prophet of Jehovah, in a decadent age, the most hopeless period in the history of the ancient people.

We now approach the final series of prophecies prior to the fall of Jerusalem, and they consist mainly of messages delivered to Zedekiah, the last and the weakest of the kings. Some of these were direct words to the king himself. Some of them consisted of repetitions, in the hearing of Zedekiah, of prophecies which Jeremiah had uttered in previous reigns, with such applications as the immediate need demanded.

At the commencement of the reign of Zedekiah a Chaldean army approached Jerusalem, and the king immediately sent to the prophet to ask what the outcome would be. We must remember that at the time Jerusalem was filled with prophets; prophets who were urging King Zedekiah to what they were pleased to think of, and to describe as a national movement against Babylon for the freeing of Judah from its oppression. The reply of Jeremiah was that the king of Babylon would be victorious, and that the political wisdom of Judah would be manifested by bending the neck to the yoke. In giving this advice Jeremiah was acting in the light of the ultimate fact. It is for us to remember that seven or more years passed before the city fell; but Jeremiah knew and was commissioned to declare the fact of that ultimate fall. This necessarily brought him into conflict with the rulers and the prophets; and his insistence was the cause of very much suffering, indeed ultimately of terrible experiences in prison.

We have now to do with his messages during this period. His immediate answer to the messengers of Zedekiah was devoid of all hesitancy or uncertainty. He first foretold the disaster in detail; and declared to them that the only alternative offered to them was that of death or captivity. His final word had to do with the house of the king. He called that royal house to return to paths of rectitude in government. The hopelessness of the situation was evident in the fact that in spite of this call, the last word of his message was one of sentence pronounced, and the clearest declaration that the doom must fall by the will and the act of Jehovah.

But this message of Jeremiah, delivered to the deputation, was not sufficient. He was commanded to go himself to the house of the king. This he did, and what he said there occupies these chapters, up to and including chapter twenty-seven. Arrived at the court, he first of all repeated at greater length his call to repentance, and his warning. He charged the king to remember that the way of repentance is the way of restoration, that the way of disobedience is the way of destruction; and then he reviewed in three movements, characterized by brevity and clarity, the history of the three predecessors of Zedekiah. First concerning Jehoahaz he declared that there was no need for men to weep for Josiah, who had died, but rather for Jehoahaz (that is, Shallum), who had been carried away to die in captivity. Moving on to the reign of Jehoiakim he described the sin of his unrighteous reign, which was characterized by injustice and oppression. For this sin he had been judged and flung out of Jerusalem. Yet his influence remained. Finally the prophet described the doom of his son Jehoiachin (or Coniah), and its reason; and throughout the messages which followed that brief survey of the immediately preceding history of the kings, the burden was that of the causes of the national failure and disaster.

The two quotations which I have selected give us the key to the teaching. The nation was under the domination of evil rulers, civil and spiritual. Shepherds, the civil rulers; and prophets, the spiritual rulers; were exercising a false authority, and debasing national life and character. In these great burdens therefore Jeremiah denounced the sins of kings and of prophets, and in so doing laid bare the causes of the national ruin.

With that rapid survey of the situation we may approach the theme which is suggested by these prophecies, and by these texts. The theme is that of the elements which are destructive in civil and in spiritual authority; the relation of national life to authority, the necessity that authority in the life of the nation should be true, that it should be spiritual; the peril that threatens a nation when there is a coalition between civil and spiritual rulers, in which each yields something to the other upon the basis of compromise, and so pollutes the springs of national life, and defiles the streams that flow therefrom.

Glancing back over these chapters then, we shall consider their revelation of the sins of kings, and the sins of prophets; the inter-relation between these things; and the effects produced.

First then, the revelation here of the sins of kings. The term "shepherds" is the arresting one. "Woe unto the shepherds." Jeremiah used the term after his reference to those principal reigns, describing the central iniquity in the reign of Jehoahaz, the successor of Josiah; in the reign of Jehoiakim; and in the reign of

Jehoiachin. In referring to them he broke out into this cry, "Woe to the shepherds." This term is used as the true figure of civil authority in the Bible. Kings and all civil rulers were thus referred to; not the kings upon the throne only, but the principals in Judah, those who, united with the king, had oversight of the affairs of the realm.

In the Biblical literature the idea of the shepherd as king, first emerged in the great final song or prophecy of Jacob, in which, in a parenthesis—a little difficult to interpret, I admit,—he referred to Joseph and said, "From thence is the shepherd, the stone of Israel." From that figurative use of the word, the idea runs on through the literature. If we follow it historically, or in that progressive movement which is discoverable in prophetic utterance, the thought of authority is always symbolized by that of the shepherd relation. The supreme illustration is found in the twenty-third psalm. We are all familiar with that psalm. We love its music. It is the psalm of the infinite rest and the infinite quietness, of the care of Jehovah, of the leading by still waters, of the rejoicing in the palace of God; but it is the psalm of sovereignty, it is the interpretation of the Kingship of Jehovah. When sang the psalmist, "Jehovah is my Shepherd, I shall not want" he was rejoicing in the character and activity of God in His Kingship.

The same truth becomes yet more apparent when we turn to these prophetic writings, and see how constantly the great outstanding prophets protested against false civil authority under this selfsame figure. It becomes clearest yet and most remarkable in Jeremiah's great disciple in exile, Ezekiel; and in Zechariah it emerges again.

Crossing into the New Testament, we find that our Lord's perpetual invective against the rulers, borrowed the figure of false shepherds, the result of whose false rule was that the people were scattered as sheep having no shepherd. That great idea is discoverable not only in our Bible, but in all great thinking. It was Homer who declared, All kings are shepherds of the people.

The denunciation here of shepherds then is the denunciation of kings and those in civil authority. Particularly, the mind of the prophet was resting upon Jehoahaz, Jehoiakim, Jehoiachin, and Zedekiah, the last and weakest of them, whom he did not name; and inclusively his charge against them was this, that their sin consisted in their failure to realize the shepherd character, and fulfil the shepherd function in the life of the nation.

With that general thought in mind we turn to the message of the prophet, and find three phases of the sin definitely described. He first charged these false rulers with self-interest as the inspiration of all their government. He charged them in the second place, in a very notable word, with refusing to hear the word of Jehovah in the day of prosperity. He charged them finally with that which resulted from their self-interest and their refusal to hear the word of the Lord in the day of prosperity; neglect of the people, and scattering of the people who should have been consolidated into strong national life.

He charged them with self-interest:

"Woe unto him that buildeth his house by unrighteousness, and his chambers by injustice; that useth his neighbour's service without wages, and giveth him not his hire; that saith, I will build me a wide house and spacious chambers, and cutteth him out windows; and it is ceiled with cedar, and painted with vermilion."

That is so graphic a picture that very little needs to be said about it. It is the picture of kings and those in civil authority strengthening their own house, and seeking their own greatness, and compelling the people to minister to them; and all the while doing injustice to the very men who build their house, refusing to pay the hire of the neighbour who builds. The prophet's word is very suggestive; not the *labourer*, but the "*neighbour*." This prophet of God saw through all the false conditions of human life, and watched the kings beautifying their own houses, that particular action being symbolic of their own attitude, making it glorious with cedar, making it gorgeous with vermilion. This prophet-priest Jeremiah of Anathoth, watching the process, saw the men who hewed the cedar, and carved the cedar, and placed it, and put on the vermilion, not as hands employed, but as neighbours in coöperation. The civil authorities had no care for the workmen, but much for the work; and much for the work, because the work contributed to their own self-aggrandizement. Absorbed in this ministry to self, and this consequent injustice to neighbours who coöperated, they were failing to administer judgment and justice, forgetting the method of the father of these kings, Josiah, who did judgment and justice, so that it was well with him; forgetting his constant care to judge the cause of the poor and the needy, and that so it was well with him, for then he was acting in coöperation with God. That is the first sin of the kings as Jeremiah saw it; self-interest the purpose of their authority, seeking only their own enrichment, their own security, their own comfort; the employment of their neighbours to minister to them; and the neglect of judgment, justice, mercy, and truth in their dealing with these men.

A little further on Jeremiah touched another and yet deeper note:

"I spake unto thee in thy prosperity; but thou saidst, I will not hear. This hath been thy manner from thy youth, that thou obeyedst not My voice."

Speaking undoubtedly at the moment to one particular king, but speaking to him as the representative of other kings, and as representative of all these civil rulers who were united to him, the prophet said to him: This is the central sin of thy persistent failure; from thy youth upwards thou dost not hear when God speaks to thee in thy prosperity. Presently in a great outburst the prophet cried:

"O earth, earth, earth, hear the word of Jehovah."

If we link that final cry of the prophet in that particular connection with this central charge, we discover how he saw this to be the supreme sin of the civil ruler, that in the midst of prosperity he refused to listen to the word of Jehovah.

That is the second phase of sin in kings, and in civil rulers; trust in material things, forgetfulness therefore of the spiritual in such hours of trust; the very failure which that far-seeing prophet law-giver of this self-same economy foresaw, when in his final messages to the children of Israel, he said to them:

"Lest, when thou hast eaten and art full, and hast built goodly houses, and dwelt therein; and when thy herds and thy flocks multiply . . . thou say in thine heart, My power and the might of mine hand hath gotten me this wealth. But thou shalt remember Jehovah thy God, for it is He that giveth thee power to get wealth."

These were illuminative words, spoken at the commencement of their history, and now being fulfilled in the case of the rulers in the day of prosperity, who were declining to hear the word of God, saying, Our own hand hath gotten us this wealth, this is the result of our own policies, of our own skill, and of our own devotion to toil; forgetting that all the original capital of man—his keenness of understanding, his strength of limb, and dexterity of fingers—is a Divine gift. The civil rulers are seen forgetting the spiritual, and trusting in material prosperity.

I pick up no newspaper without trembling, in which I read of unprecedented Trade Returns. I have little care, less care than ever, to account for these things. It is the fact of them that constitutes national peril, for it is in the hour of prosperity that we are at least in danger of forgetting that it is God Who has given us power to get wealth. It is in the hour of prosperity that we are least likely to be listening to the voice of God. As we look at this picture in this mirror of prophetic revelation, as we look at this distant scene in Judah, of kings prosperous materially, as they certainly had been in a wonderful succession, and we hear the prophet speaking to them in the name of God, charging them, I spake to thee in thy prosperity, and thou wouldst not hear; what a picture it is of the degradation of all life under the influence of an authority that forgets spiritual things. From the height of the sanctuary, looking on such life, whether in Judah or here, whether in that far gone century, or in the immediate present, one feels that the trail of the serpent is everywhere. When I say, the trail of the serpent, I am referring to that old story in Genesis, where the whole activity of godless life was expressed in the terrific language addressed to the serpent, "Upon thy belly shalt thou go, and dust shalt thou eat." That is the story of all national greatness that forgets God both in its method and in its issue.

Glancing once more at this prophetic page, I discover the issue, so far as the nation is concerned, of the sin of the rulers; the sin of the rulers who act in selfish interest and forgetfulness of the Word of God. That issue is neglect and scattering of the people; first contempt for them, the holding of them in a low estimate; the terrible conception that the people, the masses, are in some senses inferior; that they are, to use that terrific and damnable word that came into our own speech from the sensualism of the French Revolution, the *Canaille*. When rulers think of the people so, they are sinning against God; and all their authority will result in disintegration, and the break-up of national life. To the rulers the prophet said: You have neglected the people if you have failed to visit them; if you have not paid them their hire; if you have not administered judgment and justice. Their essential needs are unmet. Much may be done for the accidental needs of the people while their essential needs are unmet. Their inherent rights are neglected. Their persistent wrongs are unrighted. The word of Jeremiah became the word of Jesus, a very practical and immediate and actual word; and we may rob it of its true spiritual significance by spiritualizing it too far. You have scattered the people, said Jeremiah. The people are scattered, said Jesus. When Jeremiah said, scattered, he was referring to the deportations of people from Judah, through the political intrigue and trickery between these kings and foreign rulers. Take one glaring instance from the standpoint of Jeremiah. Ezekiel, his own disciple, was gone, and with him others of the best men of the nation; they were scattered, and the nation impoverished; they had been neglected, and men had been trusting in their own cunning, rather than in the living God. I confess that I mourn whenever I read of emigration from my own country. It may be a great necessity, but it is created by false conditions. When the best of our young manhood have to go out to other parts of the world to live, we are weakening our national strength; we are scattering our people. It would be well for us to read once more an old poem:

" Sweet Auburn! loveliest village of the plain,
  Where health and plenty cheered the labouring swain,
  Where smiling spring its earliest visit paid,
  And parting summer's lingering blooms delayed."

Let us read a brief quotation:

" Princes and lords may flourish, or may fade;
  A breath can make them, as a breath has made;
  But a bold peasantry, their country's pride,
  When once destroyed, can never be supplied.

" A time there was, 'ere England's griefs began,
When every rood of ground maintained its man;
For him light Labour spread her wholesome store,
Just gave what life required, but gave no more;

" His best companions, innocence and health;
And his best riches, ignorance of wealth.

" But times are altered; trade's unfeeling train
Usurp the land and dispossess the swain;
Along the lawn, where scattered hamlets rose,
Unwieldy wealth and cumbrous pomp repose."

That is the old Hebrew conception; it is the Divine conception that any policy which scatters a nation weakens national life; and any form of civil authority based upon self-interest, refusing to listen to these voices of the ancient prophets, and the perpetual voice of God, must issue in the harm of the nation.

The prophet passed on, and said not only, " Woe unto the shepherds," but in the name of the Lord God, " I am against the prophets." The place of the prophets in the national life in the Bible is a very interesting one. I but recall it to your memory. The prophets were men of God, delivering the word of God. The prophets were not essentially, or necessarily men who foretold events; and whenever the element in prophecy was predictive, it was subservient to the moral and immediate. In the history of these people, in the economy of God, the king was superseded by the prophet. God ceased to deal with kings, and began to deal with prophets, and expressed His word through them. That meant the growing up of the schools of the prophets; and I cannot read the Old Testament without feeling that this was a great disaster, for it made the prophetic office professional, and as it became professional, it lost its power. That is why Amos was so particular not to be called a prophet. In effect he said, I have nothing to do with the schools of the prophets, and professionalism in prophetic work. Jeremiah was at war with crowds of prophets in Jerusalem. His chief trouble came from them. Of them he said, "Both prophet and priest are profane." The word profane there has not the peculiar sense of our word profane; neither has it the sense of the word profane in the New Testament. It simply means defiled. Jeremiah declared that the prophets were defiled. To put that into another form briefly; the teachers of truth were untruthful; the teachers of purity were impure; the teachers of right were unrighteous; the teachers of morality were immoral. In that terrible day of Judah's final decay the prophets were characterized by the loss of that aloofness of character which creates power to touch national life healingly. They were themselves profane.

He charged them secondly with vanity: "Thus saith Jehovah of hosts, Hearken not unto the words of the prophets that prophesy unto you; they teach you vanity," or a little more bluntly, they fool you! "They speak a vision of their own heart, and not out of the mouth of Jehovah." "How long shall this be in the heart of the prophets that prophesy lies; even the prophets of the deceit of their own heart?" In other words, or in another word already used, they were professional. The prophets of Jeremiah's days were political time-servers. Their message came out of their own heart, out of the result of their own thinking, and the result was that they were lowering moral standards. As distinctly declared, they said, "Ye shall have peace; and unto every one that walketh in the stubbornness of his own heart they say, No evil shall come upon you." They were lowering moral standards simply because they were getting their message out of their own heart, and as the result of their own observation of the times.

No prophet of God ever finds his message by the observation of the times in which he lives. No prophet of God can neglect his times; but the work of the prophet is not to devise a message from the imagination of his heart. After observation of the times, the work of the prophet is to declare the Word of God to the times for their correction. We, who are in the Christian ministry, are sometimes told, that what we need in order to be successful is to catch the spirit of the age. Nothing of the kind; our work is to correct the spirit of the age, and never to catch it; to know it, and to correct it. Here was the curse of the hour. The prophets had become professionalists, students of political economy weaving out of their own imagination their messages; and God Almighty had set Jeremiah to work to bow the neck of mere professionalism.

The last charge was the most serious of all. They were profane in another sense of the word. They were profane in that they claimed to speak with Divine authority. They said, This is the utterance of God. They said, This is the word of Jehovah. They said, This is the burden of Jehovah. God forbade the use of the great formula of expression, because men had abused it! The false prophets were using the phrase, the burden of Jehovah, so God said, We will drop it out of Our vocabulary. This was the last sin of these prophets, the debasing of spiritual formulæ, the using of the language of orthodoxy, but in a false way, the claiming to speak in the name of Jehovah, while they were seeking no message from God.

If this prophecy teaches us anything, it teaches that it is better to have no kings at all than kings uninspired; better to be without any civil authority than a civil authority based upon the dust. It is better to let the world plunge itself into anarchy, and fight its way through. Old Carlyle was a wonderful seer, when he reminded us in his *French Revolution* that we talk of the reign of terror when we speak of the Revolution, and forget the longer and more deadly reign of terror of a millennium that had preceded it. There are hours when the French

Revolution is the only way. Better red anarchy out of which God will lead lines of order, than a people content to be ruled by men who have lost their vision of God.

The other thing is also true. Better no prophets than prophets patronized and muzzled. Better have no word of God than the Word of God which is merely a professional claim, and lacks vision, authority, and force.

And why so? Kings under the influence of false prophets, what is the issue? The arrangement of conduct uninspired by the Word of God is the most deadly and ghastly failure. Prophets under the influence of false kings, what have you? Motive—for the prophet has to do with motive—polluted by complicity with evil. Such prophets become politicians in the base sense of the word, men who merely manipulate matters, and do not include the supreme matter which it is their business to deal with. Wherever in the life of a nation we have this strange and appalling mixture of false rule, the result is the pollution of the springs of national life; the true principles are forgotten, perverted, distorted; and the ultimate is the defilement of the streams of national life; the people without vision, and consequently perishing.

The central word of this study in the life of a nation is found in that outcry of Jeremiah, which is parenthetical, and yet terrific, to which I have already referred:

" O earth, earth, earth, hear the word of Jehovah."

The central word of this study to the Church of God is found in that selfsame chapter: " Thus shalt thou say to the prophet, What hath Jehovah answered thee? and, What hath Jehovah spoken?" That is the question which the man who governs the nation is to ask of the prophet. The responsibility of the Church of God is that of answering that question. While the earth is to seek the word of God; the business of the prophet of God, the witness, is to answer the enquiry, and proclaim the word of Jehovah.

[133]

XII

THE CALL OF COMPASSION

Preparatory Readings: 2 Chronicles 36: 14-16; Jeremiah 24-26.

" Now therefore amend your ways and your doings, and obey the voice of Jehovah your God; and Jehovah will repent Him of the evil that He hath pronounced against you."—JEREMIAH 26: 13.

THESE words were uttered by Jeremiah under strange circumstances. He was on trial for heresy. As we saw in our last study, when Jerusalem was threatened by an invasion on the part of Babylon, Zedekiah sent messengers to Jeremiah. To them he declared that the victory of Babylon over Judah would ultimately be complete, and that the true policy of the king was that of submission. In obedience to the Divine command Jeremiah then went to the house of Zedekiah, and delivered his messages, first denouncing the sins of shepherds and prophets as being the cause of national degradation. As I read the prophecy, Jeremiah—still speaking to Zedekiah—repeated three prophecies from the past, the first being that of a vision which came to him after Jeconiah's captivity; the second, a message delivered in the fourth year of Jehoiakim; and the last, a yet earlier one, having been delivered in the beginning of Jehoiakim's reign.

The vision after Jeconiah's captivity was that of two baskets of figs, the first containing very good, and the second very bad figs. The basket of good figs, said the prophet, symbolized the captives who had been taken away to the land of the Chaldeans. From them in the future Jehovah would restore His own. The basket of

bad figs represented those who remained in the land.
These, in the economy of God, were devoted to judgment. The remainder of this earlier vision would serve
to make plain to Zedekiah the burden which the prophet
was commissioned to deliver to him.

Still speaking to him, Jeremiah reminded him of the
word which came in the fourth year of Jehoiakim. It
was a message which announced the judgment of God
as determined against Judah, Babylon, the nations, and
the world at large.

With regard to Judah, the reason of the judgment was
that of her persistent sin. Notwithstanding the fact
that Jehovah had spoken constantly, and called them
to return to obedience, they had not hearkened. The
judgment foretold was that of the conquest of Judah by
Babylon, and her captivity for a period of seventy years.

The prophecy, moreover, foretold the judgment of
Babylon itself after the seventy years by a confederacy
of nations and kings; and indeed, the prophet looked yet
further afield, and saw that the judgment of God would
ultimately fall upon all the nations, and that there would
be no escape therefrom. Judgment would go forth from
nation to nation, said he, until a great tempest would be
raised from the uttermost part of the earth. The severest strokes of this judgment would fall upon the shepherds, that is, upon the kings, upon the rulers. Thus
again Zedekiah was reminded of the prophecy delivered
in the fourth year of Jehoiakim, and was thus warned
how inevitable was the doom now threatening himself
and Jerusalem.

Once more Jeremiah repeated a previous message, one
delivered yet earlier, as he said, in the beginning of the
reign of Jehoiakim. He had then been instructed to
stand in the court of Jehovah's house, and deliver his
message, in order to give the people an opportunity to
return to God. The message had been one which had
warned them against refusing to hearken, and declared

their persistent refusal, and the consequent judgment decided against them.

The delivery of this message was followed by the hostility of priests, prophets, and people. Jeremiah had been seized, and condemned to die, by what, for want of a better term, we may describe as the ecclesiastical court. The princes of Judah however interfered, and he was placed upon his trial before a civil court. The priests and the prophets charged him with speaking against the city of God. The interference of the princes, and the defence of the prophet, won the people to his side for a moment; and they, with the princes, declared to priests and prophets that he was not worthy of death. Certain of the elders declared that to slay the prophet of Jehovah would be sin, instancing the illustrations of Micaiah and Uriah; and Jeremiah was preserved by Ahikam.

Thus the words of the text, first spoken in essence in the reign of Josiah (see 7: 1–7) and then in the reign of Jehoiakim, were now repeated to Zedekiah. Let us endeavour to understand the mood of the people at this time, and then consider this declaration of the prophet.

We need give no further consideration to the difference between the reigns of Jehoiakim and Zedekiah. The conditions were practically the same through all that period. From the death of Josiah until the capture of Jerusalem the conditions varied little. What then were these conditions? First, the nation was conscious of perils upon the frontier. Egypt was an uncertain quantity. There were politicians who desired to secure an alliance with her, in order to save them from the peril threatening them in the North. But Egypt could not be depended upon, and even these politicians were uncertain of what action she would take. There in the North was this strange, restless, Chaldean movement threatening Judah perpetually. Within the Nation, councils were divided. There was what we may term a popular party, clamouring for national independence, clamouring for breaking loose from the restraint of Babylon; suggesting that by an appeal to Egypt and an alliance therewith, this national independence might be secured. And there was Jeremiah, the lonely, heroic prophet-priest of Anathoth, persistently declaring that the Chaldeans were not only at hand, but that they would capture the city, and all this, moreover, as within the government of God; persistently affirming that the true policy of king and rulers and people was that of bending the neck to the yoke of Babylon. There also was Zedekiah, a nominee of Nebuchadnezzar; weak, vacillating, desiring to break with his master, and establish national freedom; desiring to be true to the prophetic word; the tool of the princes, the plaything of the priests, the object of Jeremiah's persistent attack in the name of Jehovah. The civil and spiritual degradation of the hour was marked and terrible. In our last meditation we spoke of the sin of the shepherds or civil rulers, and the sin of the prophets, or spiritual rulers; and then we glanced at the whole nation; at the unrest of an oppressed people, a people like sheep having no shepherd; and at the false security of a polluted people, a people who were being misled by the voices of the false prophets. We observed also the false religious conception that moved priest and prophet, and so largely swayed the national will. They were under the sway of the Temple fetish, and of the city pride.

The Temple fetish was the idea that this Temple was the house of Jehovah, and therefore it could not be destroyed. The false civic pride was the conviction that this city was the city of the King, and that therefore to speak a word against it was more than treason, it was religious heresy. This first conviction that the Temple was indeed the house of Jehovah, and could not be destroyed, was in itself an evidence of the divorce between religion and morality which characterized the thinking of Judah at that particular time. This conception that the city was the city of the King, and therefore must not be spoken against was an evidence of their forgetfulness of the true strength of a city. These men had entirely forgotten the burden of Isaiah's teaching; which teaching may be summarized by one brief quotation from chapter twelve, in our arrangement of his prophecy. He was looking on to the far-off day of victory, when the people of God shall fulfil the purpose of God; and he closed with these significant words:

" Cry aloud and shout, thou inhabitant of Zion: for great in the midst of thee is the Holy One of Israel."

Isaiah was referring to Jehovah, nevertheless the implicate of such a reference is patent. Cry aloud, O Zion, rejoice in this, O city, that greatness in thee is holiness; great in the midst of thee is the Holy One of Israel. The nation had forgotten that; perchance did not believe it when Isaiah declared it; and had certainly not acted upon it for long. To them the greatness of the city was traditional, and not the greatness of character.

And yet, look again, and more closely at the picture presented. The action of the priests and prophets in arresting Jeremiah was an acknowledgment of their fear that perhaps he was right. The very fact that they had formally arrested him, and formally set him on trial, and did that in the presence of the people, and drew attention to his words, is an irresistible proof that down in the deepest of their heart they were at least afraid that after all, this strange voice sounding so long and so persistently in the midst of the national life, was uttering the very truth of God. The action of the princes was an open avowal of their conviction that he was indeed the messenger of God. All this is of vital importance. Truth can never be robbed of its power. This underlying sense of the human soul is one of the most wonderful things in human history. Men and nations will fight against truth, refuse to obey it, even by argument almost persuade themselves that they do not believe in its message; but it is persistent, and there is always that in the human heart which is conscious of the truth of truth. This trial of Jeremiah presents a very remarkable picture. The priests and the prophets, hot and angry, protesting against him for heresy, for daring to suggest that the Temple of God could be destroyed, or the city of God become a desolation; angry with an apparently religious heat; and all the while doing these things in answer to an underlying suspicion and fear that after all he was right, and thus unconsciously paying tribute to the irresistible appeal of truth in the human soul.

Glancing once more at the picture, we observe that the priests and the prophets were consistent in their opposition to Jeremiah; the princes acquitted him; while the people first sided with the priests, and then with the princes. Priests, prophets, and people laid hold of him, and put him on his trial. Priests and prophets never wavered. The princes were willing to hear the story, willing to consider it, willing to arbitrate, and at last, answering the conviction of their own souls, acquitted him; and immediately the people crossed to the popular side, and were with the princes.

This is more than history, it is revelation; and these are some of the things that the picture reveals; first, debased spiritual authority is far more evil in the national life than debased civil authority. The only consistent people in the New Testament narratives of the life of Jesus were the priests, the Pharisees, and the religious rulers. Do not make your boast that you are a consistent man! Your consistency may be your bigotry, and your doom!

Secondly the picture is a denial of the fallacy *vox populi vox Dei.* The voice of the people is by no means always the voice of God. Fickle, moved by passing emotion, responsive to the loudest voice, so the people vote.

God deliver me from putting my trust in the people, unless the people are instructed and inspired by the voice of God. Another voice is needed, which shall not be the voice of the people, which shall not be the voice of princes, which shall not be the voice of priests or prophets; and where the other voice is not heard, then the chaos will continue.

In this atmosphere we listen to the text: "Amend your ways and your doings, and obey the voice of Jehovah your God." Jeremiah was the one true statesman in all the political chaos, speaking not merely in the interest of the life hereafter, but in the interest of the present moment; addressing himself to the strange international complication and internal political chaos, with only one word; Amend your ways, and amend your doings; and amend your ways and your doings by doing one thing; obey the voice of Jehovah your God.

In connection with that great call of the prophet, he made this, may I say, strange declaration;—not strange really, and yet very strange to our thinking oftentimes, —that if men will amend their ways and their doings in listening to the voice of their God, then Jehovah will repent Him of the evil that He hath pronounced against them. The attitude of God toward a people in this mental mood is revealed in an earlier paragraph, in which we find the instruction that was given to Jeremiah concerning the burden of his ministry:

"And thou shalt say unto them, Thus saith Jehovah: If ye will not hearken to Me, to walk in My law, which I have set before you, to hearken to the words of My servants the prophets, whom I send unto you, even rising up early and sending them, but ye have not hearkened; then will I make this house like Shiloh; and will make this city a curse to all the nations of the earth."

The picture of the Divine attitude is that of God rising up early,—mark the daring of the figure,—to send the messengers in the interest of the national life.

STUDIES IN THE PROPHECY OF JEREMIAH

Jeremiah called upon the people to respond to this Divine attitude by an actual and external change, to amend. The Hebrew word translated *amend* is a strong and suggestive one. Make well your ways and doings! Make them sound, make them healthy, make them beautiful! Amend them in that sense. Amend your ways, that is, the habitual order of your life, its set and direction, the high road along which you are travelling; change that. Amend it, heal it, make it sound, make it true, make it noble, make it beautiful. "And your doings," the positive acts, not merely the habitual poise, set, direction, but the activities which result from that poise, that set, that direction, of the life.

Jeremiah on an earlier occasion had stood at the gate of the king's house, and had charged them with folly; Say not, The temple of Jehovah, but amend your ways and your doings, and amend your ways and your doings by ceasing to oppress and to tyrannize and to neglect the need that exists in the life of the nation; and amend your doings by walking no longer after false gods, but after the true God.

At last we come to the central thing of this demand made upon the nation, "And obey the voice of Jehovah your God." Now the difficulty of this is its simplicity and self-evident truth. Let our imagination help us. Get back into Judah. Get back into the very atmosphere of the hour and listen. This man had nothing else to say. He had been exercising his ministry now for many years, he had startled the people by saying that the temple was to be destroyed, and the city made a desolation. Now he was upon his trial. He made his appeal to them again, and in effect declared that the one trouble with the national life was that the nation, while attentive to other voices, did not listen for God.

In the year 1912, in the midst of trouble in the Balkans, a striking article appeared in the *London Daily Telegraph*, from which let me give you a quotation:

"No chapter of European history more closely resembles fiction than that which chronicles the present phase of the Near Eastern crisis. It is a bundle of wild incongruities, to which the future historian will seek a clue in vain. How, for example, will he explain on the one hand the will of each of the European States to maintain the general peace, even at a heavy sacrifice; and on the other hand, the fear felt by them all that something—they know not what—may at any moment occur which will precipitate a sanguinary war? For if one and all they are resolved to keep the peace, it is manifest that they wield the requisite power to carry out that resolve. Why, then, should Europe at the present moment be living on the tenterhooks of seemingly groundless hope and dread?"

The writer, Dr. Dillon, then answered his own question, so let me read you his answer:

"One cause of this unparalleled impotency is the lack of a leading European statesman, capable of storing up and utilizing the vast peace forces at present scattered over Europe. We lack a Cavour or a Bismarck. There are, indeed, one or two in the ranks of diplomacy, French and British, with whom the world is, and will probably remain unacquainted. But at the head of public affairs there is none; one looks in vain for the leader of men. And at this moment of storm and stress, when in southeastern Europe decay and dissolution have overtaken the old order of things, and a new political and social fabric is a-building, this deficiency is felt as an international disaster."

But here is the sentence that arrested me:

"*Above the babel of fearsome and mistrustful tongues one hears no far-resonant voice to reassure and cheer.*"

That is the significant word. I am quite willing to make no further application of it to statecraft; but in that word Dr. Dillon put his finger on the central agony of the moment. Mark the significant picture; the distrustfulness of the great Powers:—Great Powers, forsooth, " Great Impotencies " rather, as Chesterton has named them—unable to secure peace, afraid of war, and not knowing whence the haunting spectre comes that makes them fear. What was wanted was a resonant Voice. And for lack of that Voice then, the Great War followed in two years.

And yet the Voice was sounding, the Voice had spoken: " God, having of old time spoken unto the fathers in the prophets by divers portions and in divers manners, hath at the end of these days spoken unto us in His Son." Until the nations hear the voice of the Son and obey, they will never settle their difficulties, or bring cosmos out of chaos.

We may leave the surrounding nations, Assyria, Babylon, and Egypt, or Germany, France, Russia; and after the habit of our national pride believing ourselves to be the people of God. Then to us the voice has one message: Amend your ways, the general set of your life; and your doings, your relationship to all the crying need of the scattered peoples that are going without shepherding; and do it, do it all, by obeying the voice of Jehovah. That is the call to the nation.

If we will, what then? Then Jehovah your God " will repent Him of the evil that He hath pronounced against you." That is not a figure of speech, although you will find almost invariably expositors suggest that it is. It is no figure of speech. It is a fact. Jehovah will repent Him. The word repent does not here mean change His mind. That we may understand the prophetic word, let us notice first that the root meaning is that of a sigh. Jehovah will sigh. But we must also consider the use of the word. It is a word that always presupposes sorrow, of which sighing is an expression, but in its use it is a word that suggests an activity of sorrow on behalf of some one else. It was constantly used not merely of sighing, not merely of sorrow, but of consolation growing out of sorrow.

The form of the verb moreover is reflexive, " He will repent Him." The suggestion is that of a people listening for God, and so amending ways and doings, turning back to God; and God—do not be afraid of this, it is human speech, but that is the only way in which we can express truth concerning Him,—God sighing with relief, and releasing His sorrow in order to console and deal with a people that turn back to Him. " Jehovah will repent Him." It is not merely that He will change His mind; it is not that He will change His mind at all. It is that He will change His activity, because He cannot change His mind. His mind is the mind of compassion, of love, of tenderness. The supreme desire of the heart of God is never to smite, but always to heal; never to afflict, but always to bless. If men have turned from Him, they have made their own whips and sufferings. When they turn back, He will repent Him. That is an unveiling by reverent suggestion, of the sorrow of the heart of God, of the breathing sigh of relief when the penitent man or nation turns back to Him; and of the activity out of sorrow which is for the healing, and the consolation of the people that turn. There is no greater word in all the Bible, Old or New, than this. Amend your ways and your doings; listen to the voice of God, and God will repent Him of the calamity that He appointed; and out of that sorrow in activity, will turn back the forces that are marching against you, and deliver and heal and take you to Himself!

Let us attempt to gather up, in a closing word, some of the essential things of the meditation. The story teaches us that national calamity comes by Divine appointment; that it is always the result of national sin; and that it is poetic, or judgment in kind; that which Gilbert wove into a sort of half humorous idea in one of his operas: He "makes the punishment fit the crime." That is God's method. It is poetic justice.

But that act of God in punishment, is ever the "strange act" of God. Now that is not a phrase of my own. I would not dare to use it. Isaiah used it. When the drunkards were mocking at him, and saying Who is this that talks to us, who speaks to us line upon line, precept upon precept, here a little and there a little; the prophet answered them, and finally told them God must visit them in judgment, and he called it "His strange act." It is the act that is foreign to the nature of God, that which is not within His deepest purpose for man or nation. "He doth not willingly afflict . . . the children of men." That is Jeremiah's word; we find it in the Lamentations; but hear it even more literally translated: "He doth not afflict *from the heart* the children of men." His heart is against it. When men turn back to Him, He sighs and repents. How are we to escape the calamity which God appoints? Directly there is true and thorough return to Him, He repents. Apart from such return on our part, there can be no Divine repentance.

What then, is the immediate need? The voice of Jehovah. If the nation will seek God, and seek to know His way and will, and conform its policies and life to the eternal standards, then for the nation there is healing; and if the nation will refuse that voice, listen not for it, or hearing it obey it not, then nothing can prevent the ultimate disaster.

XIII

THE KNOWLEDGE AND WITNESS OF GOD

Preparatory Readings: 2 Kings 24:18–20; 2 Chronicles 32:11–16; Jeremiah 27–29.

" I am He that knoweth, and am Witness, saith Jehovah."—JEREMIAH 29:23.

THE immediate application of these words of Jeremiah was that of their reference to the case of Ahab and Zedekiah, two prophets nowhere else referred to, who had joined in the false prediction of victory over Babylon. They were men of immoral character, who had used the Name of God as giving authority to their lying messages. In view of the evil character of these men and the falseness of their predictions, the prophet Jeremiah declared, as the spokesman of Jehovah, that He, Jehovah, was at once the One Who knew, and the One making known. "I am He that knoweth, and am Witness, saith Jehovah."

These men were of the number of the false prophets against whom Jeremiah had uttered his protest to Zedekiah. Chapters twenty-seven to twenty-nine reveal the prophet's conflict with these men, especially as it had its final manifestation in Jerusalem, in his conflict with Hananiah. Babylon was threatening not Judah only, but also all the nations in their neighbourhood. Representatives of the kings of Moab, Ammon, Tyre, and Sidon had come to Jerusalem to consult with Zedekiah, evidently with a view to forming a confederacy to act against Babylon. From the standpoint of the mere politician in Jerusalem, it was a hopeful sign that the kings

[146]

were willing thus to act with Zedekiah. Jeremiah, however, whose outlook was that of fellowship with God, and who therefore saw the situation from His standpoint, declared to these ambassadors the sovereignty of God, announced to them the coming victory of Nebuchadnezzar over all of them, and accompanied his declaration by the weird sign of bands and bars, or yokes, one of which he wore upon his own neck, and others of which he sent by the ambassadors back to their kings. He warned them against believing either their prophets, diviners, dreams, soothsayers, or sorcerers.

He then delivered the same message to Zedekiah, king of Judah, but with greater emphasis, warning him against the words of the false prophets, and urging him to bend the neck to Nebuchadnezzar, and thus save himself and his people from death. This insistent teaching could not fail to stir up the enmity of the prophets, and the politicians, or that political party in Jerusalem at the hour clamouring for the adoption of means to ensure national independence.

It was at this time that Hananiah publicly protested against Jeremiah's ministry, and predicted the breaking of the power of Babylon in two years. Jeremiah calmly appealed to time as the test of Hananiah's prediction, and of his own.

During the whole of this strange period, Jeremiah emphasized the messages he delivered by the wearing of the yoke upon his neck. This yoke Hananiah broke, and declared that its breaking was a sign of the coming deliverance from Babylon. The Divine response to this was, that if the yoke of wood was thus broken, it would be replaced by a yoke of iron. There could be no escape from the Divine decree, and this teaching was emphasized by the death of Hananiah.

This spirit of unrest and uncertainty filling Jerusalem at the time, was prevalent also among the exiles in Babylonia. There false prophets were uttering the same predictions, and giving the same political advice. To these, therefore, Jeremiah sent a letter, urging them to remain under the yoke, to give themselves to their own strengthening, because they were the people from whom, after seventy years, God would bring back a remnant to the city, to carry out His purposes.

This then is the historic background of the text, roughly sketched. Babylon was threatening this group of smaller nations. They were perturbed, and sought strength by attempting to make common cause with each other. This line of action was inspired and encouraged by the false spiritual rulers. There was great uncertainty. What would Nebuchadnezzar do in the long issue? How far could these different nations be trusted? In what measure were the prophets to be trusted? And above all, what was the true, deep meaning of the strange and troublesome ministry of this man Jeremiah? These, and similar questions were subjects of debate, and causes of turmoil. The supreme need of the hour was that of some one who knew all the facts of the situation, and who knowing, would declare them, and so indicate the true line of action.

That supreme need of that troubled hour was that to which the prophet appealed in these words, in the utterance of which he stood as the spokesman of Jehovah: " I am He that knoweth, and am Witness." In this declaration we have an argument for obedience to the appeal which Jeremiah had already made to the princes and the people, to obey the voice of Jehovah.

Sound policy demands a complete knowledge of facts, and wisdom as to how they bear upon the situation; how therefore they ought to be dealt with. It follows that Dr. Gunsaulus was perfectly right when he said:

" Statesmanship is the art of finding out in what direction Almighty God is going, and in getting things out of His way."

"I am He that knoweth, and am Witness," said Jehovah by the prophet to the people perturbed and perplexed, and seeking some true line of policy. If you would know all the facts of the case, if you would understand what you ought to do; I am He that knoweth, and I am Witness!

Let us then consider the double statement of the text, not to defend it, but to illustrate it, in order that we may learn the lessons which it teaches. Let us attempt this along two lines of consideration: first, God as the One Who knows, and Who makes known; and secondly, man in his relation to that knowledge.

First, then, the declaration of the text, that God is the One Who knows, and Who makes known. That is the real meaning of this declaration, its simplest intention. "I am He that knoweth." The word knoweth suggests quite simply the ascertaining of facts by the seeing of them; and consequently in common, simple, everyday use, it is the word that declares the knowledge of all the facts, because the facts are under observation. It is a very simple word, one that these Hebrews would constantly be using as among themselves, and of themselves; just as to-day we may constantly make use of this word as among ourselves, and of ourselves. In such use, however, there must be limitations. In the last analysis, I know, and I am He that knoweth, is only finally, and accurately true when God says it. It is a little difficult in the text to decide as to the tense, or mood. It is quite clear, however, that the statement suggested a contrast. "I am He that knoweth," said Jehovah to the troubled age. These ambassadors that have come from kings have come seeking knowledge; "I am He that knoweth." These politicians in your midst are attempting to formulate a policy which shall render the nation safe; "I am He that knoweth." These prophets who are making their predictions, and are using My Name, are after all but guessing; "I am He that knoweth." The declaration thus reminded the nation that this knowledge, which is the knowledge resulting from observation, can only be finally postulated of God, and never of man, because man's observation is limited, and incomplete in range and intensity.

"I am Witness." The word witness means to repeat, that is to say, Here are the facts never proclaimed. God repeats them in words, that is, bears witness concerning them, and makes them known. We may catch the very inner meaning of the declaration by rendering it: "I am He that knoweth, and He that maketh known." It is indeed the exact language that might have been used by one upon the watch-tower, one elevated to a position from which further distances could be observed. To the inquiries of those beneath the watch-tower, the watcher might answer, I am he that seeth, and I make known the thing I see, thus describing his office.

This is what Jeremiah said of God, in the midst of the turmoil, in the hour of perplexity and difficulty, when men hardly knew which way to turn, and false prophets were almost believing that they were inspired, and becoming nearly religious in their devotion to their hope of deliverance: "I am He that knoweth, and I make known."

Let us observe the Divine knowledge as illustrated in this particular history. The knowledge of God as here revealed was that of all the patent facts, and that of all the latent forces. The knowledge of God was that of Himself, and what He Himself would do in the presence of the difficulties by which His people were at the hour confronted.

He had perfect knowledge of the whole national situation, and of the private life of public men. Two prophets had made themselves notorious in their prophetic-political ministry. Ahab and Zedekiah had been in opposition to the ministry of Jeremiah; and Jehovah declared that He knew their immoral life, hidden away behind their public position. It was closely in connection with that unmasking of the immorality of two prophets that the declaration was made, "For I am He that knoweth, and am Witness." He knew all the patent facts; the national situation, the private life of public men, and all the scheming of the politicians.

He knew all the latent forces, the pride of heart, the ambitions of individual men, the secret purposes unconfessed in councils for publication, but remaining as inspirations.

But the word is a profounder word than that. The knowledge was knowledge of Himself, and of what He purposed to do. He not only knew the facts and the forces; He held them all in His own power, and He knew therefore what would become of them. " I am He that knoweth."

All that becomes immediately practical, when we listen to the word that follows it, " I am witness." Not only does God claim to be the One Who knows. He also claims to be the One Who witnesses, Who makes known. Again illustrating the declaration by this page of history, and by all the history that is related thereto, we find God's method of making known. How does God make known to men the things He knows on man's behalf? He makes known first by history. He makes known secondly, by direct inspired messages spoken in the midst of the circumstances which demand revelation. He makes known thirdly, by bringing men into circumstances which will reveal secrets, not concerning Himself, but concerning themselves. As God has perfect knowledge of all patent facts and latent forces, and of Himself, and of His intention; He makes these things known to the sons of men in these ways.

First, by history. Here is something which the Hebrew understood, while we to-day are perhaps a little in danger of undervaluing, or even of forgetting. God teaches men by the history of the past. Call to mind that simplest division of the Old Testament Scriptures, with which every Jew in the days of our Lord was perfectly familiar; the law, and the prophets, and the hagiographa, or sacred writings; and then remember that the central division in the Hebrew Bible, the prophets, contained two parts. The Hebrews spoke of the former prophets, and the later prophets. The "former prophets" consisted of some of the historical books, and not the books that we call prophetic. The "later prophets" was the term they used mainly to describe those books of prophecy which we describe as prophetic books. By all of which I am simply attempting to illustrate a matter of importance in the understanding of this method of God. Prophecy is always forth-telling, teaching, declaration, revelation of the will of God. Consequently, when these Hebrews arranged their Bible, they used the term the Prophets, as applying not merely to Isaiah, Jeremiah, Ezekiel, major and minor prophets, as our modern division runs; but also to some of the historic books. This they did in recognition of the fact that God teaches men by history; and that in any given hour, if a man would know what God intends to reveal to him for that hour, one sure method is that he shall take time to remember the past, and consider the lessons which the past has been intended to teach. That was ever, and still is a method of God in making known to men exactly what they fain would know at any given moment. Dr. Edersheim says, "History never repeats itself." What happens is, that some principle obtaining at a certain moment, obtains and works at a later moment; and so the later may be illustrated and understood by the former. In the hour of perplexity we should first look back, and see what God taught men in similar hours of perplexity. It is an evil thing for a nation when it has no time to think of the warnings that came, and the catastrophes that followed failure; of the deliverances that have been wrought, the deliverances following loyalty. The history of our own land is as truly full of God as the history of Judah or of Israel. Through history He is for ever speaking to men; and in every hour of difficulty men should listen for the yesterday of experience and of teaching.

But God not only makes known by history; He makes known by inspired messages. When I make use of that term, I do it in no narrow sense. I do it in the sense in which Peter described God's method of making known His will. In his second letter, the apostle declared that no writing, no Scripture—he was then referring to the sacred writings,—" No prophecy of Scripture is of private interpretation," by which he did not for a moment mean to declare that no writing is of private exposition. He did not mean to declare that no man has any right or authority to give his private interpretation of a Scripture that is given. That is to miss the meaning of the passage. He declared that no writing was of private interpretation, as to its origin; that these writings did not come by private interpretation; that the messages the prophets wrote and spoke in the olden time were not the result of their observation of the times in which they lived. He then proceeds to tell us how these men wrote, and how they spoke. He says, " Men spake from God, being moved by the Holy Spirit; and the word " moved " is a very inadequate word at that point. The word of which it is a translation is picturesque. They spoke as they were borne along by the Spirit of God. The word suggests exactly what we see when a ship is caught by the wind, and carried across the sea. It suggests the Divine afflatus filling the soul, and bearing it beyond its age. Holy men of old spoke as they were borne along by the Spirit, upward to a height of more accurate understanding, outward toward the boundaries of the Divine government, inward to the heart and wisdom of God. In such hours men spoke things far more wonderful than they themselves knew, although they spake things directly for the meeting of the immediate need.

That is the story of Jeremiah's ministry from beginning to end, and if we take this prophecy, and glance through it, letting the eye run over the page, we shall discover how persistently and perpetually he proclaimed it. Five-and-forty times in the course of this one brief book, he says, " The word of Jehovah that came to Jeremiah." So God speaks to every age. I am not arguing now for the inspiration of the Bible, but for the inspiration of the prophets, immediate, and direct. Over and over again the prophet at the moment is not conscious of his inspiration, not conscious of any mechanical process; so that he never can, and never will be able to describe it. It is a remarkable fact, that nowhere in the Bible is there any description of the method by which God possessing a man, bears him beyond the limited and mechanical observation of men, and whispers the secret to his soul, which he is to proclaim to men. That is not of the past alone. It is of to-day, if men are but in such relationship with God as to receive the message. When we are inclined to say, We can believe all that of Jeremiah; then let us go back and live in Jeremiah's time, and we shall discover how the men of his day were saying: We do *not* believe this of Jeremiah! We can always believe a prophet is a prophet when he has been dead long enough! The difficulty is to recognize him, and believe him, in the day of his living message.

But the Divine method of making known, is not that of history and that of inspired message alone; it is also that of circumstances which reveal secrets. This great principle, I think, is first manifested in the Biblical record in words recorded as falling from the lips of Moses, in the book of Deuteronomy. He there reminded the people that God had led them in the great and terrible wilderness, and fed them with manna, which they knew not, neither did their fathers know; that He might make them know that man doth not live by bread only, but by everything that proceedeth out of the mouth of Jehovah doth man live. He declared that God led them in the wilderness to prove what was in their heart, whether they would keep the commandments of Jehovah their God. It is hardly necessary to say that the passage does not mean that God led these men into the wilderness in order that He, God, might find out what was in their heart. " I am He that knoweth," but " I am Witness " ; I make known to you; and I do it by leading you into circumstances in which there will be manifested to yourselves the truth concerning yourselves. That again is a perpetual method of God. It is so in the case of a man. It is so in the case of a nation. God is for evermore leading a man into some place where the fact concerning him is forced upon his own recognition. Unless he obey the light, it will be made manifest before the world, but it is first brought to his own consciousness. Here is one of the strange and yet wonderful words of the New Testament, which may help us. " Judas was a thief, and he had the bag " ; and Christ gave it to him; and as surely as there is in me the making of a thief, I shall be put into circumstances where I shall discover it. You say, Then do you suggest that Christ was tripping this man, and putting temptation in his way? The answer is that we must not measure Christ by human standards. Christ's method with the man was that of discovering the man to himself, in order that he might escape from evil by casting himself upon the power of his Master. He is always doing it. If there is the making of a traitor in me, I shall certainly be placed in circumstances which will give me the opportunity to discover it, to yield to it; or to master it by flight to the refuge and the strength of my Lord's love. So with the nations. Whatever unholy thing there be incipient in the life of a nation, circumstances will conduce to its discovery, or its manifestation, in order to its putting away. Thus God makes known by overruling circumstances, so that men discover, not Him, but themselves, and what their profound need may be.

We turn in conclusion, to a statement which may be brief, but is of importance; a consideration of man in his relation to this knowledge. We may think of the individual, we may think of society, or we may think of the nation; I care very little. Let us make the term generic, and speak of man, in his relation to this knowledge of God.

First, in relation to the knowledge itself, to the fact that God is the One Who knows. If that fact is recognized, it must inevitably call for and should create a certain attitude of mind on the part of man. Fundamentally and simply, in all true policy, whether it be for the arrangement of my own personal life, or whether it be for the ordering of my family, or whether it be for the ordering of my city, or whether it be for the conduct of the national life, if this thing be true, that God knows, and witnesses, or makes known, then the first thing of importance is the acceptance of the fact. That is fundamental, and apart from it there can be no application of this text whatever.

It may be that at this point some one will fall out, intellectually, and perhaps honestly. I am not going to stay to argue, save to say one thing. It may be some one will say, We cannot accept this position, we do not believe God knows; or if we believe God knows, we do not believe that He makes known, that He is in any sense revealing either Himself or other things to men. Then I can only say to the man who takes up this position, anything else I may have to say will not affect him at all; he must drop out of my argument, and appeal; only I would remind him that the claim is so tremendous, that his solemn business is to settle once and for ever, as to whether it be true. I can understand the man who cannot accept it immediately; I can understand the man who says, I am not sure of a God Who knows. I can understand the man who says, Oh, I know there is a God Who knows in this way, but I am not sure that He reveals Himself. I can understand the man who is facing that difficulty, and can sympathize with him, and believe in him. But the one man that I cannot understand is the man who drifts for years, contented with that ignorance, and with no serious attempt to settle the question. It is fundamental. Either God is, or He is not. Either God knows, or there is no infinite or final knowledge. Either there is a God Who knows, or there is no final knowledge; for knowledge is partial in you and in me; and in this school and in that school; and in this philosophy and in that philosophy. There is no final knowledge unless it is in God. We must settle this, because if we are living in a world where there is no final and complete knowledge, things are different; we shall live differently, entirely. That is the first thing to be settled.

But if the statements of the text are true, then immediately I may urge the importance of this recognition of the fact of the Divine knowledge, for if I may use a word somewhat unequal in this connection, God's knowledge is not merely academic. God's knowledge produces action always, and such action is consonant with Himself; righteous action, love-inspired action. All that He knows is the reason of His activity; and what He is in Himself is the reason of the method of His activity.

Now if all this be true, the first question we have to settle about everything in life is, What has God to say? This is the first question for the nation, before it discusses frontiers, or home affairs. Submission to the authority of this Divine One Who perfectly knows is a reasonable sequence. Submission to His authority is simply the acceptance on the part of the individual of the eternal order, and conformity thereto. Submission to His knowledge is the finding of the place of the man or the nation in the rhythmic order of the universe.

What then is man's responsibility with regard to the making known of His knowledge on the part of God? The discovery of what God makes known is the first matter of importance in all human life; the consideration of history from that standpoint; the study of revelation, already made in times past, through prophets, seers and psalmists, and centrally, in the ministry of the Incarnate Word; and finally the understanding of circumstance.

The great word of the prophet Isaiah concerning the Servant of God, "He shall be of quick understanding in the fear of Jehovah," I never now can read, without hearing the almost overwhelming note of incisiveness that came with Dr. George Adam Smith's translation of it, "He shall be keen of scent in the fear of Jehovah"; that is, keen and quick to understand what God is saying, by this *now* of circumstance. This is the first matter in all individual and national life, that we should find out what God has to say.

There must be, not only the discovery of what God says; there must also be acceptance of its accuracy; assurance of the Divine wisdom. That means the renunciation of private judgment. We Protestants have talked of private judgment, and often it is private nonsense, and very often public nonsense. If we are comparing human opinions, and you ask me to accept your interpretation, then I assert the right of private judgment. But there is a moment when a man has to say, Oh God, who am I that I should presume to judge Thee with this intellect of mine? I want Thy judgment, not my own. That is the crucial point of all religious experience. That is the point where the cross confronts you, and confronts me;

"I lay in dust life's glory dead!" Life's glory is not the occasional pleasure, the thing men call worldliness.

Life's glory is life's pride, and man's opinion that he can arrange for himself, his independence, his right;

"I lay in dust life's glory dead!"

That is the first thing. When a man has done that, yielded his judgment and his will to the infinite wisdom of God, to be revealed to him immediately; then he becomes independent of human opinion, he is no longer mastered by the thought of another man, or swayed with the fashions of an hour. He has made adjustment of relationship toward the final, the ultimate, the central, the innermost wisdom; and when a man's life is there, or the nation's life is adjusted toward that centre, then the secret of strength is found.

And not alone, discovery of the revelation, or acceptance of its accuracy is necessary; but necessarily and finally, in a word, obedience to its demands; immediate, complete, effective.

And so, even in this hour, believe me; this hour of confusion and strife, and wondering, and difficulty, this is the voice to which men need to listen; the voice of God which says: "I am He that knoweth, and I make known." Be it ours in our national life somehow—and God show us how—to recover ourselves of our madness, that we may take time to find out what God has to say to us.

XIV

THE EVERLASTING LOVE

Preparatory Readings: Jeremiah 30–31 : 3.

*" Yea, I have loved thee with an everlasting love:
therefore with lovingkindness have I drawn thee."*
                                    —JEREMIAH 31 : 3b.

IN our survey of the prophecy of Jeremiah we now
come to four chapters (30–33), which stand out in striking contrast to the general tone of the book. In these
chapters the tone is that of hope, the burden of the prophetic message being that of coming restoration. In the
first two of these chapters we find no historic note. They
form one whole, which is a song full of confidence,
described by Hengstenberg as " the triumphal hymn of
Israel's salvation."

The second two chapters are clearly dated as in the
tenth year of Zedekiah's reign, and deal with matters
which took place while the prophet Jeremiah was in
prison. It is generally agreed that these four chapters
belong to the same period, for they are most evidently
unified by the note of confident hope to which we have
referred.

They were dark days indeed. The army of Nebuchadnezzar was outside the city walls. The prophet was
shut up in the court of the guard. Nearly seven years
had passed since the conflict with the false prophets.
Events had quietly moved on, every hour contributing
fresh evidence of the Divine authority of Jeremiah's
teaching. Hananiah had predicted that within two years
the power of Babylon would be broken; the vessels of

Jehovah's house would be restored to the Temple; and Jeconiah, together with the captives of Judah, returned to the city. The prediction had been demonstrated false. Things had gone from bad to worse in the life of the nation, and now the foe was at the gates; Jerusalem was already imprisoned within the might of Babylon; and the prophet of Jehovah was held captive by the rebellious spirit of the sinning nation. Could any hour be darker, or any circumstances more calculated to fill the heart with despair?

It was in this hour, and under these circumstances, that the prophetic note rose to the high music of perfect confidence and buoyant hopefulness.

The movement of these particular prophecies is threefold. First we have the song of coming deliverance in chapters thirty and thirty-one; then the story of how the prophet had purchased land in his native place of Anathoth, with an explanation of the meaning of the act in chapter thirty-two. Finally, in chapter thirty-three, we have a glorious promise of a final restoration under the Righteous Branch, when Zion's name would be Jehovah-Tsidkenu, the Lord our Righteousness.

Our present study is concerned with the song, and I have selected this declaration of love for text, because in it we have the secret of this song. The word came to Jeremiah, as to the true representative of the national idea and the national purpose at that moment. It was a revelation to him of the deepest thing in the heart of God, the reason of all His dealings with His people; and so it became the inspiration of the prophet's song, the foundation of his hope.

The whole song is worthy of the closest study, for it is full of beauty and of permanent values. We must content ourselves with endeavouring to catch its spirit. There are certain general things that may help in our study. The first is that of the inclusiveness of its outlook. The key-note is found in the introductory word of Jehovah, " I will turn again the captivity of My people Israel and Judah." The first period of the song contains words concerning Judah and concerning Israel, and the whole nation is in view to the end of chapter thirty. The second period had special reference to Israel, which though then scattered, would ultimately be gathered. The third period deals with Judah alone, and the fact of the restoration of her cities to prosperity; while the fourth and last had to do with Israel and Judah, and speaks of the new covenant which God will establish with His people. Here it is well to remember that the fulfilment of these glorious foretellings will come by the way of this new covenant, and in no other way.

The second fact to be noted in a general survey of the song is that of the minor and major passages in the music. The note of sorrow upon sorrow is here; but the ultimate is always that of joy. Moreover these are closely related. It is through trouble that the people of God are to be brought to triumph, and by the lonely pathway of utter friendlessness, they are at last to reach the highway of favour.

The third and last fact is that of the clear system of the song. It first declares the Divine purpose to restore. Then the process of restoration is described. Through tribulation and affliction, peace and joy must come. Jacob's trouble is the means for ensuring Israel's triumph. Finally, the issues of restoration are gloriously set forth. The city is to be built, the people to be regathered, sorrow is to pass away; and all this will be followed by a new contentment, allied with a new covenant.

Thus the whole song becomes the interpretation of our text, as the text is the revelation of the inspiration of the song. In the text itself then, we have a double declaration, the first part of which is that of the fact of the Divine Love, " I have loved thee with an everlasting love "; and the second is that of the relation of that fact of the Divine Love to God's dealings with His people, " Therefore with lovingkindness have I drawn thee."

Let us therefore consider, first, this everlasting love of God; and secondly, the activity of that love as declared in the text, and illustrated in the context.

The everlasting love of God is really too vast a matter for interpretation. The Bible has never attempted to explain it. It declares it; it sings of it; it celebrates it; it illustrates it; but nothing more. The greatest passages in the Bible dealing with it, are those that lead us to the realm of mystery, and leave us without final explanation. The text is no exception to this general rule. I suppose in all the Old Testament Scriptures there is no one passage more familiar to men and women of faith, pilgrims of the night, warriors in the great campaign, than this simple and yet perpetually sublime word, " I have loved thee with an everlasting love." Indeed our very familiarity with it may make it difficult for us to grasp its suggestiveness. Therefore let us be children, and begin at the beginning. Let us consider the terms that are made use of in this brief and yet remarkable declaration, " I have loved thee with an everlasting love." The terms taken separately were ordinary and everyday terms. By that I mean they were terms with which these Hebrew people were perfectly familiar in their everyday converse. It is the grouping of them which is remarkable; and especially so if we pause in the presence of the very first formula of personality, " *I* have loved thee with an everlasting love.'

" I have *loved* thee." The word employed to make this declaration was the everyday word of the Hebrew for love; the word that husband used of wife, and wife of husband; that parents used of children, and children of parents. It was the ordinary and everyday word of the common speech of the people, a word indicating desire for. inclination toward. affection centred upon. " I have loved thee," said Jehovah; as many a father had said to his child, as many a bridegroom had said to his bride.

"*Everlasting* love." Everlasting is another of the baffling words to which we come over and over again attempting to find its suggestiveness; only to discover that its supreme value is that it introduces us to the realm of mystery. "Everlasting" is the concealed, the veiled; not necessarily concealed, not necessarily veiled; but concealed and veiled to the observer, because the observer's sight cannot penetrate far enough to know the ultimate. Quite literally everlasting means the vanishing point, the point beyond which sight cannot penetrate. When used of time, it means time out of mind. If we travel back through all the perplexing ages of history, we reach at last some point where there is no history, but the mind immediately affirms times beyond that limit. That is the everlasting; the veiled, but not the unreal. Or if our mind travel forward, and we attempt to construct for ourselves, as all healthy souls will, the ages that are yet to come;—placing upon to-morrow the measurement of yesterday, discovering the principles of the past, and thinking how they will operate in the future; thus dreaming dreams, and seeing visions, the great ministry of prophecy and of poetry;—we inevitably reach a limit, a haziness, a vanishing point; that is the everlasting.

Or if we use the term, as we may quite rightly do, in the realm of dimension, height and depth,—two relative terms only used by reason of the place that we occupy at the moment; for I gaze to the height and climb to it, but the height is still above me; or I gaze into the depth and descend to it, but the profundities are still beneath me;—then when I have seen the height beyond, and the depth beneath, neither reached nor fathomed, these are the everlasting.

The last term, *love*, is also the common everyday word

STUDIES IN THE PROPHECY OF JEREMIAH

that these men were using all the time, but in the Hebrew Bible the word love in this text is in the feminine
form. This is another of the great texts in which that
supreme and too often forgotten fact of the Motherhood
of God gleams out through the sacred declaration, " I
have loved thee with an everlasting Mother-love."

The terms taken thus separately are arresting and interesting; but they are all intensified in meaning by the
Personality Who employs them. It is when we allow
ourselves to listen to them, conscious of the One Who
utters them, that they create the greatest amazement; " *I*
have loved thee with an everlasting love." We may interpret the suggestiveness of the pronoun by returning
to the commencement of the song, and listening to these
words: " Thus speaketh Jehovah, the God of Israel."
We are simply attempting to hear these words as Jeremiah heard them, as the men of his time heard them, if
they were attentive to them; and we are immediately
reminded that the One speaking was Jehovah, the becoming One, the One Who was for evermore becoming
what man needed. The speaker moreover was the One
they had come to know by that majestic and intensive
Hebrew plural, Elohim. All this may mean little to us
of the mechanical, and insufficient, Anglo-Saxon speech;
but in this Hebrew language every word was pictorial,
poetic, and suggestive. If we literally translate we are
immediately shocked at our own attempts; *strengths*, in
that there is no music; *powers*, that is quite inadequate.
Strength is, however, the essential thought, but it is expressive, by this adoption of the plural, of limitless and
all-sufficient strength. The same idea was expressed in
another way when they added to the word for God, the
word that declares Him to be. All-sufficient. Thus by
these words of the Hebrew speech, conveying ideas
which had come to them by revelation, we are introduced to the presence of the Person. I, Jehovah, the
Elohim of Israel, the God Who becomes what man

needs, in order to the perfecting of man, " *I* have loved thee with an everlasting love."

" The conjunction which is in itself an amazement, is that of the word " everlasting " with " love "; " I have loved thee with an everlasting love." In other words: I have loved thee with a love that has no beginning; I have loved thee with a love that can have no ending; I have loved thee with a love that knows no change.

The amazement grows upon the soul when the object is considered. Take the case in view, that of Israel, using the word not of the Northern Kingdom, but of the whole of the people. Think of their history. Once more pass back into the historic atmosphere, and remember these days, in which Jeremiah was fulfilling his heroic ministry; a ministry of forlorn hope, a ministry, by all human standards, foredoomed to failure from its very first utterance; and think what that means as to the condition of these people. Look at them in all their wantonness and waywardness and wickedness; and as we look on them,—not in criticism, but seeing mirrored in their history the story of our own wickedness,—we hear the Divine word, " I have loved thee with an everlasting love."

Or take the wider outlook, and think of humanity at large. I affirm that apart from this declaration of God's love, and apart from sympathy with that love of God, humanity in the mass is loveless. Or leave the larger outlook, and let each think of himself or herself, and then comes the most amazing thing of all, and growingly so, the fact that He can see anything in us to love.

Well did Faber sing:

" How Thou canst think so well of us
   Yet be the God Thou art,
Is darkness to my intellect
   But sunshine to my heart."

But if when I look at the object, Israel, humanity, myself, I am amazed; when my eyes are turned from the object to the Lover, using the word with all reverence, then there is a sense in which my amazement is at an end. I immediately see the naturalness of it. I will be utterly superlative in what I now affirm. In spite of what I am, in spite of what humanity is, in spite of what Israel was, God can none other. Well did John write, " Herein is love; not that we loved God, but that He loved us." This indeed is Love. Cramer has this comment on this very text:

" The love of God toward us comes from love, and has no other cause above or beside itself, but is in God, and remains in God, so that Christ Who is in God is its Centre."

He hath loved, He hath loved, I cannot tell why! That is, when I look at myself. But when I know Him, and look at Him as He has been unveiled in the Son of His love; then I say, O God, had I been ten thousand times more polluted than I am, Thou couldest not have helped loving me. So I am constrained to say in addition to Faber:

" Yet Thou dost think so well of us,
        Because of what Thou art;
    Thy love illumines our intellect,
        Yet fills with fear our heart."

That is the implicate of that word of Jesus in the Sermon on the Mount, when He said to His disciples, " I say unto you, Love your enemies." In connection with that command He said, Your Father " maketh His sun to shine on the evil and the good. . . . If ye love them that love you, what reward have ye? do not even the publicans the same? . . . Ye therefore shall be perfect, as your heavenly Father is perfect." That per-

[167]

fection is the perfection of love, in spite of anything that man can be.

Jeremiah discovered this truth in the darkest day of all. The place of revelation was that of darkness, of disaster, and of distress. It was out of the horror of all that awful hour that Jeremiah lifted his voice and sang, and this was the inspiration of the song, and this the key-note of the music, " I have loved thee with an ever-lasting love." Everlasting love is love which exceeds the possibility of measurement in any dimension. The New Testament recognizes this in the language of Paul, " the breadth and length and height and depth, the love of Christ which passeth knowledge." Passeth knowl-edge, that is goes beyond the vanishing point of human observation. Whether we look up, love passeth the place where vision ends. Whether we look down, into the most appalling depths, still underneath is love.

The relation of the fact of the love of God to His dealings with His people is expressed in the words: " Therefore with lovingkindness have I drawn thee." Mark the " therefore." " *Therefore* with lovingkind-ness have I drawn thee." The first suggestion of the word *drawn,* the most simple, is the most true. It is the thought of leading, of guidance; of leading and guid-ance in spite of the will of the one led or guided. There is an element of compulsion in it. It was a word that was used in many ways; of marching, of developing; of leading the march, and compelling it; of watching the process of development, and conducting it. The declara-tion has reference not only to the moment when God put His arms about these people and drew them to His heart. It refers also to the hour when He thrust them from Him, and kept them at arm's length, and put them through trouble and travail and agony and pain. " I have drawn thee," I have been leading, guiding, march-ing, and developing, but always with lovingkindness.

The first suggestion of the word lovingkindness is

that of bending down. This we considered in a previous study. That this is the first suggestion of the word is borne out by the fact that in the Hebrew Bible once it is translated *a wicked thing,* and once *reproach.* In the text, " Sin is a reproach to any people," the word *reproach* is exactly the same word as the word lovingkindness in our text. Of course no one imagines that it means that sin is a *lovingkindness* to a people. It is evident that the word was used in that place in its first and most simple sense; sin is a bending of the neck to any people; it puts them beneath the yoke. That however is a most unusual use of the word. It is most often translated *mercy;* next in order of number, *kindness;* then *lovingkindness,* but it is also translated *goodness, favour,* and indeed in many other ways. The real meaning of the quality described may be illustrated by the conduct of the good Samaritan. He showed *the mercy.* That is lovingkindness. It is the bending over toward need, with intention of blessing. This then is the Divine declaration: Because I have loved thee with an everlasting love; therefore with lovingkindness, with mercy, with persistent bending over in goodness and in favour, I have drawn thee after Me.

But is not this examination of the statement creating strange difficulty in the mind? We have been following this prophecy of Jeremiah, attempting always to remember the background of history. What turbulent times they were; what agonies, what bruisings of the people of God; what awful sin they manifested; and with what terrific severity the prophet thundered against them. Even now, while the prophet sang his song, Nebuchadnezzar was outside, and the city was quite helpless in his grasp. How does all this square with the affirmation that God's dealings are in lovingkindness?

Let us glance at the context. "All thy lovers have forgotten thee; they seek thee not; for I have wounded thee with the wound of an enemy, with the chastisement of a cruel one; for the greatness of thine iniquity, because thy sins were increased. Why criest thou for thy hurt? thy pain is incurable; for the greatness of thine iniquity, because thy sins were increased, I have done these things unto thee." Thus God clearly declares, that when He says "With lovingkindness have I drawn thee," He includes the very travail through which His people are passing, and claims that the travail is by His own activity.

Throughout the song the claim is made, like infinite sweetness and strength, that it is by His activity that they will at last be restored, and will find their triumph. The two things are brought together in the declaration, "Hear the word of Jehovah, O ye nations, and declare it in the isles afar off, and say, He that scattered Israel will gather him." God has scattered, and will gather; and the relation between the two facts is emphasized.

A little later, in the same song. Listen to the harmony and beauty of this. "Is Ephraim My dear son? is he a darling child? for as often as I speak against him, I do earnestly remember him still: therefore my heart yearneth for him; I will surely have mercy upon him, saith Jehovah."

The claim of the declaration then is that everlasting love leads through travail as well as triumph, and that all pain and suffering are somehow or other within the compass of that love, and are intended as ministers for the making of life and the purifying of high and noble purpose. "With lovingkindness have I drawn thee." Why hast Thou afflicted us, O God, and why are we left so sore and broken? With lovingkindness have I drawn thee! Why are we bereft and hemmed in by the enemies? Why has the song of hope been silent for so long? With lovingkindness have I drawn thee! I will surely not let thee go unpunished, because I love thee! His chastisements are not joyous, but grievous; but afterward, afterward! Through processes of pain, God

[170]

resolutely, in the strength of love that is too strong to falter, leads to the fulfilment of high purpose.

What national applications can we make of a story like this? So far as the historic setting is concerned, the applications are all national. There are individual applications which must never be made in the reading of a prophecy like this, such for instance as that of the eternal state of the individual men of the olden time. God was dealing with a nation, as a nation. This was His declaration of love for that particular and peculiar nation. From the declaration then in that sense, we observe that His persistence, manifested in His faithfulness to the smallest remnant of faithful souls, is ground-work for high hope in the most dark and disastrous day. Let us never forget that God has never left Himself without witness. There have been dark hours in our own national history, when it has seemed as though God had forsaken us, or that we had forsaken God; but it has never been wholly and finally true. God has always a band of faithful souls, maintaining allegiance to Himself; and to them He speaks; and if there be at last but one man,—I am not prepared to say there was only one in Jerusalem in Jeremiah's time,—but if there was but one, if there was but a prophet-priest of Anathoth in the court of the guard, well then God will say to that man, and through him to the whole nation, " I have loved thee with an everlasting love."

Then let us learn the importance to God of our loyalty to Him on the darkest day. One man standing true to God against widespread deflection, is God's vantage ground; and through that man God will move toward the ultimate accomplishment of His purpose. Therefore the true note of the prisoners of hope is always that of a song. Just before the dawn the night is darkest, and the supreme hour for singing is the hour when all the reasons for song seem to have departed. Shut up in the dungeon, men of faith sing.

And why do they sing? Because they know, that though all else may fail, though the king be weak and vacillating, though the rulers be mere politicians trying to traffic with their own wit and wisdom, though the people are ground under the heel of false civil and spiritual authority, though everything human has failed; God's love has not failed, and in that they rest, and in that they hope.

There are personal applications that seem to me to be full of value. They are of the most general nature, but none the less valuable; and I may express them in very brief words. The first is that in the life of faith, darkness is the place of songs. Those were wonderful men who talked to old Job. Everything they said was true, only that they did not understand him, and so their applications were at fault. Elihu speaking of God said, "Who giveth songs in the night." That is true! Songs in the night. I am not saying that when we are conscious of darkness and night we are immediately to compel ourselves to sing. By no means. Moreover, if we do not feel like singing, we have no right to sing. But I am saying that when we find ourselves in such situations, if we will patiently wait for Him, suddenly we shall sing; for it is there that He unveils His heart. On that day, when the thing happened that put out the light of hope, and you were face to face with the blankness of dismay and despair; when long-cherished aspirations suddenly went out in night, and you sat in the prison-house! It was then that He gave you songs. The place of song is the place of darkness.

The inspiration of such songs is the everlasting love of God. What ails thee, O my soul, what ails thee? I am afraid of the height that I am called to climb. Have no fear! Higher than any height thou hast ever seen is Love enabling thee to climb. What ails thee, O my soul? The depth and the darkness beneath me into which I fear I may fall, into which I am already falling. Have no fear, my soul, for when thou shalt fall, thou shalt discover underneath are the everlasting arms of the everlasting love! What ails thee, O soul of mine? The illimitable length that stretches out beyond me, and which I have to travel; the appalling breadth that stretches away on every side in which unknown foes are lurking. Have no fear, O soul of mine; for His love passeth knowledge, and He is at the ultimate reach of the longest length, and encompassing the widest reaches of the most infinite breadth. What ails thee, O my soul? Oh, it is not height and depth, it is not length and breadth! These things do not appal my soul. What then? The near, the immediate, this thing right at hand, this smallness. Well then, hear the final word, " with lovingkindness I am drawing thee." This also is part of the great whole. The thing of the hour, the fretful thing, the restless thing, the hot thing, the disappointing thing, is in the Divine! So let the man and the nation see God, and trusting in His Everlasting Love, sing the songs of the coming triumph.

XV

THE SPIRITUAL COVENANT

Preparatory Reading: Jeremiah 31.

"But this is the covenant that I will make with the house of Israel after those days, saith Jehovah; I will put My law in their inward parts, and in their heart will I write it; and I will be their God, and they shall be My people. And they shall teach no more every man his neighbour, and every man his brother, saying, Know Jehovah: for they shall all know Me, from the least of them unto the greatest of them, saith Jehovah: for I will forgive their iniquity, and their sin will I remember no more."—JEREMIAH 31 : 33, 34.

THESE words are found in the great song of hope which Jeremiah wrote while he was still shut up in the court of the guard. In our last study we considered the declaration of the fact which constituted the inspiration of the song, "I have loved thee with an everlasting love; therefore with lovingkindness have I drawn thee." In the final movement of the song found in verses twenty-seven to forty of chapter thirty-one, the whole nation was in view.

Then suddenly we have that somewhat strange verse preceding the section to which I have now referred: "Upon this I awaked, and beheld; and my sleep was sweet unto me." The reference cannot be to Jehovah, and the reference cannot be to Israel. It was unquestionably to Jeremiah himself, and to the fact, either that the revelations had been made to him in a dream, or that between one revelation and another he had fallen on sleep, and had been refreshed. But now, waking from a sleep that had been sweet, that is, full of refreshment, he broke out into this final burst of song, and the keynote is found in the words, " Behold, the days come, saith Jehovah." The prophet was now lifted upon the assurance of the love of God to a height from which he saw, far beyond the mists, the days of God's ultimate victory, the victory of the Everlasting love. For him therefore all the mists were purple with the promise of the morning.

This final section falls into three parts, each one being introduced by this same formula, " Behold, the days come." The first part celebrates the ultimate prosperity of the whole nation, connecting that prosperity with a new spiritual sense of direct relationship to God, which among other things will cancel all such false and foolish proverbs as that " The fathers have eaten sour grapes, and the children's teeth are set on edge." That hint prepares the way for the second part, which reveals the nature of that new covenant which Jehovah will make with His people. Finally the song declares that this restoration will be as firmly established as the ordinances of the natural order.

In our text then, we have the revelation of the nature of the new covenant. Its first and peculiar application is to Israel, and to the fact that in the economy of God, the ideal of Israel will yet be realized. We shall deduce those larger values which we may make our own, both in application to our national life, and to our individual need.

The method of the declaration should be carefully noted, and in order to this, we must observe the recurrence of the very simple word, " for," quite easily passed over as if it were of no great moment. By doing this we shall see that the statement of the prophet concerning the covenant proceeds from effect to cause. Let us glance at it in that way, simply endeavouring to catch its argument by the observance of this word: " I will . . ."; " for . . . they shall "; " for . . . I will." " I will put My law in their inward parts. . . . I will be their God . . . they shall be My people; and they shall teach no more every man his neighbour, and every man his brother, saying, Know Jehovah: *for* they shall all know Me, from the least of them unto the greatest of them . . . *for* I will forgive their iniquity, and their sin will I remember no more."

The final covenant of relationship will be that of the clear apprehension of the will of God by individual souls, without human mediation, " I will put My law in their inward parts, and in their heart will I write it "; and no man shall say to his brother or neighbour, Know Jehovah. This apprehension of the will of God will be possible through direct and personal knowledge of God on the part of all men. This knowledge of God on the part of all will result from the putting away of moral defilement.

Let us now state this, no longer proceeding from effect to cause, but from cause to effect. There will first be the cleansing of the moral nature. Resulting therefrom there will be the clear vision of God. Resulting therefrom, there will be the accurate apprehension of His will.

In our meditation we shall follow the prophetic order of statement, considering the new covenant; first, as the covenant of spiritual discernment; secondly, as the covenant of Divine fellowship; and thirdly, as the covenant of moral cleansing.

Beginning therefore with the final effect we find it expressed in these words, " I will put My law in their inward parts, and in their heart will I write it; and I will be their God, and they shall be My people. And they shall teach no more every man his neighbour, and every man his brother, saying, Know Jehovah." The declaration needs very little by way of exposition in some senses. Jehovah declares that in this day of the new covenant, He will place His law within the individual life, that He will write it upon the individual heart; that in the day of the new covenant the law of God will be within the life. I think we should remember that we must take this term law, in its most essential sense, not as having reference to the law as given by Moses, not as having reference to any written code whatever; but to the law of Jehovah as the will of God, concerning the individual life, and concerning the national life; the law of God as the purpose of God for man and for the nation. The declaration, then, is that there shall come an hour when this law of God shall be within, written upon the heart; when the law of God shall be communicated to the individual directly, clearly, and constantly; so that it shall be ever new, so that in every hour there shall be no need to look back to the thing spoken yesterday, because of the consciousness within the life of the Divine thought and will and purpose in that particular moment.

Such knowledge will issue in the realization of the mutual relation which is described in the words, " I will be their God, and they shall be My people." " I will be their God," maintaining toward them the attitude and activities of God, as Creator, as Preserver, as Friend, as King, as Saviour; or if we may pass back into the very atmosphere of this Hebrew thinking, as Jehovah, the One Who becomes to men what they need in every moment, accommodating Himself to the necessity of His creatures; " I will be their God."

" And they shall be My people," maintaining the attitude and activities of a people to God. The outcome of the law within will be that man will understand it to be good and perfect and acceptable, and will respond to it.

This positive statement is, however, made far more forceful if we consider the negative, and observe the things which are excluded. The prophet put this new covenant into definite contrast with the old covenant. Most distinctly did he affirm that the new covenant should not be according to the covenant made with the fathers in the day that they were delivered from the bondage of Egypt; but that it should be a new covenant, something in advance of the old, and different from it. The new covenant will exclude the external letter, the commandment written upon a table of stone, the commandment written on parchment; the commandment written at all will become unnecessary; it will be excluded. It is well to remember that the written commandment—and I refer resolutely to the commandment contained in Holy Scripture, whether in the Old or the New Testaments now—the written commandment is always incomplete, and constantly obscure. The order of the scribes arose because of the obscurity of the written commandment. When I speak of obscurity I mean the difficulty of the application of the commandment to every new phase of life. The scribe was the interpreter of the moral law. The moral law was supposed to contain within it everything that was necessary for the government of human life, and so it did. But how it met certain individual needs, who should tell? The order of the scribes arose in order to interpret and apply this inclusive law to human needs. Is there any question more often asked in spiritual conversation between men and women following Christ, and those who are their responsible teachers than this? How am I to know what the will of God is? This simply means that the written word, even of the New Testament, is obscure. Life is so complex, so varied, so perpetually changing its manifestation and its need, that ever and anon we imagine enough has not been written to cover all the necessities of the case. In the new economy, so far as it is found in writing, we are still face to face with exactly the same difficulty. This is not the economy of rules but of principles, and it is in the application of principle that a man finds his difficulty. I venture to affirm that every Christian man and woman, at some hour or another, every day faces this difficulty, What are we to do in these circumstances? We have turned to our New Testament, and it has been silent, as it seemed; no rule, no regulation. In this new covenant, then, the external writing, always incomplete, perpetually obscure, is to be excluded. " I will put My law in their inward parts, and in their heart will I write it," so that there shall be no need for them to lift their eyes and look upon the writing on the tables of stone, no need for them to turn again to the writings which have been given to them.

And not only is the external letter excluded, the human interpreter is excluded also. No man in that day shall say, or have any need to say to his neighbour or to his brother, Know Jehovah. In the history of human interpretation, at the best, the human interpreter has been fallible; and at the worst, he has been false; and that abides true, until this hour. The new covenant is a covenant, in its final experience, in which the human soul shall be rendered independent of the external law, and independent of the human interpreter; the law of God within, written on the heart, apprehended immediately rather than mediately, received by the direct revelation of the will of God within the spirit, and independent of all writings, and of all human interpretation, is to be the rule of life.

This is an exact description of the covenant under which Christian people live. This is the communion of the Holy Ghost. Yet how we still hanker after laws and rules and regulations. How we of the Christian Church and the Christian dispensation still perpetually put ourselves back under the Hebrew economy, the imperfection of which was revealed by the spiritual interpretations of Christ, and declared in the holy apostolic writing, which affirms that the law made nothing perfect, nor could do so, and that it was therefore abolished.

How perpetually moreover, we give ourselves to modern legalisms, signing our pledges, or conforming our habits to the opinions of other men, looking outside for direction instead of expecting direction within. The law is interpreted by the indwelling Spirit, the law is written upon the heart; not upon one occasion, to be stored as within the memory, and referred to in every hour of need; not that to-day I am to ask what God said to me yesterday, but that now, at this moment, in this hour of need, I am to expect the voice Divine, the interpretation within the soul.

Or if we have escaped from the Hebrew economy, and are set free from modern legalisms, then we are in danger of making rules and regulations for the government of our own lives. It is all false, all unnecessary, all engaged in because we have never entered into that privilege which is ours in the communion of the Holy Spirit, wherein the law of God is within, written in the heart, interpreted to the life directly and immediately in the very hour of need. We sometimes affirm that God does not speak to men as He did to Abraham. He speaks far more directly to men if men have ears to hear, and hearts to apprehend. The spiritual covenant in which we live, is far ahead of the covenant made with Noah, or Abraham, or Moses, or Ezra. It is this very covenant that the prophet saw the glory of, while he was yet imprisoned, and expressed in the language of this triumphant song. It is the covenant of the law of God made known directly to man, without any mediation of writings, or of human interpretation. In some senses— I use the qualifying phrase, in some senses—this is the great doctrine which we owe to those mystics of the past, held tenaciously even until this hour, and sometimes, it may be, misapplied, by our friends, the Friends, the doctrine of the inner light; not an inner light found in every man by birth, but an inner light given to all such as are brought into new covenant relationship with

God, in the communion of the Holy Ghost. All written
laws fail, not because man is less than the law, but because the law is less than man, and because within human personality there is something infinitely greater
than ever can be conditioned within any law uttered at
a single moment. Human personality demands God and
His light, and the immediate communication of His will.
I will put My law within them, and write it upon their
heart, and so they shall be My people, so I will be their
God; there shall be the exclusion of all that is outside;
these things being rendered unnecessary by this inner
communion of the individual with God.

That takes us backward a step, and so we come to the
second part of the prophetic declaration: " For," or because, " they shall all know Me, from the least of them
unto the greatest of them, saith Jehovah." Everything
that we have been attempting to consider is dependent
upon this, for there is no writing of the law of God
within, no direct and immediate communication of the
will of God to a man, apart from the knowledge of God
Himself. The knowledge of the will of God is the outcome of the knowledge of God. That is always God's
order. God's order is never that of revealing Himself to
the man through law. His order is always that of revealing law to the man through Himself. That is a very
general statement, but considered in the light of past
economies, it is proved true. The Mosaic law was never
given to the people until they had found God. They did
not find Him through the law. They found the law
which came by Moses, because He had found them and
redeemed them and ransomed them. Or, to put it in
another way, the nineteenth chapter of Exodus precedes
the twentieth! The nineteenth is the chapter of a covenant; I have brought you unto Myself, a peculiar treas-
ure, a kingdom of priests. After that, the twentieth
chapter, and the law! Through every successive dispensation or economy of God, the method has been first

the knowledge of God, and then the knowledge of His will. So also in this final spiritual apprehension of the will of God, we must understand that this must grow out of a knowledge of God Himself; so that the new covenant in its deeper note is that of Divine fellowship. "They shall know Me," quite literally, they shall ascertain the truth concerning Me by seeing Me. The word *know* here indicates observation and care and recognition and immediate understanding. "They shall know Me," not merely hold an orthodox creed, but know Me personally; not merely be intellectually convinced of my existence, but have first-hand dealings with Myself. "They shall know Me."

Then mark the gracious sweep of the declaration, so much in advance of the time in which it was uttered that we are astonished, because it includes the whole Christian economy, " from the least . . . unto the greatest of them "; that is, this knowledge of God is not to be communicated to some particular section of the community through which it is to be passed on to others. It is to be the common birthright inheritance of every individual, " from the least of them unto the greatest of them." I do not desire to put undue emphasis on the method of a language, and yet I pray you notice the form and fashion of the suggestion. Not, from the greatest unto the least. " I thank Thee, O Father, Lord of heaven and earth, that thou didst hide these things from the wise and understanding, and didst reveal them unto babes." So said our Master in the days of His flesh, and the same thought is here. This knowledge of God is not to come through intellectual attainment, it is to be direct, immediate, a consciousness, which is independent of instruction by man, a great certainty of God, and familiarity with God; "they shall know Me from the least to the greatest." We may with all fairness read into our text all qualifying words, whatever least may be, least in intellectual attainment, least in influential position as among the sons of men, least in moral capacity, still it is true " From the least unto the greatest, they shall know Me."

This is an exact description of the relationship which Christ came to establish. If in the first phase we found the communion of the Holy Ghost, here we find the love of God. We fear the will of God because we do not know God; and we fail to know God because we do not acquaint ourselves with Him. All my pronouns now refer to His children. I am speaking of our failure to realize the very covenant in which we live. I repeat: we fear the will of God because we do not know God. We fail to know God because we do not acquaint ourselves with Him, by quietness, by meditation, by silence. One is tempted to think that is the peculiar failure of our own age. There is so little time taken to acquaint the life with God by quietness, by meditation, by silence. Sometimes our very Prayer Meetings are so full of our own talk that there is no room for God to talk. We are constantly so busy speaking to Him that we hardly take time to listen to what He has to say to us.

This knowledge of God, while it is direct and immediate, yet comes in its fulness, in response to the attitude of waiting and listening. To dwell within the love of God, is to know that fellowship in love cannot be one-sided; we never can express our love ultimately in giving to God in service; love finds its final and finest expression in receiving. It is more blessed to give than to receive is one application of one truth; but there is another truth that we may set over against it, for there is always the opposite to every truth expressed in an aphorism; it is also more blessed to receive than to give in the fellowship of love. I sometimes think that it takes more grace to be willing to receive than it does to be willing to give. In all this realm of fellowship with God, this fellowship of love, this knowing of God, He waits until we are quiet enough to receive His word, that

He may make Himself known to us more perfectly. It is when we have learned the secret of waiting, and of being still and quiet that we find His law within, written upon the heart, and we know the next thing to do, without the commandments on tables of stone, without the interpretation of the human teacher.

That consideration takes us back yet further to that which is initial; "*for* I will forgive their iniquity, and their sin will I remember no more." The knowledge of God is dependent upon this; and once more we may pass into the New Testament and hear from the lips of our Lord the whole truth crystallized into the beatitude, "Blessed are the pure in heart, for they shall see God." It is only by the way of moral cleansing that we can know Him. It is only by the knowledge of Him that we find His law within, and on the heart, so that we know immediately what we are to do. Where there is such immediate knowledge of the will of God, it is the result of the knowledge of God Himself. Where there is such knowledge of God Himself, it is the result of heart purity.

But mark the inevitable grace of the idea. Purity is not something which a man is to attain by struggle. It is something which he is to receive as the gift of infinite grace: "I will forgive their iniquity, and their sin will I remember no more." In this great prophetic word of the past there is the most radiant foretelling of that peculiar and central mystery and ministry of Christ, in which He does bring to the soul of man the sense and the assurance and the experience of forgiveness, the sense that is expressed in the consciousness of inward purity, and the consciousness of inward peace; the sense that has enabled countless multitudes of souls to sing,

"My God is reconciled,
His pardoning voice I hear,
He owns me for His child,

I can no longer fear;
With confidence I now draw nigh,
And Father, Abba, Father! cry."

That is the sense of moral purity, that is the sense of being forgiven, of loosing from sin. Not merely that sin is judicially put away, a minor matter, but that the soul is cleansed from its defilement, its stain, its pollution. Out of that sense of purity, and of peace resulting from the removal of pollution, lo, the vision of God! In answer to that purity of heart, not attained but received, there breaks upon the mind the certainty of God, and there comes to the individual the knowledge of His will.

If in the first phase we have the communion of the Holy Ghost, and in the second the love of God, in this last we have " the grace of our Lord Jesus Christ." In the one pamphlet in the New Testament specifically and definitely written for Hebrews, the writer makes such use of this word from Jeremiah concerning a covenant, first quoting it at length to show the superiority of this new covenant which Christ established, over all that had preceded it; and then quoting it again, so as to show that the nerve of the argument is this, " By one offering He hath perfected for ever them that are sanctified." The grace of our Lord Jesus Christ begins with us there, dealing with moral depravity and pollution; cleansing, purifying, sanctifying; and lo, to the heart thus purified there comes the vision of God; and lo, to the life thus brought into fellowship with God, there comes the immediate and constantly renewed revelation of the will of God. Such is the new covenant and we are living within that covenant. Whether we are availing ourselves of all its values who shall tell?

The prophesying of Jeremiah was national, and there are great national values which we may deduce from this marvellous song of the covenant. National regeneration must begin with moral renewal. Wherever there is moral renewal there is the restored consciousness of God. Wherever there is the restored consciousness of God there is the restored keenness of scent in the fear of the Lord. Have we lost that at all? If so it is because we have lost the vision of God. There have been hours when the vision of God was clear before the eyes of the whole people. I am not affirming that it is not so now. I am asking, and I am wondering! At any rate let us remember that if we have lost that vision, there is only one way for its renewal, and that is by moral renewal; and the business of the Church of God is to deal with the inspirational centres of human life, with man's moral nature, and its relationship to God. If indeed, we believe that God is still the Governor of the nations, and that the government of the world is in His hands; and we desire, as we do desire most earnestly, that our own nation shall take its true part in the Divine economy, and minister to the Divine end, then we shall serve our generation best when we bring men to the Cross, to individual dealing with God through Christ, in order to their moral renewal.

Yet let the last word be, as it inevitably must and should be, the personal word. This is the true order of life; purity of heart, fellowship with God, the clear shining of the inner light. However much it may rebuke us, yet let the fact be recognized, that the difficulty of knowing what God would have us do next, is the measure of our distance from God; and distance from God in experience, is in the measure in which we regard iniquity in the heart. Or to state the same truth in the positive form; heart purity, a gift of grace to be received, is the condition for the knowledge of God as here. Maintained fellowship is the condition for immediate illumination. So may we live within the covenant.

XVI

THE PURCHASE OF THE FIELD OF ANATHOTH

Preparatory Readings: Jeremiah 31:4—32; 2 Kings 25:1, 2.

" I bought the field that was in Anathoth of Hanamel mine uncle's son, and weighed him the money, even seventeen shekels of silver. And I subscribed the deed, and sealed it, and called witnesses, and weighed him the money in the balances."—JEREMIAH 32:9, 10.

THE thirty-second and thirty-third chapters of Jeremiah constitute the second movement in the prophecies of hope, uttered when the prophet was imprisoned in the court of the guard, and the armies of the Chaldeans were encamped around the city. In the two preceding chapters we have the song of hope, some of the dominant notes of which we have considered together in previous meditations.

In these two chapters we have the account of a transaction on the part of Jeremiah which was significant and suggestive, that namely of the purchase of a field in his native city of Anathoth. This took place during his imprisonment, and the prophet now told Zedekiah the story of the purchase. A rapid survey of the scheme of the two chapters will materially help us in our present study, and in that which will come next.

The first section describes briefly the condition of affairs; Jeremiah was in prison in the court of the guard; Jerusalem was imprisoned by the besieging and invading armies. It also tells us of Zedekiah's protest against the gloomy predictions of Jeremiah. The rest of the two chapters contains the prophet's answer to the pro-

test of the king. The burden of the answer was that
of restoration rather than of judgment. While Jeremiah
did not withdraw anything that he had said as to the
immediate judgment, he told this story of his own experience, and uttered a prophecy of ultimate restoration
and healing for the people.

In that story then let us observe the movement yet a
little more closely. First there came to Jeremiah the
word of Jehovah telling him that Hanamel would come
to him, and ask him to exercise his right of redemption
in the purchase of a field in Anathoth. In consonance
with this foretelling Hanamel came, and Jeremiah purchased the field. Having done so he prayed, and his
prayer consisted of a reverent statement of his sense
of the difficulty of the thing which he had done, of the
difficulty of the accomplishment of that which his action
had symbolized. Said he in his prayer: To God as
Creator, nothing is too hard. Moreover, that had been
demonstrated. His power had been seen in the history
of His people both in patience and in judgment; indeed,
in that very hour the presence of the Chaldean army
outside the city was a demonstration of the power of
God, and of the persistence of His government. Nevertheless God had instructed Jeremiah to buy land which
already was, according to his prediction, devoted to the
invaders, and could not be possessed.

To that prayer of the prophet the word of Jehovah
replied in four messages. The first commenced on the
same note as did the prophet's prayer. Jeremiah had
said, There is nothing too hard for God. Jehovah replied, Is there anything too hard for Me? and then proceeded to affirm the certainty both of judgment and of
realization.

The second movement in the answer of Jehovah yet
more distinctly foretold the way of realization, and predicted the coming of the Branch of righteousness, the
great King-Priest.

STUDIES IN THE PROPHECY OF JEREMIAH

The third and fourth sections employed the covenant of day and night as the symbol of the stability of the covenant which Jehovah had made with David.

Our present theme is that of the purchase of the field on the part of the prophet, and its revelation of the activity of faith. So far as the story is concerned it is so simply and perfectly told on the sacred page that we need not tarry with it; but the significance of the action is important. The first value of the action most evidently is, that it was an action of faith. For nearly forty years Jeremiah had been predicting the fall of the city and the loss of the land; and in fulfilment of his foretelling the armies were encamped without the walls. He knew in his heart that overthrow was imminent, and yet he bought land, which presently must inevitably pass out of his possession. It was an action of faith. I am not proposing to defend that statement, but to consider the action; and I do not know, as it seems to me at the moment, any page in my Bible that more wonderfully illustrates the activity of faith; any action which taken not merely in itself, but in its setting, more radiantly reveals what it really is to walk by faith. There are four lines of consideration that I shall ask you to follow; first the intelligence of faith; secondly the obedience of faith; thirdly the enquiry or doubt of faith; and finally the assuring of faith.

First then as to its intelligence. In the midst of all the darkness of the dark time here was a man most evidently walking in the light; light that shone in the darkness but was not of the darkness; light that shone within the darkness, but did not dissipate the darkness. This was the intelligence of faith. Here also we have a picture of the obedience of faith, of how faith acts, of the fact that its action is reasonable, cautious, legal, accurate. Faith is never fanatical. Then we come to that which it seems to me is the central thought of comfort and help in the story, that faith asks questions.

And finally, we have that mystic and wonderful ending of the story which brings us to a realm that will defy all logical statement; the fact that to such enquiry God gives His answer.

First then, as to the intelligence of faith as it is here revealed. Let us bear in mind most carefully that this hour had been prefaced by long years of fellowship with God in the experience of the prophet. We have but to recall the things we have considered, to recognize the wonderful relationship between God and this lonely soul, lonely, that is, so far as his own age was concerned; he was a man exercising a ministry foredoomed to failure from its very commencement, that is, judging a human ministry by purely human standards. It has been a story of difficulty faced by the prophet, and of deliverance wrought by Jehovah. It has been the story of an absolute loyalty on the part of Jeremiah to Jehovah. It has been the story of an absolute loyalty on the part of Jehovah to Jeremiah. It has been the story of repeated protest made by the prophet. There were hours when in agony and in anger he cried out against the intolerable and insufferable ministry he was called upon to exercise. Ever and anon at set intervals we hear the man in agony and in anger crying out against his own ministry; but ever, side by side with the angry protest, there is the unveiling of the infinite patience of God, as understanding the weakness of the human heart, and the pain it suffers, God bent over His servant, and encouraged him. Jeremiah perpetually trembled in the presence of God in view of his ministry. He never trembled in the presence of men. That long fellowship through the years had created for him a mental mood, in which faith most perfectly operated.

First of all that mental mood may be said to have been characterized by sensitiveness of mind and spirit, to the will and voice of God. Here is something that we should notice carefully. Jeremiah declared that God told him that Hanamel would come and ask him to buy this field in Anathoth. That is the sensitive mind hearing the voice of God, discovering the thought of God. When Hanamel came, making his request, then said the prophet, I knew that this was the word of Jehovah. By bringing these two things together we have a revelation first of this sensitiveness of mind which was made conscious of a purpose of God, and then of this cautiousness of mind which took no steps until that impression was vindicated by the actuality of circumstance. He knew that the impression was definite, when circumstance ratified the impression. I lay stress upon this, because sometimes men tell me to-day that God does not speak now as He spoke to Jeremiah. He speaks in exactly the same way. He spoke then by an impression upon the soul. It came perchance in some hour of loneliness. The land is devoted to destruction; it is to pass from the people of Judah. The Chaldeans will own it; and there is that field away in Anathoth. I am, as though Jeremiah had said, the goel, the redeeming kinsman; I have the right to redeem it; and Hanamel will come and offer it to me, and I shall purchase it. But he took no step until Hanamel came; and when Hanamel came he said, Then I knew that was the word of Jehovah. In that simple way of telling the story, in the very incidentals of the narrative, we have a wonderful revelation of that mental mood which is the true mood of the man of faith; the sensitive mind that receives an impression even though at the moment of its reception he is not conscious, or perfectly certain, that it is the will of God. It is received as a suggestion in harmony with larger Divine intentions; and then faith waits for the verifying circumstance that sets its seal upon the spiritual impression.

In the story we have a revelation of the fact that the conditions for the life of faith, for the exercise of faith in hours of darkness, and in all hours of life, are those of such intimacy with God as makes necessary the setting of all things in relation to His government; and on the other hand, of such intimacy with events as makes this possible. Here was a man living in Jerusalem in the court of the guard, in the imprisoned and beleaguered city; and in the natural order of events conscious that the land was forfeit; thinking of his native city of Anathoth, remembering his field, knowing that this also was forfeit. I do not think I wrong the narrative if I say that the coming of Hanamel was a desire on the part of Hanamel to realize before it was too late. He wished to sell, for he saw how things were happening. The man of faith set this commonplace incident in the light of Divine arrangements, and Divine movements. He was so intimate with God in daily life that all the events of the days were set in relation to His government. He asked of every incident and happening, What does this mean in relation to God's throne? It also reveals the fact that the man of faith must live in such intimacy with all the actualities and facts of everyday life that it is possible for him to set them in relation to the throne of God. Intelligent faith is ever quick of impression, or keen of scent, in the fear of Jehovah. Intelligent faith is ever cautious in its action, and waits for the seal of circumstance upon the impression made.

So we pass to the act itself, the obedience of faith; and here again the thought of the last suggestion that faith is never fanatical is emphasized by the care Jeremiah exercised in the purchase of the field. The passage is strictly technical in the terms employed, and in it we discover the rites and customs of the times. It was a time of stress and strain, men everywhere were conscious of the coming downfall of the city, of the passing away of the nation. Why not buy the land in faith, and do it carelessly? Faith is never careless. The deed must be drawn up, and it must be drawn up legally, and it must be drawn up indeed with a care beyond the ordinary. Two copies of the deed were made; one was sealed, that is, it was locked up; another was made, which was an open one, that is, it might be looked at; but this last must be compared with the sealed one, in order to verify and correct it. Witnesses were appointed, and all was done before the judge. When we are tempted to do some foolhardy thing in the name of faith, let us go back and read this chapter, and observe that faith is legal and faith is accurate.

Again we discover the reason of faith. Faith is never irrational. Faith is always based upon some reason. Jeremiah did not buy this field as the result of his calculation of circumstances. Jeremiah did not buy this field because he had discovered how God was going to act. Jeremiah did not buy this field because it was perfectly sure that God would at some future time give the land back. What then was the reason of the action of faith? "For thus saith Jehovah of hosts, the God of Israel." The certainty of God, and the certainty that whatever God said must be right. Not by the cleverness of politicians who forecasted the issue, not by the clear mathematical and mechanical vision of how God was going to accomplish His purpose; but upon the basis of the fact that God told him what to do in the secret of his own soul, that God spoke, he bought the land. The action of faith is taken in response to the light that shineth in the darkness. Faith is conscious of God, conscious of the light, and therefore obeys without reserve. Faith is conscious of the darkness, and therefore is cautious in its obedience. The act was characterized by all legal formality and care. The act was based upon a soul's assurance of God; and in its twofold attitude, of obedience without reserve in spite of all outward appearances, and of quiet cautious care, is a radiant revelation of the true balance and proportion and perspective of faith's obedience.

Obedience by faith does not mean that there will be

no enquiry, no question, no sense of difficulty. The whole movement reveals the presence of this very sense of difficulty in the mind of the prophet. Faith is the evidence of things not seen, the assurance of things hoped for; but the moment you speak of faith you admit doubt. If there be no risk, then there is no faith. If there be no venture, there is no faith. If there be risk, and if there be venture, there is the consciousness of risk and the consciousness of venture; and in the consciousness of risk and venture we have the element of doubt. The more profoundly we follow Bible history, or search the experience of our own attempts to live by faith, the more we discover that doubt is the evidence of faith, that apart from it there is no faith; and that outside the realm of faith there is no doubt. It is the man who believes nothing, who has no doubt and no difficulty. Everything is settled. Two and two make four. So he lives. No larger vision, and consequently no smaller question. It is Habakkuk, the prophet of faith, who believes in God most profoundly, who cries out with a sense of the difficulty. What is God doing? That is the question of a man of faith. The man who lacks faith will not ask anything about what God is doing. It is the principle of faith that gives birth to enquiry, to question, to doubt. The whole of this great prayer of Jeremiah is a demonstration of this fact.

But now let us carefully watch what Jeremiah did. First of all he said nothing about his doubt to Hanamel. He made no proclamation of the enquiry that was lurking within him, and persisting through his soul, when the elders were round about him, and he was drawing up the document. He said, " After I had delivered the deed of the purchase unto Baruch the son of Neriah, I prayed unto Jehovah." So far as men were concerned, he had already committed himself, before he gave utterance to the question in his heart. That is faith. God commands, and I do not see how this is going to be, but I obey. That is faith taking the risk, making the venture, daring everything upon the word of God.

Observe in the second place that if he did not speak of his doubt to Hanamel, or to the elders who were round about him, if he made no reference to the sense of difficulty until the deed was subscribed and sealed, he did speak of these things to God: "After I had delivered the deed . . . I prayed unto Jehovah." Now here is the distinction between the unbelief that dishonours God, and the faith that asks questions. The faith that asks questions asks them of God, asks them in the secret place. What a wonderful prayer this of Jeremiah is. It opens with a sigh, "Ah Lord Jehovah!" This man was in prison; the armies were round about the city; the city was to be destroyed and the land taken from the people; then the impression came to him that Hanamel would offer him the field in Anathoth; Hanamel came, the field was bought, the deed was subscribed, faith acted. Then he bared his soul to God: "Ah Lord Jehovah," I cannot understand this, I do not see the meaning of it, I cannot see how that which is suggested by my action can ever come to pass. After the sigh came the affirmation: "There is nothing too hard for Thee." Then the celebration of the power of God ran through the prayer with hardly a petition, until it abruptly ended in what was practically an exclamation: "And Thou hast said unto me, O Lord Jehovah, Buy thee the field for money, and call witnesses; whereas the city is given into the hand of the Chaldeans!" Thus faith, in the presence of God, spoke of its difficulty, of its enquiry, of its questioning.

Faith involves questions. Faith involves the element of risk, of venture; but faith in God asks its questions of God. The one thing we need supremely to guard against in the life of faith is the attempt to hide our lurking unbelief from God. This is an almost unnecessary thing to say in some ways, because intellectually we cannot hide anything from God. Yet, all unknowingly, we try; we come into the midst of danger and doubt and difficulty, and we sing of our trust in God, and all the while the heart is saying: What does it mean? How can God do this? Why has He done this? That is the hypocrisy that kills faith. Faith will follow resolutely and obediently and heroically; but faith will have its quiet place in which it tells God of its doubts and its questionings, and its unbeliefs. There is nothing, if I understand my Bible aright, against which God has made His protest more persistently, than that of hypocrisy of this kind. Is your heart hot and restless? You believe in God. The deepest thing in you, is your belief in God. You do desire to follow Him, even when you cannot see how this thing is going to be, or why this thing is done. Make time to tell Him your doubt; and tell it Him with absolute honesty. The prophecy of Habakkuk to which I have referred, is the central illustration of this principle in the Bible. Habakkuk said: I cry murder, and nobody answers me! What is God doing? Yes, but Habakkuk said that, in the secret place, to God; and God bent over him, and said: If I should tell you, you would not believe Me; but I will tell you what I am going to do. I am going to employ the Chaldeans to do My work. Habakkuk replied in effect: This is worse than ever! God is going to employ the Chaldeans! I will up to my watch-tower, and wait and see what God means. That is magnificent faith.

> " There lives more faith in honest doubt,
> Believe me, than in half the creeds."

If Habakkuk had not believed in God, he would not have been troubled. If Carlyle had not believed in God he would never have said to Froude that God was doing nothing. If there are any who do not know darkness, it is because they have never seen light; and if they have no doubt, it is because they do not understand belief. "Ah Lord Jehovah! . . . there is nothing too hard for Thee." Thou hast been gracious, and lovingkindness has been Thy way, and Thou hast been persistent in Thy judgment, and the armies are here; and yet Thou hast told me to buy a field, and the Chaldeans are going to possess it. I have bought it, Lord, but now I want to know something about this thing. That is the enquiry of faith.

And so the story ends with the assuring of faith. Here we reach a realm which transcends logical statement. We now move into the atmosphere of communion; and although the answer of Jehovah occupies this somewhat long section, the important matter is not what God said; it is that He spoke. " Then " ; When? When doubt had expressed itself, when the difficulty was stated, when the incipient trembling was forced into the open; " Then came the word of Jehovah unto Jeremiah " ; . . . " Moreover the word of Jehovah came unto Jeremiah the second time." Not to dwell upon the details of this great answer, let me simply gather up its twofold value. First, when the word of Jehovah came it said: " I am Jehovah, the God of all flesh: is there anything too hard for Me?" Now Jeremiah's prayer had begun, " There is nothing too hard for Thee," and Jeremiah's prayer had ended in effect; This looks too hard for Thee. Jehovah began by ratifying the fundamental affirmation of the prophet, and he did it in the form of an enquiry. Jeremiah affirmed that there was nothing too hard. He ended practically with the enquiry, Is it not a little too hard for God? God asked: Is it too hard for Me? The question seems to me to suggest an amused patience with Jeremiah. If you object to that, it is because you are neither a father nor a mother! If you are a father or a mother you know how often there is an amusement, that is full of pathos, in the way in which you talk to your child when it is in trouble. Jeremiah said: Nothing is too hard for God; but this looks too hard for Him! God said: I am going to talk to you, Jeremiah; Is it, is it too hard for Me? Is anything? That was God answering the doubt of a believing soul by expressing the doubt for the believing soul; and my doubt never sounds so unworthy as when God expresses it for me. After that God affirmed that men would yet fulfil the sign of Jeremiah, and buy land and buy houses in that very region.

Later we read: " Moreover the word of Jehovah came unto Jeremiah the second time, while he was yet shut up in the court of the guard." God had something else to say to him: " Call unto Me, and I will answer thee, and will show thee great things, and difficult, which thou knowest not." In effect God said to him: You are perfectly right in expressing your doubt. This was a vindication of the prophet's right to enquire. Then God admitted him into the deep and profound secret of the fact that presently through all this turmoil and this strife, through all this chaos and this devastation and desolation, there would grow a Branch out of the root, there would come One Who would be King and Priest, exercising authority, and mediating, so that men would be able to enter into the realization of the meaning of the Divine government.

Such was the answer of God to the soul of the man of faith, who had been honest enough to speak of his doubt in the Divine presence. By honest enquiry, we create the opportunity for confirmatory revelation; but that is never collective, it is always personal. I cannot have my deepest question answered by any man. No priest or prophet or preacher, can bring to storm-tossed souls God's answer. I can but say to you: Give God the chance to speak to you. The chance is created by the affirmation of unbelief, in His presence. The trouble of our infidelities is that we proclaim them to friends and neighbours and not to God.

All this, for present and practical purposes, is in illustration of a principle. Sometimes the activity of faith is that of selling land instead of buying it. I think I ought to say that, because we are so much in danger of laying stress on the accidental and missing the essential. Jeremiah illustrates his faith by buying land. If we cross over into the New Testament we find exactly the reverse. "Barnabas . . . having a field, sold it, and brought the money, and laid it at the apostles' feet." Do not let us confuse the essential with the accidental. It is a wonder that the Church has not had two new sects of land buyers, and land sellers; the Jeremiahites, and the Barnabasites! It is the sort of thing the Church has been doing constantly, building up a sect upon accidental things, while forgetting the essential. The principle is deeper than the buying or the selling of land. The principle is deeper than any expression at a given moment.

The principle illustrated in this story of Jeremiah's buying of the field in Anathoth, is that of the importance; first, of such maintained fellowship with God that we may understand events; and secondly, of such maintained intimacy with events, that we may be able to coöperate with God. The opportunities of expression occur in the commonplaces of life. To-morrow morning, as a man of faith, you will buy, you will sell. Faith in God is that fellowship which is so real, that every passing and incidental thing is vibrant with the forces of eternity. Faith in God makes itself so familiar with Hanamel and that little bit of ground that he is anxious to realize on because there is a catastrophe coming, that it sees in that a chance to protest and to affirm faith. This can only be cultivated toward its ultimate perfection when the soul refuses to cloak or disguise its enquiry, but states it daringly in the presence of God. To such men and women of honest faith God will tell His secret: "The secret of Jehovah is with them that fear Him."

XVII

THE METHOD AND RESULT OF RESTORATION

Preparatory Readings: Jeremiah 33; 2 Kings 25:1, 2.

" In those days, and at that time, will I cause a Branch of righteousness to grow up unto David, and He shall execute justice and righteousness in the land. In those days shall Judah be saved, and Jerusalem shall dwell safely; and this is the name whereby she shall be called, Jehovah our Righteousness."—JEREMIAH 33:15, 16.

THE prophet was still a prisoner in Jerusalem, and Jerusalem itself was imprisoned within the besieging battalions of Nebuchadnezzar. Within the purpose of God the city and the whole land were devoted to destruction and desolation. Under these conditions, and acting in response to the Divine impulse, Jeremiah had purchased a field in Anathoth as a sign of the perpetual possession of the land by the people of God. In view of the fact that it was about to pass into the power of Babylon,—a fact which Jeremiah, under Divine compulsion, had been insisting upon,—the prophet conscious of difficulty, had spoken of the matter in prayer.

The answer of God to the soul of His servant is given in four movements within this section of the prophecy. Of these the second and supreme, is that in which Jehovah distinctly foretold and described the way of His future realization of His purposes. Of that central word, the principal values are contained in these verses which we have selected as the basis for our meditation, " In those days, and at that time will I cause a Branch of Righteousness to grow up unto David, and He shall execute justice and righteousness in the land." That is the method by which the restoration is to be effected. "In those days shall Judah be saved, and Jerusalem shall dwell safely; and this is the name whereby she shall be called, Jehovah our Righteousness." That is the result.

As we read these words we are conscious that we have read them before in the course of our study of this prophecy. Turning back to the messages in denunciation of false rulers, both civil and spiritual, both kings and prophets, we find almost identical words. Those messages had been uttered by the prophet about seven years earlier than this period of his imprisonment, and the besieging of the city by the armies of Nebuchadnezzar. Turning back to those prophecies we find these words: "Behold, the days come, saith Jehovah, that I will raise unto David a righteous Branch, and He shall reign as King and deal wisely, and shall execute justice and righteousness in the land. In His days Judah shall be saved, and Israel shall dwell safely: and this is His name whereby He shall be called, Jehovah Tsidkenu." The similarity between the two passages amounts to identity so far as their main teaching is concerned, both as to the method and the result of the restoration foretold; but there is a disparity between them. The disparity simply serves to emphasize the relation between their method and result. In the earlier passage the prophet had said, "This is His name, whereby *He* shall be called, Jehovah Tsidkenu." In this later message he said, "This is the name whereby *she* shall be called, Jehovah Tsidkenu." In the first the suggestive name is borne by the King Himself. In the second it is the name of the city over which He is to reign. Jehovah Tsidkenu then as the name of the King, reveals the method of restoration. Jehovah Tsidkenu as the name of the city, reveals the result within the city of His administration.

Without dealing with the title, "the Branch," or with

the relation of the Person bearing the title to David's house, let us take the broader outlook, and consider the teaching of this passage, first concerning the name as revealing the method of the King in realization; and secondly, the name as revealing the conditions of realization, as describing the ultimate in that work which God is ever doing,—moving through judgment, by way of discipline, toward the establishment of the order which is in harmony with His will.

We will first take the name as it is found in the earlier passage, Jehovah Tsidkenu, translated suggestively, " the Lord our Righteousness," or " the Lord is our Righteousness " ; such translation being really of the nature of interpretation rather than translation. As a matter of fact the name stands quite bluntly. It is not a sentence. Jehovah the great title by which God had revealed Himself to men; and Tsidkenu, the word standing for righteousness. Jehovah Tsidkenu, the name first of all as revealing the method of the King.

As we saw in our last meditation, this declaration occurs in the second answer of Jehovah to Jeremiah. With all rapidity let us recall the situation. Jeremiah in these days of darkness had purchased a field in obedience to a Divine intimation in faith; had immediately felt the challenge of the situation, and the difficulty thereof; and had poured out his soul to God, speaking of his questioning and his difficulty, expressing the agnosticism of faith, uttering the enquiry of confidence. God now delivered to him a second message: " The word of Jehovah came unto Jeremiah the second time." It is quite evident that this part of the answer of God was intended as a special reply to his sense of difficulty; for notice these words, " Call unto Me, and I will answer thee, and will show thee great things, and difficult, which thou knowest not." In these words there is a recognition of the exact mental mood of the prophet at the moment. How could it be possible that a land, now devoted to an alien army, and an alien people, and about to be taken possession of by them, and handed over to devastation and desolation, could be restored? The problem to the mind of the prophet was that of a degraded people. And how great the degradation! For forty years Jeremiah had proclaimed the word of Jehovah in thunder and lamentation, and yet they had refused and rebelled, had gone their own way, and sunk ever lower and lower into darkness and degradation. The problem was as to how a people so degraded, and a land so desolated, could ever be restored. What is the way of realization? In this chapter we have God's particular answer to that enquiry.

In examining the answer let us follow the order of the message. In this message we have first of all a description of the processes of God toward realization. In the second place, and central to the message, we have the declaration of God concerning those facts, which will make realization possible. Finally, we have a revelation of the Divine operation in the midst of such degradation, in order to the predicted restoration.

The processes of realization are described thus: first, destruction in order to rebuilding; secondly, moral cleansing in order to spiritual joy; and thirdly, spiritual joy in order to material prosperity. That, I think, is a fair summary of the wonderful teaching of the whole chapter.

How can there be restoration of such a degraded people as this, said the prophet? What is really the use of my buying this field? I have done it in faith, but how can the land ever be restored? In reply God first declares that He will come and deal with the people in a process of swift judgment, in which there will be destruction, but destruction always in order to construction. The pulling down is in order to building up.

In that first movement of the Divine answer we are brought face to face with this method of God, that in all His judgment of men in this world, and all His judgment of nations, judgment,—using the word now in its narrower sense as chastisement, punishment, calamity—is always remedial in its intention. God declared that He would come to shut in, and through the armies of the Chaldeans to lay low the city. He said that though they were already building up their mounts of defence, it was only that the trenches should be filled with their own dead men; and yet He declared to them in the very next word, a word not separated from that primal word of judgment: " Behold, I will bring it health and cure, and I will cure them, and I will reveal unto them abundance of peace and truth. And I will cause the captivity of Judah and the captivity of Israel to return, and will build them, as at the first." Thus upon all the desolation that was coming to them, there flashed for the soul of the prophet at least, the light of the Divine intention, the Divine purpose. " I looked, and lo . . . the Waster is the Builder too." So sang old Whittier, interpreting the exact thought of the prophet, that God moving against a people in destruction and in desolation is doing that which is ever necessary toward construction and realization. It is the drastic and terrible, but necessary method, that prepares for rebuilding and for restoration.

In the second place, the process of realization is that of moral cleansing, in order to spiritual joy. He declared to these people that He would come to them, and pardon their iniquities and their sins and their transgressions; that He would cleanse them from their iniquities. Immediately following thereupon, He said that the city should be for a name of joy, for a praise and for a glory, a place of rejoicing rather than of lamentation; that is moral cleansing in order to spiritual joy. Here again we have a revelation of the Divine process toward realization. It is that of the purification of the springs of life, in order that life may become full of joy

[204]

and full of gladness. If the Biblical revelation, the whole
Biblical revelation,—and by that I mean the whole unveiling of God in the Divine Library,—teaches us anything, it teaches us that His will for man and the
race is that of abounding joy, and perfect happiness, and
persistent merriment. Tears are in the Bible from beginning to end, sorrows are multiplied to the sons of
men. The ways along which they walk are shadowed
ways, and ways of darkness; but when we follow
through the processes as suggested and revealed in the
wonderful literature, we come at last to the final truth,
and it is this, uttered in the word of the prophetic age,
and finally repeated amid the glow of the morning as
John saw it in Patmos; that God shall wipe away all
tears from human eyes, that sorrow and sighing shall
flee away, and no more place shall be found for them.
Human joy, and human gladness, human laughter and
human singing, human merriment, these are never to
pass. They constitute the ultimate purpose of God for
humanity. But in order to such spiritual joy, there must
be the purification of life. Life must be purified at its
springs, at its sources, at the places from which all its
streams flow, those intellectual, emotional and volitional
sources, which constitute the essential things of human
life; then the life becomes joyous, then the life becomes
glad.

Thus we have first the preliminary method of destruction in order to construction; a pulling down in order
to rebuilding; then we have the revelation of this central and persistent method, cleansing from iniquity, the
purification of the inward springs of life, in order that
life may express itself in songs and in gladness.

Perhaps the most surprising part of this revelation to
us is the declaration that spiritual joy is in order to
material prosperity. That is the last note. It is when
the nation is cleansed, when the men of the nation are
cleansed morally, that they are filled with spiritual joy.

It is when they are filled with spiritual joy, that they realize true material prosperity. Shepherds are seen again, leading their flocks, and counting them, and telling them; the city itself is filled with material prosperity. This is an arresting order. It is the perpetual way of righteous restoration. We constantly begin our attempt at restoration by endeavouring to secure material prosperity. God never begins so. He begins with the destruction of the things that are evil, but proceeds through the moral cleansing of human life, to the creation of spiritual joy; and wherever there is spiritual joy in human life, all the forces of the life are freed for their finest activity, and there results true and lasting material prosperity. There may be an apparent material prosperity without moral cleansing, but it never abides. It is the old story, uttered over and over again, perhaps most forcefully put a generation ago by the iron Duke of Wellington, when the education of a people was being discussed, and he said: If you educate these children apart from religion, you will make them clever devils. It was the rough uncouth language, if you like, of a man of war, but it was the language of a prophet, of a man who had perfect understanding of human nature. If you have not dealt with the inspirational centres as well as with the external things of life, the garden will become a slum again. It is only by the way of that moral cleansing which fills the life with super-abounding joy, that men will construct material conditions that are of a true and lasting prosperity, and which make for abiding and continuous peace.

In the second place, the central facts are declared. God told His servant what things in human history must be central, in order to the realization of these purposes of restoration. "In those days, and at that time, will I cause a Branch of righteousness to grow up unto David; and He shall execute justice and righteousness." His name, according to the earlier prophecy; and presently the name of the city over which He reigns, according to the present prophecy; shall be Jehovah Tsidkenu. Therein we are brought face to face with the central fact; the principle which makes for realization is righteousness. The power making that principle operative and dynamic is the power of God Himself, Jehovah as righteousness. Not God as righteousness alone. That surely yes; but also, God in that particular attitude in which He perpetually revealed Himself to His ancient people, speaking to human life, interested in human life, active in human life, facing every problem for its solution, putting Himself against every difficulty that it may be swept away, bending ever lower and lower in Almightiness until He has reached the very foundation, that He may lay it sure and strong, proceeding along all the line of development until the top stone is brought on with shoutings of Grace, Grace unto it!

Righteousness is the principle of realization. It is an old word; a common word in the speech of the preacher, in the speech of the sanctuary, in the speech of the Christian Church: and yet how we are constantly driven back to it in order to reconsider it. By reason of our very familiarity with it, we may miss its true meaning. It has been suggested that we may understand it better if we shorten it, and say *rightness;* and we may come even nearer to its true meaning, if we shorten it again, and speak of *right*. Yet that does not suffice. What is righteousness as revealed in these Scriptures of truth? I want to take some other words for its exposition. Righteousness is truth, the righteousness of any particular thing is the truth about it. All sin is a lie, all iniquity is crookedness, and all transgression is deviation from the straight path of truth. Righteousness is truth, essential truth, actual truth. Primarily, that essential truth which is in God; in application, the truth about a man; so that the most righteous thing about some men is that the facts concerning them should be brought to light, even though they are facts of crooked-ness. Righteousness operates in the life of a man when his crookedness is revealed. That is the meaning of the great sacrament of confession within the Christian Church. I do not mean confession to one another, but confession in itself. That is why if a man confesses sin, he is coming at once into the place of absolution. The confession of sin is not the telling of some one else about the sin. It is the saying within the soul, This thing is sin! When that is done, in the very realm of sin, righteous-ness is operating, because truth is being declared. God is the God of things as they are, perhaps in the sense in which Kipling made use of the phrase, but in some other sense most assuredly. God is the God of things as they are. In His presence there is always truth. A man may masquerade before his fellow men as something other than he is; but righteousness measures him, and knows him, and declares the truth concerning him. It is the standard by which the crookedness is discovered. Righteousness in its application reveals the crookedness, but the crookedness is known by that which is essen-tially right, that is truth. The lie is the contradiction of the truth. It is a lie because it contradicts the truth. Truth is the standard by which you discover the lie.

But that is not all of righteousness according to the Biblical revelation. I am inclined to think that there is no more to be said about righteousness apart from the Bible revelation. I do not think Nature has any more to say about righteousness than that. I think if you observe the laws of Nature,—I speak with care, for I am not a student in such sense as to be dogmatic;—but so far as I have observed the laws of Nature, it seems to me that in them we find the element of truth alone. Break the law and die; that is truth, that is rightness; and that is Nature. But the Bible has more to say than that about righteousness; righteousness in the Bible rev-elation is more than truth. I affirm that in the Biblical revelation, righteousness in its relation to God is love; not in contradiction of truth, not in contradistinction from truth, but in coöperation with truth. Perhaps no better illustration of this can be found than that suggested by the words of our Lord, often most carelessly quoted, when passing to the waters of baptism, in obedience to the message of the last of the Hebrew prophets. He said, " Suffer it now: for thus it becometh us to fulfil all righteousness." If we simply see His baptism as that of one among the crowd, obeying the voice of a prophet, then the fulfilment of righteousness was merely obedience to the prophetic voice. But if we see that in that baptism He was publicly identifying Himself with a sinning race, and foreshadowing that passion baptism, whereby He would redeem a sinning race, then we have discovered a new unveiling of righteousness. " It becometh us to fulfil all righteousness." Righteousness in God is not merely the standard of truth, not merely that by which a man is measured, or that which stands before a man as the standard of his action. Righteousness in God is that which cannot rest, even when the man comes short, and is iniquitous and is guilty, but must devise some means whereby the banished one shall return. Righteousness in God is love as well as truth; it is principle suffused with passion, passion ever held in check by principle, the two in coöperation. Righteousness is truth and love; and consequently, order established upon the foundations of truth and of love. The order of an individual life in righteousness is the order of a life that is mastered by truth and love. The order of society in the Kingdom of God will be the order of righteousness; that is the order of a people who are true, and yet are ever full of compassion, the law of all their truthful action being that of the inspiration of an abiding love. Righteousness has its norm in God. In man righteousness is conformity to that norm. The proportion in which a man is godly is the proportion in which he is righteous. The proportion in which a man is godly is the proportion in which he is love-mastered, and truth-expressive. There is to be a building of Jerusalem, but it is to be no slight healing of the wound of the people of God; no superficial reconstruction, leaving foundations rotten; no whitewashing of the building, leaving the walls cracked, with untempered mortar. There is first to be destruction, destruction to the foundations, that everything that is evil shall be swept away. There is then to be within the heart of the people a moral cleansing, creating a spiritual joy, energizing the life along new directions, so that all things material are realized in their fulness and in their blessedness. In other words, the central fact is that of righteousness, a righteousness operating through God Himself, Jehovah Tsidkenu; the Norm overcoming the abnormal. There is nothing in Holy Writ more wonderfully expressive of that than a word in the prophecy of Isaiah (63: 1–6):

"Who is this that cometh from Edom, with dyed garments from Bozrah? this that is glorious in His apparel, marching in the greatness of His strength? I that speak in righteousness, mighty to save. Wherefore art Thou red in Thine apparel, and Thy garments like him that treadeth in the winevat? I have trodden the winepress alone; and of the peoples there was no man with Me: yea, I trod them in Mine anger, and trampled them in My wrath; and their lifeblood is sprinkled upon My garments, and I have stained all My raiment. For the day of vengeance was in Mine heart, and the year of My redeemed is come. And I looked, and there was none to help; and I wondered that there was none to uphold: therefore Mine own arm brought salvation unto Me; and My wrath, it upheld me. And I trod down the peoples in Mine anger, and made them drunk in My fury, and I poured out their lifeblood on the earth."

Some one will say: That is a terrible passage, does that describe God? Let us read on:

" I will make mention of the lovingkindnesses of Jehovah, and the praises of Jehovah, according to all that Jehovah hath bestowed on us; and the great goodness toward the house of Israel."

God is seen destroying, sprinkling His garments with blood, destroying. But what is the end? Travelling in righteousness, mighty to save, set upon the establishment of an order in which sorrow and sighing flee away, and no room shall be found for them; a moral cleansing issuing in a spiritual joy expressing itself finally in the highest material prosperity. In our text the Prophet reveals the operation itself. A King is to come Who is to be a Priest; He is to sit on the throne of David, He is to exercise the priestly function; He is to be a King-Priest.

When we turn to our New Testament we find Him, and we see Him in that last appalling hour, pulsating with the agonizing mysteries; and we hear Pilate say to Him, puzzled and distracted and perplexed, " Art Thou a King?" and He answers, " Thou sayest that I am, a King. To this end have I been born, and to this end am I come into the world, that I should bear witness unto the truth." That is one element in righteousness.

Then they stripped Him, and robed Him, in mockery, as King; and led Him forth to the mystery of His dying; and behold the Priest, love stooping to the very uttermost depth to deal with the poison and the virus, to undermine the awful structure of evil that has been erected, in order to moral cleansing, and to the creation of spiritual joy. That is the great King-Priest in the midst of human history, King in truth, and Priest in love, and therefore Priest of truth and King of love.

In a final word, let me draw attention to the fact that as that was to be the name of the King according to the prophetic word, it was also to be the name of the city of the King; " She shall be called, Jehovah Tsidkenu."

This is a sequence, the statement of result. Under the administration of the King-Priest, whose name is Jehovah Tsidkenu, the city becomes the place of truth and love. So that she may now be called Jehovah Tsidkenu. While Jeremiah was exercising his ministry in besieged Jerusalem, in Babylonia, by the banks of the Kebar, Ezekiel was exercising his ministry; and his last great messages were concerning the city restored, and the temple restored. After poetic and graphic description both of temple and city, he brought his important prophecy to a conclusion by declaring the name of the city: "Jehovah Shammah, Jehovah is there." That includes Jeremiah's name for the city, Jehovah Tsidkenu, for when the King Himself shall dwell within the city in spiritual power and administration, the city will answer His rule, and become as He is Himself, a city full of truth, a city full of love, and therefore she also shall be named as He is named, Jehovah Tsidkenu.

Ransomed by the King as Priest in love, ruled by the Priest as King in truth; the City will reflect the glory of the King-Priest in the established order and the restored beauty. Within that city, the matter of supreme and persistent concern will be that of moral cleanness, resulting in the abounding exercise of spiritual joy. Out of that freedom and fulness of life there will come the true material prosperity, held, distributed, shared, in the impulse of love, and according to truth. Thus, the question of the prophet was answered. The restoration would be by the activity of God in righteousness.

The consummation is not yet. Literally and locally Jerusalem has never been rebuilt on this wise. Judah has never known these conditions. Israel has not yet dwelt in peace by the side of Judah, as said the prophet that she should. But the Branch has come, the King-Priest has appeared; and God is still moving surely, quietly, persistently toward that goal. I will end this meditation by the recitation of two New Testament words, the relation of which to the study I think will be apparent; two words, revealing what our attitude should be.

Hear the first from that wonderful, ethical, and practical epistle of James, " Be patient therefore, brethren, until the presence of the Lord. Behold, the husbandman waiteth for the precious fruit of the earth, being patient over it, until it receive the early and latter rain. Be ye also patient; establish your hearts: for the presence of the Lord is at hand."

In our restlessness and our feverishness, and in the very exercise of faith we are very often inclined to say, How long, O Lord, how long, how long dost Thou delay the coming of Thy Kingdom and its establishment? Here is the answer: the Husbandman is waiting for full fruition ere He gather in His harvest.

Again, hear the word of Peter in his second letter: " The Lord is not slack concerning His promise, as some count slackness; but is longsuffering to you-ward, not wishing that any should perish, but that all should come to repentance. But the day of the Lord will come as a thief; in the which the heavens shall pass away with a great noise, and the elements shall be dissolved with fervent heat, and the earth and the works that are therein shall be burned up." There is yet to be a further coming, from Edom, with garments dyed from Bozrah, of One Who, travelling in the greatness of His strength, shall destroy the things that destroy, and proceed in awful might and majesty against every form of tyranny. " Seeing that these things are thus all to be dissolved, what manner of persons ought ye to be in all holy living and godliness, looking for and hastening the coming of the day of God?"

XVIII

THE PROFANATION OF THE DIVINE NAME

Preparatory Reading: Jeremiah 34.

"Ye turned, and profaned My Name."
—JEREMIAH 34:16a.

OUR last four meditations have been occupied with the dominant notes of the prophecies of Hope which Jeremiah delivered while he was a prisoner in the court of the guard. From chapter thirty-four to chapter thirty-nine, we have a mixture of prophecy and narrative, ending at that point with the account of the fall of Jerusalem. Chapters thirty-four and thirty-five contain prophecies of the siege. The armies of Nebuchadnezzar were round about Jerusalem, and Jeremiah, at the command of Jehovah, again declared to Zedekiah that the King of Babylon would be victorious, that the city would be taken, and burned with fire, and that he himself would be carried away captive to Babylon. Nevertheless the word of Jehovah concerning Zedekiah was that he should not die by the sword, but in peace.

The next prophecy was a denunciation of the king for breaking the covenant which he had made with the menservants and the maid-servants. Freedom had been given to them, but they had been compelled to return to subjection and slavery. This was a sin against the express covenant which God had made with His people that the slaves should be set free every seventh year. On account of this breaking of the covenant and oppression of the people, the prophet declared that Jehovah would fling them out, as he satirically declared, to the liberty of the sword and the pestilence and the famine.

The words of our text occur in this connection, and constitute a revelation of the true nature of the sin which had been committed. Actually it was the sin of breaking faith with servants. Essentially it was the sin of profaning the name of God. It is an arresting word, revealing the fact that injustice on the part of man toward man, is a profanation of the name of God.

In order that we may apprehend the full significance of this declaration, let us consider first, the sin in itself, without reference to the context; the sin of profaning the name of God. Secondly, let us take this particular illustration, observing how the name was profaned in this instance. Finally, from this twofold consideration let us attempt to deduce the permanent teaching of the story.

First then, as to the sin itself, the sin of profaning the name of God. The place which the name of God occupied in the religious thinking of the Hebrews was unique, and it is, I venture to think, familiar to all of us. Even from the mechanical standpoint of observation, it is an interesting fact to discover how persistently the name of God is referred to in that way in the Old Testament writings. Constantly God spoke to His people about His name, and perpetually the singers of Israel, and the seers of the Hebrew people, spoke of the name of God. The word itself is an interesting one, signifying simply an appellation, but always that which stands as the representation of a Person. I need only remind you that in all this Eastern life, which we have revealed in our Bible, that was true perpetually. We do not pay so much attention to the value of a name to-day, as these people did; that is, we are not so careful that names should be significant of anything save our capricious choices and predilections. But men were named at this time, in order to indicate the hope of those who

named them, or presently perhaps, in order to represent
the truth concerning the men. That habit of life among
the people was one which obtained in the Divine self-
revelation to the people. In this matter as in all matters,
and as constantly in human history, God took hold of a
habit and used it, in order to reveal higher truth. He
was perpetually revealing Himself to His ancient people
through His name. The name was 'the symbol of character, of honour, of authority. There is nothing much
more interesting in the study of the Old Testament than
that of the development of Divine revelation as revealed
in the names by which God was made known; and in
the interpretation of old names, in the process of the
centuries. Every name of God found in the Old Testament, and every title of God, is in itself a suggestion, an
unveiling, a revelation. In that oldest name of all, the
name which we translate God, the Hebrew word Elohim
stood for absoluteness of strength. That was the fundamental idea and conception of God which came to these
people. On through their history He was made known
by such names or titles as *Adonahy*, the Supreme One,
or *Yahweh*, the becoming One, linked to other words,
all affording some new unveiling of truth concerning
Himself. Jehovah, or El-Shaddai, or Jehovah Tsidkenu,
—to quote one of the great names that we have found
in this prophecy,—each had special significance; and as
the name was given it went forth, as the symbol of the
One Who bore it, the revelation of His character, the
symbol of His honour; the sign of His authority.

The name of God was held in sanctity among these
people by commandment. "Thou shalt not take the
name of Jehovah thy God in vain: for Jehovah will not
hold him guiltless that taketh His name in vain." Moreover, the name of God to these ancient people was the
symbol of all their blessedness, "So shall they put My
name upon the children of Israel; and I will bless them."
"Jehovah bless thee, and keep thee: Jehovah make His

face to shine upon thee, and be gracious unto thee: Jehovah lift up His countenance upon thee, and give thee peace."

We see at once why, in the thinking of these Hebrew people, the name of God was held in reverence. They perfectly understood that the name, whatever it might be, whichever of the different titles they might employ, stood always as the sign and symbol of God Himself; to repeat the words twice already used, in character, in honour, and in authority.

What then was the sin of profaning the name? In King James' Version my text reads thus, "Ye turned, and polluted My name." The Revisers have adopted another word to express the thought of the Hebrew, "Ye turned and profaned My name." The change is a gain. Whereas at the first moment it does not seem to be so startling, so arresting a word, the soul is not filled with such a sense of fear when one reads the word *profane* about the holy name, as if one read the word *pollute*, still a careful consideration will show it to be an even more arresting word.

This word translated profane quite literally means *to bore* or *to pierce;* and by implication *to wound*, and *to wrong*. It is intimately allied to another word meaning to rub, or wear away. Involved in the word is the thought of defacing an image or superscription on a coin. The idea is accurately conveyed by our word profane, *pro fanum*, which signifies forth from the temple, that is, free from sanctity, rendered common. Indeed we are not far from the meaning of the prophetic word if we adopt that phrase, "Ye turned, and *rendered common* My name." Ye turned, and in your turning you defaced the mintage, the image, the superscription. My name stood for My character, and My honour, and My authority; but your action defaces the image, denies the superscription, debases the coinage; the attitude, as though Jehovah said to these people at this time, the attitude that you have taken up, has libelled Me, has robbed Me of My honour, has called in question My authority. That is the profanation of the Divine name.

Therefore the profanation of the Divine name is blasphemy against the One Who bears it, and wrong done to those who employ the sacred coinage. To deface the image, to obliterate the superscription, is to render the coin valueless. You have profaned My name.

Let us turn to the particular illustration. What had happened in Judah? In the Hebrew law it was provided that the house-servant, bought, that is contracted with, was to be set free after six years' service. The word of the commandment is distinctly found in the book of Exodus (21:2); and by comparison with the book of Deuteronomy (15:12) we find that it applied not to the men only, but to women also. There was another law for those who laboured in the fields. Those who laboured in the fields were never to contract themselves into service in this old Hebrew economy, and at the close of fifty years, in the year of Jubilee they were to be entirely free. This, however, is another matter. This was the case of the house-servant, the bond-servant. He was a slave, if we care to use the word; but we must always understand the word, when we read these Hebrew stories, in the Hebrew sense. The slave bought was not bought of another, but he himself contracted with his employer. It was a case of contract made; and the Hebrew law provided that there should be no contract that went beyond six years. In the seventh year there was to be freedom.

This law had been disobeyed in the history of the Hebrew people. The bond-service of contract had become the bond-service of property; and Hebrews were holding their own brethren in slavery in the sense in which we understand the word. Under stress of danger Zedekiah had made a covenant with the people to observe this ancient law. Somewhere in that wonderful

period of Jeremiah's ministry, in those final ten years of
the existence of the Southern Kingdom of Judah, Zedekiah, the halting, the afraid, the vacillating, under the
impulse of some qualm of conscience, had gathered the
people together into the temple, and had reminded them
of this broken law, and had entered into solemn covenant to give liberty to all those to whom liberty was due.
Then something happened outside the walls. The Chaldean army suddenly moved away. The army that had
been investing the city departed, as history informs us,
to meet the Egyptians of whom they were at the moment afraid. Inside Jerusalem, when the Chaldean
army thus moved away, the men of Judah felt that the
prophesying of Jeremiah was about to be falsified, that
the threatened danger was passing; and they immediately broke the covenant made with their servants, and
compelled them back into slavery. The story may be
told in the lines with which we are all familiar:

" The devil was sick, the devil a monk would be,
    The devil got well, the devil a monk was he! "

In all *that,* they profaned the holy name. The name
of Jehovah stood to the toilers as the memorial of His
care for them. In all that system of laws which had
been given to these people by their law-giver, God's care
for the toiler was evident. The proclamation of liberty
was an acknowledgment of that care. The withdrawal
of liberty profaned the name, it defamed the character
of God to the men who were wronged; it denied the
honour of God in the mind of those who were forced
back again into slavery; and it degraded His authority in
their case. These men who in His name had given the
toilers freedom, now repenting of their repentance, and
denying their freedom, were defaming the holy name;
and therefore Jehovah said: Because you have taken
away the liberty of these people I will give you to the

[219]

liberty of sword and pestilence and famine! The defaced coinage of the holy name must be reminted in the furnace of affliction.

Wherein then in this particular case lay the profanation of the holy name? First in the long perpetual disobedience which had grown into a habit; it was profanation of the holy name. These toilers had long been enslaved, and had been kept in slavery; and yet the name of God stood for their care, and His law provided that provision should be made for their liberation at the close of six years. All the way through in the history of the people, while they, the toilers, were held in bondage, God's name was profaned.

His name was still further profaned when the rulers obeyed Him from a sense of selfish fear. There was no honour paid to the name of God when they gave these men their liberty. They were simply attempting to bring themselves into a position of favour with God, in order that God might deliver them from the enemy outside. Yet, had they been true to the covenant made under such false impulse, it might have wrought its way through to something higher and nobler; for God is ever prepared to receive us when we return to Him, even though it be from unworthy motives. All the history of evangelical Christianity is a demonstration of that. Thousands of men have turned to God because they were afraid of hell. It is a mean and low and cowardly motive, but it has been the means by which men have risen to a larger life. It is never the Bible motive; but it has often been the means by which men have found their way into the larger life and the truer. If a man try and persuade men from that motive to turn to God, he is in danger of profaning the holy name as surely as did these men profane the holy name when in order to secure their own safety in the city, they liberated the slaves.

But the ultimate profanation of the name came in the violation of the covenant so made, and in the return to

disobedience. To the men thus breaking faith with
slaves Jeremiah came with his message, You have profaned the name of the Lord. Such is the ancient story.

Now what has this story to say to us? The name of
God still stands as the revelation of God in this Christian age. The principles abide. The name of God is
still the symbol of His character, of His honour, of His
authority. The value of the name is still the same. It
is a method of revelation. It is the symbol of all blessedness. It is to be hallowed. We constantly pray together
in obedience to our Lord's command, that the name of
God should be hallowed, which is always the exact opposite of profanation. We still hold the name within
the Christian Church as sacred. The name to us is a
simpler name; the name that stands as the symbol of
the character, honour, and authority of God, is the name
of Jesus. Without discussing for a single moment now
the infinite mystery of that wonderful personality, we
realize that this is the name which stands to us for God,
more simple than any of those of the past, and yet sub-
limer than the whole of them, for the light shining
through that name, and the One Who bore that name,
is far fuller and more perfect than any light men had
before He came. Nothing is lost because we use the
name Jesus. Usually and reverently and properly pref-
acing it by the titles that mark His dignity, the Lord
Christ Jesus, yet ever and anon, as the writer of the
letter to the Hebrews, and the seer of Patmos, using it
in all its human loneliness and simplicity, nothing is lost
because that is the name. All the suggestiveness of Hebrew names and titles are gathered up in what that name
stands for, to believing souls to-day. All in that name
is fulfilled and explained. It is the new name of God
to humanity. It was a common Hebrew name, of the
boys who played in Nazareth and through Judæa. It
was born in a wonderful moment in the history of that
nation, when Hoshea, the helper of Moses, was re-

named Joshua by a merging of the name of God and the word for salvation, into one. The name, Jesus, well known when the Baby of Bethlehem took it, is better known to-day throughout the world, and is the simple symbol of God the Saviour. That name is still enshrined as sacred.

Let us consider what unveilings of God His name has given to men; and especially this last and simplest human name of Jesus.

The name of God stands first of all as the symbol of the Divine respect for men; and for men as men. Our Lord's title for Himself was not Son of God. That is a perfectly true description of Him in an infinite mystery; but that was not His name for Himself. It was not Messiah. Indeed He seemed to avoid that when referring to Himself. The title He chose for Himself was that of " The Son of man," the title that linked Him intimately with humanity. The persistent poverty of the Son of man from the manger to the Cross, from babyhood to manhood, and through ministry, was the sign of the royalty of humanity. In very deed as Paul declares, in the mystic passage of the Philippian letter, He Who was in an infinite mystery, the very Word of God from the eternities, the eternal One in fellowship with the Father, emptied Himself; but the writer continues, " being found in fashion as a man He humbled Himself." He humbled Himself to the height of humanity. I go back and read the simple stories in the Gospels of His birth, and as the days pass on I come more and more to be amazed and astonished at the glory of His birth. In other days I dwelt often upon its poverty. There was no place to lay the child save the manger of charity. None to care for it save its own mother, who wrapped it herself— and do not read these stories idly, carelessly,—*who wrapped it herself in its swaddling clothes.* He was a Baby without privilege, and yet a Baby therefore in all the essential dignity of humanity, more glorious in that it lacked the accidental trappings. So we follow Him through life; no robe of priesthood; no purple of kingship; but for evermore the glory of humanity. In that way, He Who bore the name, Jesus, has made the name Jesus the symbol of God's respect for man, His recognition of the glory of humanity. He was not nurtured in a king's palace; He was not trained in a school of the prophets; He did not learn His wisdom by sitting among the priests. Stripped of all the things we value, the things upon which even until this hour, we lay so much emphasis, stripped of them all, behold Him, not an object of pity, but an object of worship. In the poverty of His humanity, taking only in the course of a generation the things absolutely essential for the sustenance of a material life, behold the final dignity of humanity. Yes, but if we admit this, then we have placed by His side in that dignity every human being. Not the kings alone, not the priests only, these also; not the prophets and the priests, not the school men and the intellectually great, these also; but not these alone; every human being is with Him, He represents all humanity! By the stripping of the Son of God and His loneliness and poverty in human life, humanity is not degraded, but revealed as noble; and that is the standard for evermore of God's outlook upon humanity, the revelation of God's respect for man.

I have sometimes, when attempting to meditate this subject and to speak of it, said that which quite literally is not true, and yet is quite true spiritually. If you think that is impossible, now listen and I will say it once more. When Jesus was in the world He never saw the phylacteries upon a Pharisee's robe or garment. He never saw the rags upon a beggar. That is not literally true. He saw everything. Yet you know exactly what I mean. He was not attracted by the phylacteries, nor by the rags. Mark that second statement. Christ is never attracted by the habiliments of poverty. Christ is no more in love with the tenement area than with the select residential suburbs. He is in love with humanity. When He met a man, whether he came from the schools in Jerusalem, or the hamlets among the hills, He respected humanity. That is the Divine attitude toward humanity, a respect for man as man.

The name of God stands not only for the Divine respect for man; it stands for the Divine care of man. God's care of man is that He will give to every man opportunity for the realization of his life. That is the meaning of salvation. Salvation is not some method of God by which He takes a man and makes him into an angel. Salvation is not some method of God by which He stoops to man in his ruined and spoiled condition, and relieves him of that condition by making another being of him, and changing his nature. Salvation is not that by which God takes hold of a man who is a beast and transforms him into an angel. Salvation is that by which God takes hold of a man and makes it possible for him to be a man. We talk of being born anew, and we need to talk of it. It is Christ's own teaching. It is the Gospel revelation. But the new birth is the way by which man is admitted into the potentialities and possibilities of his first birth. Man in his first birth is offspring of Deity. He has lost his birthright; he has lost his sense of relationship, and the powers of relationship. Then salvation comes to him that he may be restored to that which he has lost, and that he may find the meaning of his own life and realize it. That is the Divine care for man.

What bearing has all this on ourselves? If we use the name of God, let us hallow it and not profane it. There are terrible possibilities of profaning the name of God. There are thousands of people profaning the name of God to-day who imagine they are hallowing it. The man in the slum who was born with the language of vulgarity upon his lips is not profaning the name of God so terribly as the man in the sanctuary who prays and yet fails to understand that the hallowing of the name of God means the taking up of right attitudes toward his fellow men. To hallow the name is to reverence the character, to defend the honour, to obey the authority; and the test of our hallowing of the Divine name is that of our attitude toward our fellow men. We hallow the name of God when we respect humanity. We hallow the name of God when we care for men as men, and seek to serve them. Is there a more difficult injunction in all the New Testament than this apostolic injunction, " Honour all men " ? Why is it difficult? There is another injunction also in the apostolic writings, " Honour the King." That is not difficult. But " honour all men " is wider. The king is included in that. Do not neglect him. Princes and lords are included in that. Do not exclude them. But interpret the honour you owe to them by the honour you owe to all the rest; by the girls you pay wages to, who serve in your house; by the men that you employ, you masters of labour. Honour " all men " as men. If a man or a woman shall recite the Lord's Prayer and pray for the hallowing of the name, and have in the heart contempt for any man, the holy name is profaned in the hour of that praying. That is the attitude that we need to guard ourselves against as Christian souls. Find in any man or any nation a contempt for men under any circumstances, and you have found that which is profanation of the name of God, and not Christianity.

The supreme opportunity for the manifestation of our true relationship to the holy name is created in the case of those who by the exigencies of existing conditions, are supposed to be, and are, under our authority. How do we treat them? Do we respect them? Do we serve them? Oh, no, no; you say, they serve us! Then we are profaners of the holy name unless we serve them also. It is terrible how superficial we are! We talk for

[225]

instance about the domestic service problem. Yes, but there is another problem. It is the problem of the attitude of Christian women toward their servants. It is the problem of the attitude of Christian men and women toward those who are under them. If we are Christian men and women we respect them; we serve them also.

We are not in Judæa, and we are not living under these old conditions. But we are still in this world, and we are still of the same human stuff. Are we enslaving anyone? Are we treating the people to whom we pay wages as we should? Listen to this; a more terrible word was never uttered. A man says that he employs so many hundred *hands!* What blasphemy! He cannot employ hands, he is employing men! If we simply rely upon the hands doing our work, we are profaning the holy name in spite of our contribution to the Kingdom of God. Respect for humanity; service to humanity; these are the ways of hallowing the name! Lack of respect; carelessness and indifference; these are the ways of profaning the name of the Lord!

The word of Jeremiah was a national word. It remains a national word. National godliness expresses itself in human justice. Justice must be interpreted in the terms of godliness. Both justice and godliness are included in the one word, love.

To neglect national justice, is still to hear the word of the old prophet of Judah ringing across the centuries, gathering force as it comes over the holy fields and catches the inspiration of the Man of Nazareth, and the argument of His Cross. The word of the Prophet, by the way of the Cross, to the nation is this, if you neglect righteousness and justice among the people, then says God, I will give you to the liberty of the sword, and pestilence, and famine. God will remint His name through fire and furnace if the nation shall obliterate the Divine image and superscription by the neglect of humanity.

The word has also a personal application. Perhaps as all this is Old Testament, and therefore harsh and hard with the harshness and the hardness of an old economy which we may be inclined to call effete, the personal application had better be made in the language of the New Testament, which some people imagine has lost the sternness of the Old. Then let us hear in the language of the New Testament. "Come now, ye rich, weep and howl for your miseries that are coming upon you." But why? "Your riches are corrupted and your garments are moth-eaten." But why? "Your gold and your silver are rusted; and their rust shall be for a testimony against you, and shall eat your flesh as fire." But why? "Behold, the hire of the labourers who mowed your fields, which is of you kept back by fraud, crieth out: and the cries of them that reaped have entered into the ears of the Lord of Sabbaoth."

That also is hard; for that is James, the ethical writer. Then we will have one more quotation from John, the apostle of comfort, the son of thunder and love. Listen to this. "Whosoever hateth his brother is a murderer: and ye know that no murderer hath eternal life abiding in him . . . whoso hath the world's goods, and beholdeth his brother in need, and shutteth up his compassion from him, how doth the love of God abide in him? My little children, let us not love in word, neither with the tongue; but in deed and truth."

XIX

THE TRAMMELS OF TRADITION

Preparatory Reading: Jeremiah 35.

" The words of Jonadab, the son of Rechab, that he commanded his sons, not to drink wine, are performed, and unto this day they drink none, for they obey their father's commandment. But I have spoken unto you, rising up early and speaking; and ye have not hearkened unto me."—JEREMIAH 35:14.

IN chapters thirty-five and thirty-six of this book of Jeremiah, two incidents are recorded which took place at least seventeen years earlier; those of the dealing of the prophet with the Rechabites, and of the writing of the roll, both having happened in the reign of Jehoiakim. These may constitute an interpolation on the chronological course of the book, or it may be that they are inserted here because Jeremiah made use of them in messages delivered in those last days of the reign of Zedekiah, prior to the fall of the city. But the teaching of the narratives for us is not affected whichever view may be taken.

The history of the Rechabites is found in broad outline in the Old Testament. It is generally agreed that Rechab was of the Kenites, who were connected with Israel through the marriage of Moses, and who cast in their lot with them at the Exodus. They became famous by the action of Jonadab, the son of Rechab. He it was who joined Jehu in the furious driving which characterized his campaign against the house of Ahab, in order to the destruction of the worship of Baal. This man laid certain commandments on his sons; that they should drink no wine, that they should persist in their nomadic life, building no house, planting no seed, possessing no vineyard, but continuing to dwell in tents. Fearful of the corrupting tendencies of city life, of commercial activity, and of wine, he sought to secure to his descendants the greater spiritual advantages of the simpler pilgrim life. To these commandments of their father the sons of Jonadab had been true through all the years. Whether his conceptions were right is not the matter of importance in this story. I am not proposing to discuss his action. That which matters in this prophecy of Jeremiah is that his sons had obeyed him. When Nebuchadnezzar invaded the land, these people took temporary refuge in Jerusalem, and it is quite conceivable that their presence would create no small stir in the city. Acting under the command of God, Jeremiah called their representative men into the house of Jehovah, and offered them wine. Now it must be understood that this was by no means intended as a temptation to them. It was done in order to give them the opportunity to refuse, and thus prepare the way for the message which is embodied in our text that men are more loyal to the commandments of men than they are to the commandments of God. That is the theme. This is an abiding fact, and it is at once a great human folly, and the source of untold harm. It is to that subject that I would draw attention, considering first the fact; inquiring secondly, the reason of the fact; and considering finally, the folly of it.

As I have already said, we can well imagine how the presence of these Rechabites in the city aroused attention. Men of the tent and of the open country, accustomed to live the nomadic life, abstaining from all commercial exercises except those necessary to life, possessing no land, making their boast in the fact, abstaining from wine; they were a peculiar people, and in a city you can always tell when peculiar people are present.

The prophet, living in fellowship with God, and delivering his message, at once fastened upon these people for an illustration. Why were they abstaining from wine, and still living in tents? Because Jonadab, the son of Rechab, their father had so commanded them; and yet at that very moment, Jerusalem, the city of the great King, was under condemnation, was about to be destroyed, because her sons had not hearkened to the voice of Jehovah. Jehovah, said the prophet, using a fine figure of speech, had risen up early in His eagerness to reach and help and save His people. Jehovah had risen up early to arouse His prophets to bring His messages to His people. They had never been without the word of Jehovah. Even in this decadent period Jeremiah had been the mouthpiece of the word of Jehovah. But they had not hearkened, and here in the city were men of a nomadic habit, taking temporary refuge there because of Nebuchadnezzar's approach for the punishment of Jerusalem; and Jeremiah saw them. Why are they simple in their habits, why are they abstainers from wine, why do they neither plant seed nor build houses nor possess land? Simply because their father Jonadab, the son of Rechab, had commanded them so. Yet here are the sons of God, to whom God is speaking, and they will not obey Him. Because Jonadab the son of Rechab their father had commanded them, they had obeyed; but men to whom God had long been speaking, and to whom God was immediately speaking, would not obey.

This tendency of men to submit themselves to some command or idea of the past, while they refuse to listen to and to obey the living and ever-present God, is persistent. This is not a page out of the history of an obsolete condition of affairs. Let me give you one or two abstract illustrations of how tremendously men are under the tyranny of tradition, the power of precedent, the grip of the dead hand; and of how zealously and religiously they yield themselves to all these forces, sometimes with the very best effect, and sometimes with the most evil effect; while yet they will not listen to God Who is not far off or dimly distant through the centuries, but Who is where they are, speaking to them with a thousand voices. It is a persistent malady, this tyranny of tradition. The word means first the act of delivering, and presently it comes to mean the thing so delivered. Traditions of the elders are conceptions, ideas, views from the past; and men are under the tyranny of these traditions. The power of precedent is that of previous things as the rule of present action. In legal matters, acts and decisions from the past constitute the law and rule of the present. Men to-day are sometimes so much under the power of precedent that if there be no precedent they dare not act. Government will come to some situation of difficulty, and because there is no precedent for doing right, it dare not do it. The grip of the dead hand is still upon us. Curiously enough in Feudal use *manus mortua* referred to inability to make testamentary disposition, " Homines manus mortuæ," were men that could not make testamentary disposition. In process of time the phrase came to refer to the power of the Dead Hand, the hand that cannot now make testamentary disposition, that is, now lifeless and cold, but which in life made laws which are still binding. In England all the Statutes of Mortmain from Edward I to George III were aimed at restricting that power. Yet it abides to-day on property; in creeds of the Church; and in habits of life; in all these the dead hand of the past is upon us.

This is so in every department of life. In family life, habits descend from father to son, through generation after generation. In social life, distinctions are still observed that had a reason when first they were made, but which have no reason to-day. Legal enactments that were of value, and which have been abrogated, created habits which still remain. Among the mountains of Wales we still find people are most eager and anxious to bury their dead in flannel. A law was passed somewhere in previous history that it should be so in order to help the flannel industry. The law is repealed, but the grip of the tradition holds the people still. The dead hand of the past is seen in religious orders; the very garb of the monk was but the ordinary garb of the simple peasant life, but it binds and holds the man who wears it still. The dead hand of the past is felt in theology, in the persistent determination to attempt to express essential truth in language that had another meaning in olden days, and so there follows the distortion of truth, as the result of loyalty to some creed written long ago. A remarkable illustration of that emerged a few years ago in England. A minister in delivering a lecture made use of some words describing the attitude of certain preachers. He did not happen to use quotation marks in his lecture, and a layman of the Church protested in a pamphlet against what he had said. The lecturer replied that he had but quoted John Wesley, and the layman immediately apologized for criticizing him, and withdrew his criticism. If indeed, John Wesley said it in his day, it had a meaning; but it may have no meaning to-day. We are under the dead hand of the past, and we are obeying with tremendous loyalty. Men are far more bound by these things than by the laws of God. Men forget the first half of the *Gloria,* and live in the second half. They forget " Glory be to the Father, to the Son, and to the Holy Spirit," and they live in the second half, "As it was in the beginning, is now, and ever shall be, world without end."

There are certain values in this respect for the past. Let me admit this at once. Respect for the past is in itself valuable. So also is the continuity of principle which results from it. But these break down when the present is harmed by loyalty to the past, when the principle is violated. I am not saying for a single moment that these sons of Jonadab were wrong. I think, personally, that they were unutterably wrong in some things, and quite right in others. I believe there is a society of Rechabites to-day. My impression is they have fastened upon the one true thing and are true to it. But God's will for men was that they should settle in the city, and in refusing to do so they were wrong. I am not careful, however, about the illustration in detail. I am careful about the principle revealed. It is this. Men will obey the law of the past made in a time and for a season and for a purpose, religiously, and all through the years, without reason; but they will not obey God. It is a strange and mysterious fact. How are we to account for it?

First, men give themselves thus loyally to tradition, precedent, and the dead hand of the past, because of the ease of that method of life. It is simple, clear-cut, it is definite. It is the easiest thing in the world to sign a number of pledges, and then live inside them. It demands no thought, no exercise of the spirit life at the moment.

It brings a certain satisfaction also to the mind. This thing that my father said I was to do, is done. These things that tradition has marked out as necessary, are now obeyed. Oh, the indolence, the comfortable indolence of life governed by complete prescription and proscription. These things may be done; these things may not be done. Give me a complete list, and I will observe the commands, and I will be very careful not to do that which I am forbidden. That is the easiest and the laziest and the most pernicious life that any man can live.

Yet again, mark the freedom of this habit of life. All outside the territory marked by the tradition and the commandment is open ground; and thus a false sanctity is given to the areas of freedom in the case of the man who has observed tradition. The conception obtains and manifests itself in the minds of certain men to-day; every now and then we are told that if a man shall attend the morning service, he is afterwards free for the day, for golf, or anything. That man is living by tradition. It is the correct thing to assemble and worship and fulfil a form; and outside that, there is a whole area, free and open; and the sanctity of the observance of the tradition is supposed to rest upon the open area. Christianity does not begin by telling a man he shall not do this or the other. It begins by giving men what Dr. Chalmers called, "the expulsive power of a new affection." That is Christianity. That is not government by tradition. Yet men not only obey such commands, they positively lust after them. Jonadab is a benefactor. He told us what to do, and what not to do, and we will obey him. There is great rest in that. The scribes and Pharisees in Jesus' day had enormous power by reason of their traditions. I am not anxious to go back to Jonadab, or Jeremiah, or scribes and Pharisees. Even to-day, any new movement, even within Christianity, that proposes to set up a new legalism, that tells me what I am or am not to do, will be popular. Crowds of people will hasten anywhere if a man will set up commandments, human commandments.

Now I pray you think with me most seriously in conclusion of the unutterable folly of it all. The folly of it is manifested first in that it forgets the infinite nature of man. If a man shall yield himself to tradition, the precedent, the dead hand of the past; if a man yield himself to commands laid upon him by another; his unutterable folly is manifested, first of all, in his forgetfulness of the infinite marvel of his own being. Juvenal in his Satires declared that the precept, "Know thyself" descended from heaven. I am not prepared to deny it. I think it did. That ultimate word of the profoundest and mightiest of the Greek philosophers, "Man, know thyself," was indeed a great word. I think it did descend from heaven; but if so, I discuss it from the heavenly side, and I affirm that if that word descended from

[234]

heaven, it was in order that man might be brought to a consciousness of his need of God, in the discovery of the fact that he cannot know himself. It is a great thing when a man determines to know himself, when a man says, I will take time to find out who I am, what I am, what is the mystery of my being. It is a great hour when a man comes to that determination. But the greater hour is coming to him, and the greater hour is the hour when, after prolonged introspection, investigation, honest, sincere, searching examination, he cries out, I cannot know myself. What man ever did know himself? Do you remember Pope's "Essay," and these words from its second Epistle?

> "Chaos of thought and passion, all confused;
> Still by himself abused and disabused;
> Created half to rise, and half to fall;
> Great lord of all things, yet a prey to all;
> Sole judge of truth, in endless error hurled;
> The glory, jest, and riddle of the world."

Profound words, but not final words. The old psalmist of Israel was yet more profound when in that psalm, with which we are all so familiar (139), he commenced:

> "O Jehovah, Thou hast searched me, and known me,
> Thou knowest my downsitting and mine uprising,
> Thou understandest my thought afar off."

Then listen to him as in the course of the Psalm, he says:

> "Such knowledge is too wonderful for me;
> It is high, I cannot attain unto it."

Which simply means, God knows me perfectly; I cannot know myself perfectly. If it be thus true that a man cannot know himself, it follows, necessarily, that he can-

[235]

not know his brother man. " No man hath seen God at any time," is a profound truth from which no one will differ. It is equally true that No man hath seen man at any time. You have never seen your brother man. You do not know him; you cannot know him. Or let me reverse the order of statement; your neighbour has never seen you; your father has never seen you. Oh, the tragic mistakes fathers make about children, imagining that they know them, when they do not know them, nor can they. Jonadab will lay his commandments upon his children, and by his commandments will help and hinder them through all the centuries. Man in his nature is infinite, and therefore no man can legislate for himself, or for his brother man; and when a man binds himself by the traditions that have come to him from his fathers, or from other men, how does he crush and break and imprison his own soul!

I remark in the second place, that the folly of yielding thus to tradition and the commandments of men is due to the fact that men who do so, forget the perpetual change of circumstances. Every human law is a temporal expression of an eternal principle, and therefore it may have to be changed. When Arthur entered the barge, and was about to pass away, he said:

" The old order changeth, yielding place to new;
   And God fulfils Himself in many ways,
   Lest one good custom should corrupt the world."

There is a philosophy of the utmost importance in one line of Tennyson:

" Lest one good custom should corrupt the world."

Can a good custom corrupt? Yea, verily, for that which is good to-day may be entirely out of place to-morrow. If to-day I am bound by the excellent custom of my fa-

ther a generation ago, I may be spoiling myself, and pol-
luting my influence. The change of circumstance is forgotten. Man cannot legislate perfectly for to-morrow.
He must always legislate, remembering that change of
circumstance, combined with the infinite and mysterious
nature of humanity, may demand in the interest of that
which he sought in his law, the breaking of his law, and
the setting of it aside for ever.

Yet, once again, and finally, and in a sentence, though
it is the supreme thing. The folly of yielding to the traditions of the past is manifested in the fact that it forgets the God Who knows man, and knows circumstances;
and is always immediately available. That recognition
of God requires something stronger in the make-up and
the attitude and the outlook. It is much easier to do
what some one else thinks I ought to do, than to find out
what God wants me to do. Yet I shall amend that, and
declare that when a man has once resolutely set himself
to the business, it is at once easier to find out what God
wants, and easier to do it when it is found out, than to
obey the law of man. How many great souls have at
last sought refuge from the stress and strain of listening
for God and obeying God, in some system of tradition!
Is not that the story of John Henry Newman? And are
we not all in peril sometimes of longing for some authority that tabulates the order of our going? Yet, my
brethren, no such authority could be sufficient, for it is
not, neither can it be, based upon a perfect knowledge
of ourselves, or of the ever-shifting change of circumstances.

There are some practical conclusions. The first is that
we should ever be careful to distinguish between tradition and law; between that which may be the exposition
of law and its application to a certain hour, and that
which is in itself law, an abiding and eternal principle,
capable of ever-changing application, while never changing within itself. If life is to be regulated in harmony

with the Divine will, we should sift all our traditions, and find out how far they depend upon law, and how far they continue to be an expression of that which they did express upon a certain occasion, and in a certain set of circumstances.

Secondly, the meditation teaches us the necessity for violating any tradition, however excellent, when it violates law as an eternal principle. If you call in question the statement, then I shall recommend you once more to a very careful study from that standpoint of the whole public ministry of Jesus; and I do not hesitate to make an affirmation, which time forbids that I should justify by any particular argument or reference save perhaps one. I make the affirmation that from the commencement of the public ministry of Jesus—I must begin there, because I know nothing of His private life save little incidental gleams of light—from the beginning of His public ministry to its close, He resolutely set Himself to violate the traditions by which men were bound in that age. We cannot read the stories simply and naturally, without seeing that of set purpose He violated tradition. The one illustration that I shall permit myself is the supreme one, because He then spoke of the matter, and declared that men by their traditions made void the law of God. That is the very principle under consideration. We have the account of Matthew's Gospel, with I think most detail, of how He flung Himself in burning words against the traditionalism of His age; and this was His illustration. He said, The law of God says, Honour thy father and thy mother; but you have heaped tradition upon tradition, so that when a man ought to be taking care of his father and mother, you prevent him, by reason of the fact that he has devoted some portion of his wealth to the temple; and when you ask him for relief for father or mother, he says, I cannot use this, it is Corban, it is sacred. Thus by your high traditional religion, you have made contribution toward worship more important than taking care of father and mother.

With all reverence as in His holy presence, I would apologize for changing His words, but I think that is the meaning. Do not let us wander from it. If we give something to the Church which we ought to give to support father or mother, we are sinning against true religion. The tradition that we should give to a collection, must never violate the principle that we should care for those who are dependent upon us. That is Christ's illustration.

And yet how are we governed by these traditions, and how are we enslaved by precedent, and how the cold dead hand yet grips, as no living hand can! We yield ourselves to these things; and all the while, and again reverently, I shall borrow Jeremiah's great figure, God is rising early to tell us the secret of the day, to legislate for all the mystery of our nature, so vast that we cannot understand it, and that none other can understand it. We give over this strange complexity and mystery and majesty of life to the tradition of yesterday, and never listen for the whisper and the voice of God.

Oh, the reasonableness of listening for, and to God. Let the words of Jesus express it all for us. "This is life age-abiding that they should know Thee the only true God, and Him Whom Thou didst send, even Jesus Christ." The commandment of Jonadab may be excellent, but when it makes me careless of the commandment of Jehovah, or when obedience to the commandment of Jonadab shall make me disobey the living God; then, oh, the peril, and the harm, and the wrong of it! The greatest life, the age-abiding life, the life that challenges the ages, is life that realizes itself in fellowship with God, and becomes supremely, audaciously, magnificently independent of all traditions, and of human opinions. In that life there is greatness; in that life there is fulfilment.

XX

THE HOUR OF DOOM

Preparatory Readings: 2 Kings 24:18-25:7; 2 Chronicles 36:11-21; Jeremiah 52.

" In the eleventh year of Zedekiah, in the fourth month . . . a breach was made in the city."
—JEREMIAH 39:2.

THE text is part of a parenthesis, valuable as indicating the event which divided between the prophetic messages of Jeremiah during the siege, and those delivered after the fall of Jerusalem. The parenthesis in its entirety refers to the long siege of eighteen months, and the ultimate capture of the city by Babylon. Full details are found in the second book of the Kings, the second book of the Chronicles, and in the historic appendix to these prophecies in chapter fifty-two.

Our present meditation is concerned with the fact of the fall of the city. For forty years Jeremiah had proclaimed the word of Jehovah, denouncing the sins of the people, calling them to repentance, and foretelling this very catastrophe as inevitable, if they continued in their sinful courses. The nation had persisted in evil, contemning the Divine compassion, refusing the Divine call, and daring the Divine wrath. At last the long-delayed stroke fell. Babylon took possession of Jerusalem. Idolaters burned the house of God with fire. A people of strange tongue, filled with abominations, carried into captivity the people of the living God.

The story is solemn, arresting, and of grave importance. It brings us face to face with the fact of Divine vengeance, as to its reason, its slowness, its certainty.

The reason of the punishment of Judah was that of the nation's abandonment of its high ideals, its determined self-degradation, and its consequent failure to fulfil its true function in the economy of God. The slowness of the Divine method was the outcome of the Divine compassion, which gave the rebellious nation every opportunity to return, and continued to wait until, in the language of the chronicler, "there was no remedy." The certainty of the ultimate stroke was created by the determined refusal of kings and priests and people to obey the voice of Jehovah. If by reason of His pity,

"The mills of God grind slowly,"

yet,

"They grind exceeding small,"

in spite of all human opposition.

With this general sense, then, of the reason, the slowness, and the inevitability of the Divine punishment, possessing our souls, let us consider the teaching of the story as to its revelation of human folly, and Divine wisdom; considering two matters, first human attitudes toward the fact of the Divine anger, as illustrated in this particular story, but as persistent even until this time; and secondly, the fact of the Divine anger, as also illustrated in this story, and as obtaining at the present time.

First then, human attitudes toward the fact of the Divine anger. We are compelled to realize the fact of human opposition to this conception. It is a fact that humanity at large is against the idea of Divine anger; and perhaps, more so to-day than ever before, that is, within the narrower compass of those peoples who have come under the influence of the Christian fact. Now is this a true instinct, or is it a false instinct? Is it a true human attitude, this antagonism to the doctrine of Divine anger, or is it false? That is a basic question, and one that we do well very carefully to consider, for there are those who would rule out of our preaching all these Old Testament stories, simply because God is represented in them as taking vengeance, as visiting with punishment.

This human attitude of antagonism to the doctrine of the Divine anger is entirely false, and more, it is pernicious. May I first remind you that there is no revelation of God which does not include this doctrine. There may be some conception of God which has eliminated this thought of the Divine anger; but there is no revelation of God which does not include it. Admit for a single moment that God is revealed in Nature, and by the admission you have included the revelation of this element of anger, punishment, vengeance. This surely I need not stay to argue, for those who, reverently it may be, and with all honesty have turned away from the revelations of God which are found in these sacred writings, and have given themselves merely to the investigation of natural phenomena, and who perhaps will not admit that there is in them anything of Divine revelation, are nevertheless the very first to tell us that if Nature has anything to say to us it is that if we keep its laws, we live; if we break them we die. Wherever man looks in the realm of Nature, whether he considers that he have there a revelation of God or not, he is face to face with this fact of anger. Call it some other name if you will, but there it is; the fact that there is no mercy, no pity, no compassion. Rewards there are, in the fulfilment of life when laws are obeyed; but punishments or destructions as surely, inevitably following upon the breaking of law. Those of us who believe that such as discover the laws of Nature are but discovering the thoughts of God; those of us who believe with the ancient psalmist that day unto day showeth forth His praise, and night proclaims to night the glory of Jehovah; those of us who believe that all Nature is eloquent with the language of the Divine praise, wisdom, greatness, and power; affirm that the revelation of God in Nature proclaims His vengence, His anger, His punishment.

Or if we look for God in human history we find the same thing. Such a suggestion at once makes it necessary that we should admit that there are students of history who do not look for God in history. For a moment, then, let us leave the question of God, and put the matter in another form. All history testifies to the fact of vengeance, punishment, judgment, falling upon peoples who turn from high ideals, to low and base ideals. If it so please you, leave God out of the question. If it so please you, refuse to admit that God has any government of human history, and let history speak for itself. Then we are still face to face with the fact that when a nation has turned from the high ideals of purity and morality, and trusted in anything else, punishment has inevitably followed. Or if objection be taken to the word "punishment," then substitute some other; "catastrophe," for instance. The change of word does not change the fact that all through human history, in letters of fire, this truth is writ, To turn from the high and the noble is to turn the face toward deterioration, degeneration, and ultimate destruction and desolation.

Those of us who believe that God has as surely revealed Himself in human history as in Nature, recognize this operation as His operation. Those of us who believe, to quote again the oft-quoted word, that " History is His story," find in every national judgment the operation of a Divine activity, and in every national ennoblement the evidence of a Divine government, rewarding the things high and noble and of good report. Thus if we turn to history for a revelation of God, history is eloquent of the fact that He can be angry, that He has wrath, that He comes in vengeance, that He is destructive in certain lines of operation.

When we turn from Nature and from history to that

to which some will not make their appeal, but to which we make our special appeal, the sacred Oracles; then we find that there can be no acceptation of their teaching which does not include the anger of God, the wrath of God, the destructive activity of God, the vengeance of God.

This is not peculiar to the Old Testament. If I am not to preach this Old Testament because it speaks of God in terms of anger, then I must not preach the New, for the fire of the New is fiercer than that of the Old; the anger of Jesus was a far more terrible thing than the anger of Moses; the God of the New Testament is yet more clearly a God of wrath and a God of anger, than He of the Old Economy.

Let us remember in the second place that all active opposition to the doctrine of the Divine anger is accompanied by degeneration. No nation has ever turned away from it, no Church has ever turned away from it, no individual has ever banished it from the compass of his intellectual conception, without suffering degeneration sooner or later.

Finally, the fact of punishment continues even when God is eliminated, or His anger denied. The hour arrives, and the breach is made in the city, however much the city may decline to believe that God ever can punish, or that catastrophe can overtake it. If the city persist in unfaithfulness, if the nation persist in idolatry; then there will always arrive some eleventh year, and fourth month, and ninth day of the month, or some equally well definable date, upon which a breach will be made in the city walls, and the long-threatened devastation will sweep upon the city.

We thus see that this fact of human opposition to the conception of the Divine anger is false; and the reason for holding that view will be yet made more apparent, as we observe the methods of opposition.

Opposition to the doctrine of the Divine vengeance

sometimes expresses itself in denial of the doctrine, and persecution of the messengers. That was the story of Jeremiah, imprisoned in the house of the guard, dropped into the pit, hounded from message to message with unbelief through long and weary years; he persistently declared the fact of the Divine judgment, side by side with the fact of the Divine mercy and the Divine compassion. The message of the Divine mercy, and the Divine compassion, was persistently refused because men were in open opposition to the declaration of impending doom.

Another method of opposition is that of attempting to deal with situations by intrigues and by policies, which can only be cured by righteousness. That also is the story here. Babylon was threatening the city, and had been doing so for long years. Ever and anon some army marched across the horizon, and Judah attempted to arrange some league with Egypt to baffle Babylon. Jeremiah continued to thunder against Egypt, and to declare that no league with Egypt could make Judah safe against Babylon, because Babylon's victory would be a Divine chastisement for Judah's sin. Yet Judah continued her intrigues and policies and attempts to prevent a catastrophe thereby, which could only be prevented as she abandoned her iniquity, and lifted her face in penitence to the God of all grace.

Another method is that of efforts at compromise with God; wherein God is offered, and even given, everything except the one thing He asks. The temple was rebuilt, the temple was cleansed, the sacrifices were restored, the priesthood was set in order! All the outward forms and ceremonies of religion were attended to! So, a sinning people attempted to compromise with God, never turning back to Him in penitence, never putting away sin, never healing oppressions as within the nation, never squaring its life with His requirements. That is another method by which men constantly show their antagonism to the anger of God.

STUDIES IN THE PROPHECY OF JEREMIAH

There is yet one other method; that of refusal to think
on the subject under any circumstances, and that of re-
course to the aid of narcotics. During this last eighteen
months in Jerusalem there was very much of this, for
the city was hemmed in. Let us remember that at last,
the city capitulated, not to Babylon, but to famine. In
Isaiah we have his great denunciation of the drunkards
of Ephraim, who were making merry in luxury and lust,
while the things destructive of the nation were finding
their way into any and every corner and crevice of the
national life. This is the last way in which men attempt
to get away from God and the fact of His anger. They
refuse to think of it, and they give themselves up to all
the things that will enable them not to think of it. But
the hour arrives; some eleventh year and fourth month,
and tenth day of the month; and the walls are broken
down, and the enemy sweeps in, and the fire destroys
the very house of God.

There is one attitude which averts the Divine vengeance. It is that of returning to God in penitence. It
is that of true humiliation before Him. It is that of the
abandonment of all intrigue and policy which attempt to
circumvent Him. It is that of the giving up of all compromise which attempts to trick Him. It is that of the
going down before Him in penitence, confessing sin, and
turning from it resolutely. Wherever that attitude is
taken up by a nation, God takes all responsibility, both
for the sin and the wrong of the past; in some mystery
of mercy and compassion putting it away, and providing
for the restoration of the people. In spite of all degeneration, He restores the years that the cankerworm
has eaten, and gives the nation again its true place in
His regard and in His holy service. When the nation
will not take that attitude, then the hour arrives, the
breach is made in the city, and there is no averting the
catastrophe.

And so we press reverently, and for our own help and

profit, a little nearer to this subject, speaking no longer of the human attitudes toward the Divine anger, but of the fact of the Divine anger. In our thinking of this we must first eliminate entirely the vindictive element. God never willingly afflicts, and when there is no remedy, and God is compelled to visit with anger and with destruction, He never rejoices over the doom. The final and most radiant revelation of that truth is found in that oft-repeated illustration, the full depth and value of which has never yet been perfectly apprehended, even by those of us who bear the holy name of the Son of God; in that illustration wherein we see Him inevitably, resolutely, without any flinching, pronouncing doom upon this very city of Jerusalem. As we listen to Him, the voice is tremulous with emotion, and the sentence of doom is prefaced by the tears of an infinite compassion: " O Jerusalem, Jerusalem, that killeth the prophets, and stoneth them that are sent unto her! How often would I have gathered thy children together, even as a hen gathereth her chickens under her wings, and ye would not! Behold, your house is left unto you desolate." That is the language of God; and we have no right to speak of the Divine anger, until we have been in the presence of the Cross, and have been baptized with the Divine Compassion. My mind travels back to the earlier days of my ministry, to a notable conversation in the study of Robert William Dale of Birmingham. He said to me, " I never heard Dwight Lyman Moody speak of hell without feeling he had a right to do it, because I never heard him speak of hell except in a voice tremulous with emotion." Men have no right to speak of the anger of God as though they delighted in it, when God delighteth in mercy and never in judgment; when punishment, vengeance, is always His strange act.

Nevertheless God's anger is anger, it is wrath, and the more terrible because it is always inspired by love. God is angry when love's purposes are frustrated. God

[247]

is angry when love's objects are harmed. We have no higher court of appeal than the New Testament, and no clearer revelation than that of Jesus. If we observe carefully the occasions of the anger of Jesus, we have the whole truth revealed to us as to the reason of God's anger. He was angry. He said things that at the distance of two millenniums scorch and burn the soul. "Woe unto you, Woe unto you scribes and Pharisees, hypocrites." Why? "Ye devour widows' houses." God can only explain Himself to us by coming to the level of the commonplace. Thus Jesus drew attention to prevailing iniquities, simple, everyday, so common that men thought nothing of them; the devouring of widows' houses, and the putting of traditional burdens upon men, which they were not able to carry, the wronging of humanity; and on these He pronounced His fierce woes. This was the revelation of God's anger.

This is a supreme necessity in the interest of the universe. Prisons are in the interest of the free. Hell is the safeguard of heaven. A State that cannot punish crime is doomed; and a God Who tolerates evil is not good. Deny me my Biblical revelation of the anger of God, and I am insecure in the universe. But reveal to me this Throne established, occupied by One Whose heart is full of tenderness, Whose bowels yearn with love; then am I assured that He will not tolerate that which blights and blasts and damns; but will destroy it, and all its instruments, in the interest of that which is high and noble and pure.

If that be the nature of the Divine anger, let us remember in the second place that in its method it is just; and the deepest human conscience agrees with its operation. The chronicler declares that these people mocked the messengers of God, and despised His words, and scoffed at His prophets, until the wrath of God arose, until there was no remedy. The stroke of God never falls until there be no remedy. Human consciousness agrees with the justness of the Divine punishment, because the Divine punishment need never be, in spite of the sin that merits it, seeing that God has provided a way by which His banished ones may return.

If there be no Cross, then it seems to me God cannot punish. But because there is a Cross, a ransom, a regeneration made possible, then there can be no excuse for continuity in human sin; and that becomes the ultimate reason of the Divine judgment, and a vindication of the operation of the Divine wrath.

Again, its method is not only just; within that fact of justice, we may include and declare another; the judgment of God is always discriminative. I need not stay to argue that. Abraham debated that with God long since, and the record of the great debate is preserved for us in our Old Testament. Abraham under the oaks of Mamre said to Him, communing with Him in the secret of his soul, " Shall not the judge of all the earth do right?" Wilt Thou " slay the righteous with the wicked?" In prolonged and gracious intercession he sought to have proof in his own soul of the righteousness of God in judgment. Then the story tells how the action of God outran the intercession of Abraham, in that Sodom was not smitten to its ultimate doom, until the last righteous one had been delivered. God's wrath in its method, is just and discriminative.

The Divine anger, the Divine vengeance when it falls upon a man, or a nation is poetic in its operation. Some of you remember the lilt of Gilbert's lines, full of humour according to his intention,

" I shall achieve in time, my object all sublime,
    To make the punishment fit the crime, the punishment
        fit the crime."

I wonder if Gilbert at the moment knew that in trifling language he was declaring a great method of God. That

is what God always does. The city that refuses God,
God refuses; withdraws Himself from it, upon its own
vote. The temple prostituted is burned; which is but
the ultimate carrying out of man's own action. The
people misrepresenting God are silenced in the interest
of those to whom the misrepresentation is given. The
eyes of King Zedekiah that refused to see for others,
were put out.

Yet again the Divine judgment is progressive. Destruction prepares for construction. Exile is the only
way of return. Fires are for cleansing. He shall thoroughly purge His floor, the chaff He will burn with fire
unquenchable, but the wheat He will gather into His
garner.

The nation that forgets the fact of the Divine anger
is in grave peril. Paul, writing his letter to the Romans
—a letter to Christian men in the then capital of the
world, a letter to a company of saints, living in the midst
of all the conditions obtaining in Rome; dealing with
sin, with Gentile sin, and with Jewish sin, reduced the
sin of Jew and Gentile to a common denominator, discovering that which is fundamental in each case; the sin
of the men within the covenant, who had had the revelation and the oracles; the sin of the men without the covenant, who had had the light of Nature only. He gathered up all the story of the manifestations of sin by a
selection of passages from the Hebrew Psalter. Listen
to it:

" There is none that understandeth,
There is none that seeketh after God;
They have all turned aside, they are together become
    unprofitable;
There is none that doeth good, no, not so much as
    one:
Their throat is an open sepulchre;
With their tongues they have used deceit:
The poison of asps is under their lips:

Whose mouth is full of cursing and bitterness:
Their feet are swift to shed blood:
Destruction and misery are in their ways:
And the way of peace have they not known."

Then he came to the profound and deep secret of all
these outward manifestations:

"There is no fear of God before their eyes."

When the nation, whatever it be, our own, if so be that
this is true, has lost its fear of God, then in the wake of
that lack of fear, follow all these evil things.

Look once again at the letter to the Romans, and in
the selfsame chapter we find certain questions of Paul:
"Is God unrighteous Who visiteth with wrath? . . .
God forbid: for then how shall God judge the world?"

Where there is departure from high ideals there is
but one way of averting disaster, and that is the way of
return to God, and nothing else is sufficient. It is not
sufficient to deny the Divine anger, for there is the judgment of the moth and the mildew as well as that of the
lion! These things are upon us ere we know it; the
subtle, insidious, silent working of forces that sap the
life. The denial of judgment will not avert the ultimate
catastrophe; and no policy will avert it. No political
trick in the name of revenue, will avert a Divine judgment. Neither can we compromise with God by the
multiplication of our religious observances, if we are not
true to Him in heart. Our indifference is not enough.
The narcotics of our wealth are useless.

"Lest we forget, lest we forget." We in our security
need to be reminded that for us also there may come the
eleventh year, and the fourth month, and the tenth day
of the month, when God will hurl us from our place of
privilege, as He surely will, unless we are true to Him.

XXI

BACK TO EGYPT

Preparatory Readings: Jeremiah 40–43.

" They came into the land of Egypt; for they obeyed not the voice of Jehovah: and they came unto Tahpanhes. Then came the word of Jehovah unto Jeremiah in Tahpanhes."—JEREMIAH 43:7, 8.

THUS the descendants of Abraham returned to Egypt after nine hundred years. That is the fact recorded in the words of our text. It carries the mind involuntarily back to the night much to be remembered, when with a high hand, and outstretched arm God had delivered them from the yoke of Pharaoh. That night, dark and mysterious and wonderful in its revelation of the Divine power, had been followed by the morning of liberty; and the triumph song of deliverance had rung across the waters:

" Sound the loud timbrel o'er Egypt's dark sea!
Jehovah has triumphed—His people are free.
Sing, for the pride of the tyrant is broken,
His chariots, his horsemen, all splendid and brave.
How vain was their boast; for the Lord had but
      spoken,
And chariot and horseman are sunk in the wave.
Sound the loud timbrel o'er Egypt's dark sea!
Jehovah has triumphed—His people are free."

And now after nine hundred years they returned, a remnant of exiles, fleeing in fear and in rebellion, the very act of their coming to Egypt one of definite disobedience to the most recent message of the prophet of God.

STUDIES IN THE PROPHECY OF JEREMIAH

Chapters forty to forty-five in this prophecy contain the story of the events following the fall of the city, together with the prophetic utterances of Jeremiah during that period. The king of Babylon had appointed Gedaliah governor over the cities of Judah, and Jeremiah went to him, and dwelt among the people that were left in the land. For a brief period everything seemed to promise well. Troublous times speedily followed. Gedaliah was murdered by Ishmael, who, adding crime to crime, at last fled from Mizpah, taking with him all the residue of the people, even the king's daughters, and apparently Jeremiah. Johanan gathered his scattered forces, and pursued, overtaking the fugitives by "the great waters that are in Gibeon."

Having thus rescued the captives, Johanan did not return to Mizpah, but in fear of the Chaldeans halted at Chimham, intending to go to Egypt. Here they inquired of Jeremiah what the will of God for them was, promising obedience to whatsoever Jehovah might say. After an interval of ten days the prophet declared that the will of God was that they should remain in the land, and solemnly warned them against going into Egypt. Unmindful of their covenant, Azariah, Johanan, and those who were with them, refused to obey, and set out for Egypt, taking all the remnant of Judah, the men, the women, the children, all the king's daughters, and also Jeremiah and Baruch. "They came into the land of Egypt; for they obeyed not the voice of Jehovah: and they came unto Tahpanhes. Then came the word of Jehovah unto Jeremiah in Tahpanhes."

The story is full of suggestiveness, revealing as it does a peril which threatens every man and every nation. From tyranny, suffering, degradation, a people was delivered and found freedom, and ennoblement, only at last to return to the place from which they escaped in conditions far more hopeless and helpless than those of the days before their deliverance. It is the story of the rise and fall of nations, kingdoms, empires through all time. It is the story of Egypt itself, of Assyria, of Babylon, of Greece, of Rome, in all of which greatness resulted from certain elements of essential goodness, and destruction followed upon degradation. In the case of the people most irradiated, the height was great, and the depths to which they sank were profound.

Let us then consider what this text suggests concerning the return to Egypt, the reason of such return, and the persistence of the word of God, even in such an hour.

So far as the return to Egypt is concerned, the fact is perfectly plain. It was a return on the part of these people to those who had enslaved and oppressed them. This is a strange and continuous tendency in human life and human history in degenerate days, a forgetfulness of the lessons of history, and a turning back in spite of all those lessons, to the places and conditions of past oppression and degradation. They went back to Egypt. Through all the history of these people, from the founder Abraham, there had been this curious tendency to go to Egypt. Even Abraham himself, the man of high venture and heroic soul, who turned his back upon Ur of the Chaldees in order to seek a city built by God, when famine threatened him in the new land, went down to Egypt with disastrous results. His son Isaac repeated the blunder. Jeroboam in a crucial hour in the national history, had looked toward Egypt for help. Even Hezekiah, in some senses the finest of the kings that sat upon the throne of David, at one period in his life was busy with his politicians, endeavouring to arrange for some intrigue with Egypt in order to secure safety; and against that intrigue Isaiah had thundered with all the wonderful fierceness of his person and message. All this is illustrative of the same principle, the return of a great people, an emancipated and illuminated people, to the things from which they seem to have emerged, which in themselves were things of disaster and destruction and evil. A strange tendency persists on the part of nations, to go back after a period,—during which the nation has been attempting to secure its strength and safety by the methods of right and the methods of reason, by all those higher forces of human life, the mental forces and the spiritual forces— to those savage conditions in which men depend for safety upon physical force. There is a tendency in national life to return to frivolous licence from those spiritual and mental attitudes of serious concern, which make for stability and strength and greatness. There is in our own times a tendency to mock at the narrowness of the Puritans, and to lust after a licentious freedom from all restraint; a going back to Egypt; a tendency to return from the higher ideals of spiritual religion, in which men are rendered largely independent of that which is external, to elaborate ceremonials; a tendency to forget history, and to go back again to conditions from which it seemed the people had entirely been set free.

What was the motive in this going back to Egypt? These people were seeking safety from danger. Surely they had passed through trying times. For a long period Chaldea had threatened them, and at last had settled its armies round about their city, and hemmed them in, until that day when the breach was made in the city, and Jerusalem was a heap, the very house of God a charred and blackened ruin. There had been the marching away of great companies of their kinsmen into captivity, and they were but a scattered remnant left in the land of their fathers. They were afraid of the Chaldeans, afraid of new oppressions; and in order to secure their own safety these people turned toward Egypt, an evidence in itself of degeneracy; an evidence of their own consciousness,—if not expressed, still most potently active in their lives,—of their lack of inherent strength; an evidence of the fact that they knew, even though they would hardly perchance have confessed it, that they had in themselves no power to resist any oppression that might be brought to bear upon them. So they fain would render themselves safe from the oppression of Chaldea, by bending their neck to Egypt.

The fear that to-day prompts conspiracy for conscription is a confession of national degeneracy, a loss of the sense of inherent strength. I have made use of the phrase "conspiracy for conscription" of set purpose. Mr. Chesterton writing on the subject a few years ago, declared that men who talk of conspiracy for conscription are making use of a good word without understanding its meaning. He reminded us that a conspiracy is a breathing together, consequently if there be a conspiracy for conscription, it is the breathing together of the nation, and its desire for it. If that be so, the conspiracy is the panting, breathing of a fear that is dishonourable; and is a revelation of the fact that men are in danger, in the midst of prosperity, of a motive that is unworthy of all the things that have made nations really great.

The frivolous licence with which we are confronted on every hand to-day is the result of the haunting dread of the human soul, that demands an excitement in order that it may escape from itself.

The motive that lies behind the turning back again from the high ideals of religion which are spiritual, to a merely elaborate form, is but the superstition that expresses a sense of fear, and is attempting to put into the place of vital, definite, first-hand, naked relationship between the souls of men and God, all the things that may ease the conscience, and deaden the sensibility.

They went back to Egypt, these men of the olden time, and we read the story, and pity them. Are we not marching toward Egypt to-day?

This method of going back to Egypt is the method of policy, and that not in the high sense of the word, but in the baser sense; human manipulation of events, instead of Divine guidance; intrigue instead of intercession; all of which means cowardice instead of courage; all of which is evidence of degeneracy, of failure.

Let us inquire what is the reason of such return to Egypt, to the conditions of the past, from which we had hoped we were set free for ever. We have said that the reason in the case of these people was the carrying out of a policy in order to secure safety; but in view of the nature of the departure from Egypt nine hundred years before, how are we to account for the necessity for such a method? With that history behind them, the history of the Divine deliverance, the history of how, without strength of their own, they had found strength in God, and had become a people mightily strong, how is it that now we see of this people a merely scattered remnant, haunted by fear, and returning to the very conditions from which they had escaped, in order that in Egypt they may find some kind of security? What is the true story? The answer is found in the text: " They obeyed not the voice of Jehovah." It was failure of faith; it was consequently the degeneration of desire; it was finally therefore corruption of conscience. These are the facts that lie behind the method that turns back to Egypt. Let me repeat them, and ask you as I do so to notice that I am following a course and a sequence. Failure of faith, issuing in degeneration of desire, and that finally issuing in such corruption of conscience that these men had lost that which is the supreme thing in the life of a nation or the life of a man, a conscience, keen, sensitive, quick, and ready.

When in this sense we speak of failure of faith, we are face to face with the constantly recurring fact that faith is more than intellectual apprehension. " They obeyed not the voice of Jehovah." In that great epistle concerning faith in the New Testament, we find the one master idea of faith sometimes expressed in one way, and sometimes in another. Faith is obedience. Conviction never becomes faith, until it becomes the inspiration of activity. There may be belief, in a certain intellectual sense, that a thing is true; but that is not faith until it produces in the will of the man who believes it true, an answer that harmonizes with its claims. When we speak of failure of faith on the part of these people, and on the part of all people who turn back to things from which God has delivered them, it is always true that somewhere there has been disobedience to the light received. Faith and fear are mutually exclusive. Wherever there is faith fear is absent. All panic is evidence of the loss of certainty about God. The loss of certainty about God is always the outcome of failure to obey the law of God at some point. I say at some point, and I abide by my phrase, for the failure to obey may at the moment have appeared to be a very small matter, some apparently trivial deflection from the pathway of strict obedience to the law of God, the ethic of heaven; but wherever there is such deflection on the part of a man, or of a nation, the issue is the clouding of the vision of God, and the tremor of uncertainty vibrating through the soul as to God Himself; until presently, no longer sure of God, panic fills the heart, and men turn to Egypt, from which once they escaped, and over which in the might and strength of Jehovah they were the proud conquerors; and they ask to be sheltered by the power of Egypt. That is always failure of faith.

Failure of faith produces degeneration of desire. In that forty-second chapter, Jeremiah told these people exactly what they themselves were thinking. He put into the mouth of the rulers imaginatively, words expressing their decision, and he was quite right: "We will go into the land of Egypt, where we shall see no war, nor hear the sound of the trumpet, nor have hunger of bread; and there will we dwell." That is a searching and illuminative word! What were these people desiring?

What were their desires? They were lusting for ease and bread; and wherever a nation comes to the point of a supreme desire for ease and bread, we have degenerate desire working every manner of disintegration and dissolution in the life of that nation. What is it these people wanted? They wanted peace at any price, except the price of war and hunger. They were supremely anxious not to have to maintain a position of strenuous resistance. If they might no longer hear the trumpet of war, or have to fight, and might have all fulness of bread, that was everything they desired. I can quite imagine some one will say to me with some surprise: Are you arguing for war? Well, I am feeling what William James said is very true—that what we supremely need in the life of our own nation to-day is the moral equivalent of war. Not for war am I pleading, but for that heroic attitude of soul and life that stands for right, even though it may eventuate in war; rather than for that weak and beggarly and cowardly attitude, which to avert war, will stoop to any iniquity. We are constantly being told to-day that we must be ready for war in the interest of peace. That philosophy was born in hell. The only true position of those who have seen God and have believed in God is that men stand heroically foursquare to every wind that blows, upon the foundations of right and truth and love. Then, if war shall come, we may expect that God will be, not on the side of big battalions, but on the side of truth and justice and righteousness. Robert William Dale in strenuous times of a generation and more ago was asked, " Do you believe in peace at any price? " He said, " I certainly do, sometimes at the price of war." It was so profound a saying that there are very many who have never understood it. When a nation has dropped into the attitude of perpetual panic lest there should be war, and stoops to every manner of intrigue to avert it, even in methods more calamitous and costly than those of war, that nation proves that it has lost its faith in God, and is suffering from degenerate desires.

Finally we come to that which is the most hopeless thing, corruption of conscience. All its fine sensitiveness is gone. There is no high idealism, in national outlook and national thought. Or, to use the almost terrific word of the Bible, the conscience is hardened; so that there is no blanching with fear, and no blushing with shame. There is cynicism instead of faith, pessimism instead of hope, utilitarianism instead of love.

Some one may say: Do you object to utilitarianism? It depends entirely upon what is meant by the term. John Stuart Mill gave a special significance to the word in our language; and writing of this he said:

" I did not invent the word, but found it in one of Galt's novels, *The Annals of the Parish*, in which the Scotch clergyman of whom the book is a supposed auto-biography, is represented as warning his parishioners not to leave the Gospel, and become utilitarians."

John Stuart Mill fastened upon the word, and protesting against the advice of the Scotch clergyman founded the school of the utilitarians. Utilitarians, according to John Stuart Mill, are those who say that the greatest good of the greatest number is the true secret of all policy; and who say that morality is to be tested by the result it produces; and that where an action shall make a man happy, it is therefore right. That may be the profoundest truth of revelation, or the direst heresy that was ever propagated against humanity. Gradually it has become a heresy, until the standard of truth is not the standard of action; and love, well, love is out of court. Men do not talk about love in business. Then in the name of God, why do they not give up Christianity and go back to the paganism to which they belong? There is no place for compassion in legislation. Is there not? Then we are surely drifting to another decline and fall, more terrific than that of the Roman Empire. A corrupt conscience, no faith, but cynicism; no hope, but pessimism; no love, but hard, mechanical utilitarianism. That is back to Egypt; all essential grandeur gone, all the elements of strenuous heroism passed away. We are afraid of the Chaldeans; let us go to Egypt. We are afraid of . . . No, no, I will fill in no such gap! Let us make a new treaty with . . . No, I will not fill in the blank! But let us know that those at whom wise men scoff are sometimes great Christians.

And so we come to the last thing, the persistence of the word of God. "Then came the word of Jehovah unto Jeremiah in Tahpanhes." The fact that I would first ask you to observe is, that the word of God still comes. When we started these meditations, that was our key-note. The word of Jehovah came to Jeremiah in the dark days. These days were yet darker. All his prophesying had now been fulfilled after forty years. The city was a ruin; the house of God was burned; the captives were carried away; those that remained were fleeing in abject fear to Egypt. At last they came to Tahpanhes, the frontier fortress of the forbidden ground. The word of Jehovah came to them there.

God never leaves Himself without witness. There are always those who lift up the voice against war, against frivolity, against superstition. They are persecuted, often destroyed, but their message will continue. The voice may be heard no more, but the word of Jehovah is persistent. What a remarkable illustration of the truth we have in the New Testament. When Herod beheaded John, Jesus invaded his territory. Have you observed that? The synoptists begin with that public ministry in Galilee, and in every case the coming of Jesus into Galilee is associated with the imprisonment of John. I am afraid that sometimes we have imagined as we have read, that when He knew John was imprisoned, and went into Galilee, He was moving away from the zone of danger. Nay, verily; He was moving into the zone of danger. It was in Galilee John was arrested, and Herod was its tetrarch; and when Jesus knew John was arrested, He went into Galilee. The voice of John had been sounding, Repent, for the Kingdom of heaven is at hand. Herod, who once heard Him gladly, who came very near to the border land of the Kingdom of God under the ministry of the great Hebrew, at last beheaded him in order to silence his voice. Herod, ah, Herod, you may silence the voice of John, but you cannot silence the word of Jehovah! " The word of Jehovah came unto Jeremiah in Taphanhes."

Then observe the authority which it affirms and exercises. This was the word of Jehovah to Jeremiah, and to these people when they came to Tahpanhes: " I will take Nebuchadnezzar, the king of Babylon, My servant, and set his throne upon these stones." They had come to Egypt to escape from Babylon. Babylon was marching upon Egypt to master it. This is an ancient record. What really did happen after all? A few years ago, Professon Flinders Petrie discovered at Tel Defenneh a large brickwork pavement with great stones buried underneath. Jeremiah's stones! Right there ultimately Babylon set up the throne, and Egypt was despoiled.

The word of God is for ever proclaiming a fact, and producing it. All the false things in which men hope to find safety are doomed. When men, disobedient to the voice of Jehovah, turn back to the things from which they have escaped, in order that these things that once oppressed may now help, they find that these things also are doomed.

There is no refuge for the soul of man, no harbour of safety for national life, other than the throne of God. When men have lost their sense of it and their relationship to it, and turn to mountains and rocks to hide them, the mountains are rent in twain, and the rocks are ground to powder, and the naked soul of the man, or the spirit of the nation, finds itself unclothed, unhidden from the throne of the Eternal.

The persistence of the word of God had a purpose of grace. It always created, and still always creates an opportunity, an opportunity of repentance, an opportunity of return, an opportunity of renewal. The most terrible thunder of the voice of God is always intended to turn men back to Him, that they may hear the tender whisper of His love. The stroke of judgment that falls upon a nation, be it war, or famine, or blight, or those more terrible and insidious enemies of the moth and the rust, the easy, quiet, insidious, deadly forces of degeneration; these things are only intended to make men turn their faces again to God, for He is in Himself the God of the infinite and unfailing compassion, always willing to receive us as we will turn our faces back to Him.

Let us conclude our meditation in the language of Scripture itself. I pray you listen to Isaiah. " Woe to them that go down to Egypt for help, and rely on horses; and trust in chariots because they are many, and in horsemen because they are very strong; but they look not to the Holy One of Israel, neither seek Jehovah."

That word of Isaiah in the olden times may need some amendment to-day, not in its essential teaching, not in the principle that it reveals, but in the instructions it describes. When we read it next we will no longer read horses or chariots. We will read armies and aircraft! But the essential principle is this, Woe to the nation that goes back to the things from which it has been delivered, in order to make itself safe, and forgets the Lord.

A little later the prophet in words that seem to me to be full of profound meaning, and of immediate importance, declared: " The Egyptians are men, and not God; and their horses flesh and not spirit; and when Jehovah shall stretch out His hand, both he that helpeth shall stumble, and he that is helped shall fall, and they all shall be consumed together."

[263]

Once again, let us turn from Isaiah, and take up the words of the psalmist, and with these words in our hearts let us ponder.

" Some trust in chariots, and some in horses;
But we will make mention of the name of Jehovah our
God."

That is the test for to-day and for the hour. Is that so? Dare we say that? Are we prepared to abide by that? Is not that a little out of date, a little foolish, that any man should suggest that, in this hour of national life? If it be, then in that fact is the revelation of our degeneracy.

" Some trust in chariots, and some in horses;
But *we* will make mention of the name of Jehovah our
God."

Dare we stand there? Then let us hear how the psalmist continued:

" They (that trust in chariots and horses) are bowed
down and fallen;
But we (who make mention of the name of Jehovah
our God) are risen and stand upright."

All trust in the things material ends in ruin. Trust in God is still the one condition of permanence and of strength.

XXII

DEGENERATE WOMANHOOD

Preparatory Reading: Jeremiah 44.

" Moreover Jeremiah said unto all the people, and to all the women, Hear the word of Jehovah, all Judah that are in the land of Egypt: thus saith Jehovah of hosts, the God of Israel, saying: Ye and your wives have both spoken with your mouths, and with your hands have fulfilled it, saying, We will surely perform our vows that we have vowed, to burn incense to the queen of heaven, and to pour out drink offerings unto her; establish then your vows, and perform your vows."
—JEREMIAH 44:24, 25.

IN this chapter we have the last prophecy of Jeremiah concerning the peculiar people of God. Those which follow have to do with the surrounding nations. This particular message would seem to have been uttered in connection with some great idolatrous festival at which the scattered remnants of the Hebrew people were gathered together, and in which they were evidently taking part.

A considerable time must have elapsed since the departure to Tahpanhes, for the people were widely scattered. They came from Migdol on the northeastern boundary, from Tahpanhes, the frontier fortress where they had first settled, from Noph on the Nile, south of Cairo, and from Pathros, in all probability the whole region of Upper Egypt.

We are not told where this particular gathering was held, but the fact of it was enough to ensure the presence of the prophet, and to compel him once again to utter the word of Jehovah to the people who had so sadly wandered from Him. This he did first, by reminding them of the desolation of Jerusalem and the cities of Judah, and declaring that such desolation resulted from their own wickedness in serving other gods. He then protested against the unutterable folly of repeating these very sins in the land of Egypt; and declared that if they persisted in their wickedness, the same calamities would overtake them in Egypt as those from which they had suffered in their own land. To this message the people, both men and women, replied with appalling unanimity, affirming their determination to fulfil their vows to burn incense to the queen of heaven. To that attitude of mind the prophet uttered his last sad word concerning the final judgment of God upon them, giving them a sign, as he foretold the coming defeat of Pharaoh Hophra by his enemies, a prediction which was fulfilled within a very few years.

This last picture of Jeremiah proclaiming the word of Jehovah to His people is indeed full of sadness. Yet it completes the terrible movement which began with the clear declaration to the prophet that his ministry would be a failure so far as the immediate saving of the Kingdom of Judah was concerned. The attitude of the people at the hour is seen in the words, " Ye and your wives have both spoken with your mouths, and with your hands have fulfilled it, saying, We will surely perform our vows that we have vowed, to burn incense to the queen of heaven, and to pour out drink offerings unto her." The answering attitude of God is revealed in the words, " Establish then your vows, and perform your vows. Therefore," and all that remains of the chapter is necessary to complete the revelation of that attitude. Their last decision was that of wilful, emphatic turning from God. His last decision was that of ratifying their choice, and proceeding to deal with them accordingly.

That, then, is our theme; the ultimate in rebellion, and

the ultimate in punishment. The first application, and the only one, I now propose is national; for in all our meditations on this prophecy of Jeremiah which contains the record of how the Word of Jehovah came to a decadent age, national applications have necessarily been in view.

We have here then, first of all, the revelation of the ultimate in national rebellion. Its elements are of an insidious character, and even in their manifestation seem to be so natural that we hardly realize at first how utterly destructive they are. They may thus be grouped, first, the participation of women in open defiance of the word of God; secondly, a perversion of the moral and religious sense which declared itself in inability to understand the true causes of adversity and prosperity; and thirdly, that which is the ultimate and final in expression, the open and avowed prostitution of the will whereby these people did thus plainly transfer their allegiance from God to the queen of heaven.

Perhaps the most striking and remarkable element revealed in this chapter is that to which I have referred as the participation of the women in open defiance of the word of God.

The fact is distinctly referred to, more than once. In the fifteenth verse the record declares: " That all the men which knew that their wives burned incense unto other gods, and all the women that stood by, a great assembly . . . answered Jeremiah." In the twentieth verse the statement is equally explicit: " Jeremiah said unto all the people, to the men, and to the women." In the twenty-fourth verse again: " Jeremiah said unto all the people and to all the women." And in the verses constituting our text: " Ye and your wives have both spoken with your mouths, and with your hands have fulfilled it." In the language of the people declaring their final apostasy and rebellion, there are words which prove that the women were speaking: " When we burned incense to the queen of heaven, and poured out drink offerings unto her, did we make her cakes to worship her, and pour out drink offerings unto her, without our husbands?" It is a little difficult in the interpretation of this passage to know at what point in verses fifteen to nineteen, the language became that of the women only. I should personally place the dividing line at the commencement of the nineteenth verse. In that verse we have the actual record of what they said. It was full of a strange subtlety, and yet remarkably revealing of their attitude. Attempting to exonerate themselves from blame, they declared that the share they had taken in idolatry had been with the consent of their husbands. Throughout the prophecy of Jeremiah until now there is no record of the speech of the women, and no special word spoken to them.

Let us glance back, however, at the seventh chapter. In the record of how God prepared Jeremiah for his prophetic ministry, among the things that were said to him at that time was this: "Seest thou not what they do in the cities of Judah and in the streets of Jerusalem? The children gather wood and the fathers kindle the fire, and the women knead the dough, to make cakes to the queen of heaven, and to pour out drink offerings unto other gods, that they may provoke Me to anger." There in the earliest stages of the prophetic ministry, we have a revelation of the fact of the complicity of the women of the community in the idolatrous practices which the prophet was sent to denounce.

In chapter nine we have something else demanding notice: "Thus saith Jehovah of hosts, Consider ye, and call for the mourning women, that they may come; and send for the skilful women, that they may come: and let them make haste, and take up a wailing for us, that our eyes may run down with tears, and our eyelids gush out with waters. For a voice of wailing is heard out of Zion, How are we ruined! we are greatly confounded, because we have forsaken the land, because they have cast down our dwellings. Yet hear the word of Jehovah, O ye women, and let your ear receive the word of His mouth, and teach your daughters wailing, and every one her neighbour lamentation."

Rosenmüller suggests, and I think with true insight, that the women were called upon here to lament, not because it was their usual office in hours of sorrow, but because they had been the leaders in the idolatry which brought the calamity.

In the thirty-eighth chapter, when the prophet was warning Zedekiah that if he persisted in the policy he was pursuing, judgment must inevitably overtake him, he said, " If thou refuse to go forth, this is the word that Jehovah hath showed me: Behold, all the women that are left in the king of Judah's house shall be brought forth to the king of Babylon's princes, and those women shall say, Thy familiar friends have set thee on, and have prevailed over thee: now that thy feet are sunk in the mire, they are turned away back."

An examination of the context will show that Jeremiah was foretelling that the women would reproach the men whose maladministration had brought the ruin.

These are the only references in the prophecy to the women, until this strange chapter, containing the very last message of Jeremiah, to these people, a scattered remnant gathered together in Egypt for the celebration of idolatrous worship. In these messages we see the power and the influence of the women in the life of the nation.

Before giving any reflections upon the revelation, it may be well to remember how in earlier days in the history of these selfsame people, Isaiah had uttered some of the strangest, sternest, severest things on this subject that are to be found anywhere in the Biblical literature. The prophecy was uttered in the reign of Uzziah, a period of wonderful material prosperity in the history of the

Southern Kingdom. In the third chapter, I find the particular passage to which I am now referring:

" Jehovah will enter into judgment with the elders of His people, and the princes thereof; It is ye that have eaten up the vineyard; the spoil of the poor is in your houses: what mean ye that ye crush My people, and grind the face of the poor? saith the Lord, Jehovah of hosts. Moreover, Jehovah said, Because the daughters of Zion are haughty, and walk with outstretched necks and wanton eyes, walking and mincing as they go, and making a tinkling with their feet: therefore the Lord will smite with a scab the crown of the head of the daughters of Zion, and Jehovah will lay bare their nakedness. In that day the Lord will take away the bravery of their anklets, and the cauls, and the crescents; the pendants, and the bracelets, and the mufflers; the headtires, and the ankle chains, and the sashes, and the perfume boxes, and the amulets; the rings and the nose jewels; the festival robes, and the mantles, and the shawls, and the satchels; the hand mirrors, and the fine linen, and the turbans, and the veils. And it shall come to pass, that instead of sweet spices there shall be rottenness; and instead of a girdle, a rope; and instead of well-set hair, baldness; and instead of a robe, a girding of sackcloth: branding instead of beauty."

If a man preached like that to-day, what would happen? Yet all who have spiritual discernment will see that this is a description, not of a past condition merely, but also of a present condition. It is sufficient for our present purpose that we observe that Isaiah recognized, Jeremiah discovered, and the whole history of this particular people illustrates the fact of the close and appalling connection between corrupt rulers, and polluted and frivolous womanhood. If we close the Divine Library, and pass outside that history, and think of all the great peoples that have fallen, we have the same story. The corruption and degradation of Egypt itself; that of Rome and of Greece; and in more modern times of other peoples, has behind it the appalling story of the corruption of womanhood, and its dire and awful effect upon those in high authority.

Let us make some reflections on the suggestion which this chapter creates concerning ultimate rebellion in national life, as it finds expression in the participation of women in open defiance of the things of religion and the things of God.

There can be no exaggeration of the importance of the place that women occupy in national life. First of all I declare, judging not now from the standpoint of original Divine design, but from the standpoint of experience and observation, that the realm over which women rule is that of manhood. This is a fact; whether it be right or wrong I am not now discussing. The old and simple saying, so often quoted, sometimes with pathos and tenderness and sincerity, sometimes quite idly, is profounder than we imagine when we actually make use of it, that the hand that rocks the cradle rules the world; that the influence of motherhood upon manhood is something from which manhood never wholly escapes. I think I need not argue it. It will be granted. Think of the influence of wife upon husband, beginning from those first movements that culminate in marriage. I have no desire to speak lightly or carelessly on this matter. It is far too important and serious. Beginning from those moments when man is captured by woman; —that is the true word in ideal marriage;—through all the years that follow, man is far more than perhaps he thinks or understands, under the dominion of woman. It is almost an amazing thing how daughters begin a new influence in the life of their fathers. The realm over which woman reigns is that of manhood.

But follow me further. Women are influenced by the territory over which they reign in the most remarkable and subtle way. Buckle's philosophy is that you may account for the character, or characteristics, or temperament of man, by his natural surroundings. Let me borrow the intention of that philosophy and declare here, that it is not only true that woman in her reign over man influences him; it is also true that she is influenced, —and perhaps this is the deeper and profounder truth, —by the territory over which she reigns. She is influenced either to noble ends by the manhood she masters, or by that manhood which she does assuredly master, she is influenced to base issues; thus reigning, she is yet being reigned over. The manhood of a nation is perpetually under the dominion of its womanhood; and yet the womanhood of the nation is influenced by what the manhood of the nation is. The peculiar power which womanhood exercises over the life of manhood in the national life, is that of confirming, intensifying, solidifying the facts they find. If we look back again at this old-time picture, we see men turning toward idolatries and political intrigues; and women in the beginning of the movement baking the cakes that are to be offered to the queen of heaven; until at last in this final scene in the book of Jeremiah, the whole reason of the men in determined hostility to Jeremiah, and the whole purpose of their affirming their intention of offering incense to the queen of heaven, is declared to be the fact that the women burn incense to the queen of heaven.

Here we are brought face to face with one of the most profound things in national life. I am referring to the widespread influence of woman in national life; and I affirm that it is the most potent factor in the life of a nation; its potency consisting in the fact not so much that it initiates policies as that it confirms, intensifies, solidifies the directions and attitudes of men.

In proportion as we men see this, we shall never be guilty of sharing the initial cowardice of Adam, blaming women for our own failures; but in proportion as women see this, they will stand trembling in the presence of the enormous responsibility that rests upon them, in view of the strange and mystic relationship that exists between them and the manhood of a nation, and therefore between them and the whole life of a nation.

Is it at all possible to give expression to the responsibility that rests upon womanhood? I feel the difficulty of doing it. I submit, however, that the first responsibility of womanhood is that women should discover their personal rights in God, should realize that they bear to God a relationship which man does not affect, nor can; that théy have a right of access to God, for the realization of that which they are in themselves, without the interference of man in any way. Or to go back, to the figurative and poetic, and yet most truthful suggestions of the earliest part of our Bible, it is for women to realize that in them is perfected, for manifestation in the cosmos, the image and the likeness of God; that when God said, according to these ancient records, " Let Us make man in Our own image, after Our likeness," it is also recorded He made man in His likeness and after His image, *" male and female created He them."* I know the difficulty of stating this and yet it is one of the most profound truths in the Bible if we are to understand God, and if we are to understand humanity; that in womanhood we have a revelation of that in God which does not find expression in man. In proportion as woman comes to a recognition of this fact, that there is given to her, as a separate and sacred responsibility, that into which no man can ever enter for the unveiling of profound truth concerning God; as she comes to the discovery of that personal right in God, she is being prepared for the exercise of her power in the life of man, and in the life of the nation.

What is it? How shall I express it other than by saying that not only is it true that God is Father, it is also true that God is Mother? If the great doctrine of the Fatherhood of God is taught in the Bible, quite clearly also, and quite as clearly, the doctrine of the Motherhood of God is taught in the Bible. In womanhood it is intended that there shall be the unveiling of those mystic and mysterious depths of tenderness, which are of the very essence of eternal strength, which can best be understood by such mortals as we are, by the holy and sacred mystery and wonder and power of motherhood.

I am not referring merely to the actuality of motherhood, for there are women who have never been in any actual sense mothers, who nevertheless are exercising all the mother function of tenderness and care and strength that covers and guards and heals and helps. It is that strong quality, strong with the delicate weaving of infinite tendernesses and gentlenesses and beauty, which is the supreme glory of womanhood. May God deliver us from a day when anything rough-and-tumble shall spoil the finer delicacies of womanhood. It is in all these things that she is to represent God. In that side of His nature that defies human words; of which we can only speak as motherhood;—and mothers will be the first to admit that it is a rough vesture this, to express the finer facts concerning God—God is to find expression in womanhood. In proportion as women come to a discovery of these personal rights in God, and set themselves to the exercise of their matchless power for God, then still reigning over manhood, they will no longer be so entirely under the dominion of what they find as to become enslaved by it, if it be low; but they will descend to its level to permeate it, to cleanse it, to lift it, to refine it, to ennoble it.

If I have spoken of the corruption of peoples as the result of the corruption of womanhood, or the coincidence of corrupt government with frivolous womanhood; if I have felt profound sympathy with the almost unutterable roughness of the prophetic description of frivolous womanhood; I have not forgotten that which is the obverse truth, that wherever there has been high and noble uplifting in the national life, it has come, not as the result of strident political propaganda, which degrades womanhood, but as the result of this God-consecrated influence, mastering and sweetening and subduing and ennobling all the life of manhood, until man has been compelled to finer attitudes, nobler ambitions, and more glorious issues. John Ruskin said that when true womanhood throughout the world shall say that war must cease, war will cease.

It is to the fine and beautiful womanhood that has discovered its relationship to God, and goes forth to exercise that power of motherhood, that the nation must look. But on the other hand, if these finer things, these more wonderful things, these more delicate things of womanhood, are once bent and degraded they become a blight, a mildew, and a blasting, more terrible than clash of arms, or sweeping of plague. If the women are openly defying Jehovah, then there is no hope.

We may traverse the rest of the ground quite rapidly. Another manifestation of final degeneracy is that of the perversion of the moral and religious sense, the attributing of benefits to wrong causes. "Then had we plenty of victuals, and were well, and saw no evil," said they of the days when they offered incense to the queen of heaven; blind to the fact that the benefits had resulted from previous loyalty, and that the idolatry was now producing the harvest of want. They attributed the calamity to God, without recognizing the reason. They said, "We have wanted all things, and have been consumed by the sword, and by the famine"; blaming God for their calamity. It was perfectly true that their calamity had come from God; but why had it come? They had lost the sense of sin.

The modern expressions of this perversion are somewhat different, but the fact is the same. This perversion is expressing itself in the declaration to-day, that there is no actual relation between religion and prosperity. Indeed, we are sometimes told that men are more prosperous without God than with God. There is an element of truth in this; but the peril of this perversion lies in the conception of what prosperity really is. Listen to these people as they spoke of their prosperity when they sacrificed to the queen of heaven. How did they describe it? Victuals! I am glad the revisers have retained the objectionable word; even a French menu does not rob that of its significance—victuals! And what else? Physical well-being. Freedom from sorrow. Here are the conceptions of prosperity; victuals, physical well-being, and immunity from trouble. All history gives the lie to that conception, for hours of greatest prosperity in national life have often been the hours when there was hunger for bread, and famine, and plague, and pestilence, and sorrow upon sorrow. Out of these things men have found the elements of real greatness. How terribly, at this very hour we are in danger of this perverted view of religion and morality, and the relationship between religion and prosperity!

The first stage in the renunciation of allegiance to God is that of open propaganda which denies His existence. We have left that behind us long ago. The second stage is that of neglect. The third, last, and most hopeless stage, is that of forgetfulness. First, men openly fight against God; then they do not think it worth while to fight any longer; until there comes a day when they forget God. That is the ultimate renunciation of allegiance to Him.

But when a nation forgets God, it never escapes from God. If this God is not to be worshipped, then the queen of heaven must be worshipped. There are differences of opinion as to who this queen of heaven was. Personally, I have no doubt that it was the worship of the moon, worship of the receptive power in Nature. That was a mere incident which ended when the captivity ended; but the principle persisted. When God was dethroned, presently they erected the pride of race, and worshipped that. In Greece they erected altars to beauty, and worshipped that. In Rome they worshipped the power of government. Other nations dethrone God, but they always enthrone something. Commercial supremacy; a nation may make a god of that, and go back into spiritual bankruptcy and beggary; mere comfort; or sensation; something always takes the place of God.

What is the ultimate in the punishment of such conditions? I confess to you as I read this, and ponder it, and look at it again and yet again, my wonder grows. For the ultimate in punishment has two notes.

The first is a strange one, the passing of the name of God from the speech of men. How many punishments there had been in the history of these people on the way; armies and plague and famine and desolation and bereavement, but what is the last? "The men of Judah shall not use My name at all." That is the last punishment that God gives to a people. When the name of God is not mentioned, what have men lost? They have lost the synonym for purity, peace, pity, and power; and they are on the highway to the loss of purity, and of peace and of compassion and of real power. Are we in danger of losing the name of God? We certainly are, even within the Church! Time was when we said, If the Lord will, we will go here or there. To-day if we say it, some minister, some clergyman, some office-bearer will laugh at us, and tell us that kind of thing is worn out. James, the practical, the ethical writer of the New Testament says: "To-day or to-morrow we will go into this city . . . and trade and get gain." "Ye ought to say, If the Lord will, we shall both live, and do this or that." That is not an easy thing for me to say, because I am one of those who dread the man who talks glibly of the leading of the Lord. I know how much of cant there may be in such speech. Yet are we not losing something in ceasing thus to season our speech? Is not there some way of restoring a robust and healthy tone? If we are in danger of losing the name of God within the Church, how do we expect it to persist in the life of the nation?

But the last note is this: " I watch over them for evil, and not for good." That is, I will watch over them for calamity, for punishment, and not for blessing. Yes, but it is " I will watch over them." My mind travels on to the last prophetic fragment of my Old Testament, to the last prophetic message of the old economy. Malachi, the messenger, sees God thus, " He shall sit as a refiner and purifier of silver." Now I pray you, get the true picture suggested by that. I suppose no man detects the mistakes of expositors, like the man who tries to be an expositor. I turned up perhaps the greatest of expositors on these prophecies, to see what Dr. Pusey had to say about that, and this is what I read: " He shall sit as a refiner and purifier of silver," that means He shall sit as judge and king. It means nothing of the kind! Go and see how the refiner sits, watching the fires as well as the silver, until the dross be destroyed and the silver be pure. God watching above in the hour of punishment means that national chastisement is leading to national purity. Calamities are the very fires over which God watches, in order that at last He may realize His purpose in the nation, not on behalf of the nation only, but through the nation also.

So the last word for me at least, and I cannot go beyond the thing I see, the last word is not ultimate rebellion; the last word is ultimate discipline; a discipline of love that persists until He perfect that which concerneth the sons of men. There my heart finds rest.

XXIII

JEREMIAH IN THE NEW TESTAMENT

In our previous study we found ourselves at the close of Jeremiah's messages to the peculiar people of God. The rest of the book consists of a supplementary note by Baruch (chapter 45); a collection of Jeremiah's messages concerning surrounding nations (chapters 46 to 51); and a page of history (chapter 52). These messages concerning the nations may have been delivered at various times during the long period of his ministry. It is interesting that in the Septuagint, they are found after chapter 25, verse 13; and are not there given in the same order. With these messages we are not concerned. Having completed our series of meditations on some of the focal points of light, we turn in conclusion to one meditation on a matter, which is at least interesting.

All Bible students are familiar with the way in which the Scriptures of the Old and New Testaments are interwoven. This is so in a broad and general sense. As a matter of fact it is impossible to read the New intelligently, without knowledge of, or reference to, the Old. From beginning to end the writers of the New, proceed upon the accuracy of the history of the Old, and the authority of its teaching. Nowhere is there any deviation from this attitude. When our Lord sets aside the form of the Mosaic commands, it is by assuring their realization in a yet higher law; and when the writer of the letter to the Hebrews writes of the passing away of the ancient ritual, it is because all its moral and spiritual values are perfectly realized and fulfilled in the Chris-

tian economy. But it is not only true in this broader
sense. The two Testaments are wonderfully interwoven
by quotation, reference, allusion, to the Old in the New.
In the last analysis the unity is supernatural and Christo-
centric; but it is natural also, in that the Old Testament
was the Bible of all New Testament writers, even as it
was that of our Lord Himself. The exception may be
Luke, who certainly was a Greek, but his training as a
Christian was under Hebrew Christians, especially Paul;
and his writings show an equal familiarity with the Old
Testament.

We turn then with interest to consider the place this
book of the prophet Jeremiah has in the New Testament. In doing this let us first state the broad facts,
and then briefly consider the outstanding quotations.

As to the broad facts. Jeremiah is twice mentioned,
each time by Matthew (2:17; 16:14). In our versions
there is a third reference (27:9), but this is evidently
an erratum of some early copyist. Concerning it Calvin
said: " How the name Jeremiah crept in I confess I do
not know, nor do I concern myself anxiously to enquire.
It is certain that the word Jeremiah has been put down
by mistake for Zechariah." Of those two occasions the
first is in connection with a direct quotation, to which
we shall come presently; the second is in the record of
what men were saying about Jesus, as reported to our
Lord by His disciples at Cæsarea Philippi. Beyond those
two references by name, there are 41 quotations from, or
allusions to, the prophecy in the New Testament. Of
these, arrestingly enough, 26 are found in the Apocalypse. It is evident that John was familiar with the
great prophet of Judgment in the Old Economy.

Of these, seven are direct quotations, and are found
in this order: Matt. 2:17; Matt. 21:13 (this is found
also in Mark 11:17 and Luke 19:46); Acts 15:16;
Rom. 9:20; 1 Cor. 1:31 (this is repeated in 2 Cor.
10:17); Heb. 8:8–10 (and again in Heb. 10:16, 17);

[280]

STUDIES IN THE PROPHECY OF JEREMIAH

and Rev. 18:2. All now attempted will be the rapid review of these quotations as to their place in Jeremiah, and in the New Testament. The study is really an introduction to what might be a much fuller treatment.

Matthew 2:17. From Jeremiah 31:15, 16.

In the prophecy, the words are found in the Messages of Hope, which came while the prophet was a prisoner in the house of the guard. It is part of the message dealing with the action of God resulting from His everlasting love. The sorrows of the nation are there recognized, but the words immediately following tell of Jehovah's pity—"Refrain thy voice from weeping and thine eyes from tears"—and so on. Matthew quotes them in connection with the murder of the innocents by Herod. The wail of the women over their slain babies, was to him symbolic and symptomatic of the sorrows of the nation resulting from sin, and surely of humanity also. These were sorrows directly resulting from the action of evil, but involving the guiltless also. He ended the quotation with the wail of sorrow, but in close connection told the story of the Divine intervention, and the consequent preservation of the life of "the young Child." We may therefore go back to Jeremiah and complete Matthew's citation, for though the coming of this Child into human history was in every way accompanied by sorrow, His coming was in order to the ending of sorrow, and the wiping away of all tears from human eyes. In Jeremiah the gloom was evident, but the gleam shone through it. Jesus came into the gloom of human history at its densest, but when He came the gleam of prophecy became the glory of fulfilment, "He pitched His tent among us, and we beheld His glory—full of grace and truth." The minor wailing of humanity's sorrow merges into the major anthem of its perfect joy.

[281]

STUDIES IN THE PROPHECY OF JEREMIAH

Matthew 21:13. From Jeremiah 7:11.

These words fell from the lips of the prophet in a dramatic and strange hour. Under the influence of Josiah, the Temple had been restored, and the whole nation was exultant. The people were crowding its courts and giving expression to their emotions by the reiteration of the cry " The Temple of Jehovah, The Temple of Jehovah, The Temple of Jehovah." Moreover they were exultant because they really believed that the restoration of the Temple ensured national safety. They were also saying " We are delivered." In the midst of these jubilations the young prophet-priest from Anathoth stood in the gate of the Temple, as they thronged in, denouncing the whole proceeding as being unreal and of no significance, because, all the while they were guilty of every form of evil, theft, murder, impurity, lying, idolatry. Their religion was divorced from morality, and so devoid of all value. Therefore the Temple was a " den of robbers." A most significant and revealing phrase, showing how a holy place can be turned into a refuge and safeguard for marauders, and those who are wronging their fellow men. The centuries had run their course. During that time, the first Temple had been destroyed by fire. After a while the Temple of Zerubbabel had taken its place. That, in time, had been ransacked and devastated. Then came Herod, whose Temple superseded the old one. In material magnificence it exceeded its predecessors. Work on it lasted many years. When Jesus began His ministry it had been going on for forty-six years (John 2:20), and indeed the work was not completed till 64 A. D., not more than six years before its destruction by the Romans. This was the Temple whose courts were trodden by the feet of Jesus. There He had often taught. At the beginning of His ministry He cleansed it. Then at its close, He did so again, and in doing so quoted from Jeremiah,

declaring it to be " a den of robbers." The slight change
in the form of quotation is significant. Jeremiah made
it a searching question, " Is this house, which is called
by My name, become a den of robbers in your eyes?"
Jesus uttered it as a final finding—" Ye make it a den
of robbers." So He had found it. The spiritual and
moral rulers of the Temple were despoiling the people,
and were guilty of every evil thing. Very beautiful, in
this connection, is Matthew's statement that then and
there He healed in the Temple courts, to the accompani-
ment of the Hosannas of the children. Thus the dese-
cration of holy things denounced by Jeremiah was denounced by Jesus, but He revealed His ability to restore
the desecrated place to its true functioning.

Acts 15: 16. From Jeremiah 12: 15.

After the death of Josiah, Jeremiah faced a more difficult period in his ministry. During the reign of the
reforming King, he had been largely protected. With
his death the time of comparative peace for him ceased.
Under these circumstances he communed with God, and
was strengthened for all that lay before him. In the
course of that communion Jehovah assured him that
while it was true that He had forsaken His house, the
end would be restoration and realization. This was done
by the use of the words " I will return," accompanied
by the promise of future realization. When James gave
his " judgment " at the council in Jerusalem, concerning
the Gentile believers, he quoted—as he said—from " the
prophets." His more direct quotation was from Amos
(9: 11, 12); but the essential promise " I will return "
is found here also, and in the same general sense. This
would seem to be why he used the plural form
" prophets " instead of the singular " prophet." The
results of the " return " in both cases are the same, the
ultimate realization of the Divine purpose. The signifi-

cant fact is that the New Testament emphasis is on the fact that the Gentiles are included in that ultimate realization. Thus in Christ, the middle wall of partition is broken down, and the purposes of God are realized in the new entity which is the Church.

Romans 9:20. From Jeremiah 18:6.

In the midst of dark days, when in circumstances there seemed to be no gleam of light or hope, Jeremiah had a vision of the secret of security and certainty as to the issue of all things. It was that of the Throne of God. This he expressed in the words " A glorious Throne, on high from the beginning, is the place of our sanctuary " (Jer. 17:12). He found assurance of ultimate realization in the fact of the Sovereignty of God. In the course of the prophecy, the next chapter tells how he was commanded of God to go to the house of the potter, and of what he there saw and heard. It was a great and gracious interpretation of the Sovereignty of God. There he saw God as Sovereign, fashioning His work; and there he saw sovereignty acting in Grace in that " when the vessel that he made of the clay was marred in the hand of the potter, he made it again another vessel, as seemed good to the potter to make it." Paul's reference to this is not exactly a direct quotation, but a reference which involves the whole story as found in Jeremiah with its interpretation of the Divine Sovereignty. Let it be carefully observed that he employed it in exactly the same realm of truth, as that in which James had alluded to " the prophets," at the Jerusalem Council, that namely of the place of the Gentiles in the economy of God through Christ. In the course of his argument he had distinctly said already " They are not all Israel, that are of Israel; neither, because they are Abraham's seed, are they all children " (vv. 6, 7). Arguing for God's sovereign right to adopt His own method

[284]

to fulfil His purpose, he used the figure of the potter and the clay. Here then we see how God makes again the vessel marred in His hand. He does it by creating a new instrument, not from the Jews only, but also from the Gentiles.

1 Cor. 1: 31 and 2 Cor. 10: 17. From Jeremiah 9: 24.

In Jeremiah the quoted words are found in a passage of rare light and beauty. The prophet was denouncing the nation for its sins, and special reference to the sins of its supposed statesmen, or politicians, who were trusting to false securities for national safety. Those false securities were those of human wisdom, physical power, and material wealth. From these he called them to the true elements of national strength and security, those of the things which God exercises in the earth, lovingkindness, justice and righteousness. Or briefly, he called them from confidence in all things merely human, and bade them glory in the knowledge and understanding of God. Paul quotes this call in both of his letters to the Church at Corinth. In the first he was dealing with the contrast between human philosophy or wisdom, and the Word of the Cross. "The world through its wisdom knew not God," therefore God gave it Christ, at once "The Wisdom of God" and "The Power of God." That, and that alone is man's way of strength and security; there alone is the possibility of realization for humanity. Therefore let there be no trust in false things, but only in Him, "Christ Jesus Who was made unto us Wisdom from God; righteousness, and sanctification, and redemption"—"He that glorieth let him glory in the Lord." In the second letter he was dealing with a very personal matter, that of the contempt in which he was held by some in the Church. He appealed to them to look away from the personality of himself or of others, and to test his authority by the Gospel he had preached to them, and to others, for that Gospel was wholly of the Lord. Therefore "He that glorieth, let him glory in the Lord." Thus the great principle enunciated by Jeremiah in application to national affairs is applied by Paul to the Church in which God's purposes are being fulfilled; and the application is made both in regard to the life of the Church—its wisdom and power, and to its service in the world.

Heb. 8: 8–12 and 10: 16, 17. From Jeremiah 31: 31–34.

Here again the passage quoted is from the section in Jeremiah containing the messages of Hope. The particular section is that in which the prophet in prison awakes from a sleep which had brought refreshment to him, and breaks out into a song the burden of which is revealed in the way each of its three strophes begins. "Behold the days come." Through all the gloom of surrounding conditions he is looking to the consummation of the purpose of God. He speaks of that consummation in the terms of "the house of Judah" and "the house of Israel." In the second chapter he declares that Jehovah says that He "will make a new covenant with the house of Israel, and with the house of Judah." Moreover he distinctly declares that the new covenant will be different from that which Jehovah made with the fathers when He brought them out of the land of Egypt. It will be a covenant based upon immediate knowledge of God, through which the law or will of God will be perfectly known. This moreover will result from cleansing of the moral nature. The writer of the letter to the Hebrews twice quotes these words. First, when dealing with the perfect priesthood of the Son as compared with the failing Levitical priesthood. Here then is the fulfilment of the words of Jeremiah, and it is found that the new covenant with the house of Israel and the house of

Judah, is that which is created through the Priesthood
of Christ. Therefore the old covenant vanishes away.
This surely was in the mind of the Lord Himself when
He said " This cup is the New Covenant in My blood."
The second quotation of the passage is in the same realm
of revelation, being cited in connection with the statement: " By one offering He hath perfected for ever them
that are sanctified." " Them that are sanctified " are all
those who believe in Christ, both Jews and Gentiles.
Thus, and in no other way, will come the realization of
the Divine purpose, and here is the consummation of the
Divine program.

Revelation 18: 2. From Jeremiah 51: 8.

The last of the oracles concerning the nations had to
do with Babylon. Throughout all Biblical history from
Genesis 11 Babylon stood as the antithesis of Israel. It
was ever the embodiment of rebellion opposed to obedience. Through all Jeremiah's ministry it had moved
around the land in antagonism. He had seen God over-
rule its arrogance, and press it into His punitive dealing
with His people. It had ever remained the foe of faith,
the enemy of the Divine. In this oracle he declares that
in spite of her long apparent victory she is doomed, and
that because, though she might have been healed, she has
never been healed. Therefore the prophet, seeing through
all the intervening times, exclaimed " Babylon is suddenly
fallen and destroyed." All the dreams of Biblical history
converge and end in the Apocalypse. In chapter 19 we
have the songs of the ultimate victory of God, ushering
in the final establishment of His reign, and the building
of the City of God. In the preceding chapter John sees
the vision of that which precedes that consummation. It
is what Jeremiah had seen so long before, the fall of
Babylon, and the angel announces it in almost the words
of Jeremiah, " Fallen, fallen, is Babylon the great." Thus

the heroic prophet of the days of Judah's decadence saw not only the fulfilment of God's purpose in and through His people of the New Covenant, but also the inevitable issue in the complete rout and defeat and destruction of all that opposes itself to God. It was a great word from Jeremiah. This word of prophecy also is made more sure to us through our Lord Jesus Christ, Who " received from God the Father honour and glory when there was borne to Him such a voice by the Majestic Glory, This is My beloved Son in Whom I am well pleased."

Thus we see Jeremiah in the New Testament. Our study is fragmentary and incomplete, but it may help us to realize the unity of the Scriptures, and what is more, the unity and continuity of the enterprise of God. The book of Jeremiah is characterized in some ways by an almost appalling gloom. The history in the background is that of human failure, due to persistent arrogance and rebellion against the Throne of God. On the other hand, as we stand by the side of this prophet of God, the onward look is never hopeless. Here God is ever seen " Keeping watch above His own," that is, above His own purposes, and ever moving toward their full and glorious realization. The New Testament is of the same nature, and in it we see the onward march of God toward the fulfilment of the purposes of His everlasting love. To walk in the light of His revelation is to find no room for despair, but to march, even through tribulation and overwhelming darkness, with songs of the coming triumph for ever on our lips, and the light of the City of God for ever shining in our eyes.